Strategy Guide

PATHFINDER
ROLEPLAYING GAME

STRATEGY GUIDE

Credits

Authors • Wolfgang Baur, Jason Bulmahn, John Compton, Jessica Price, and Sean K Reynolds
Lead Designer • Jason Bulmahn
Designers • Logan Bonner, Stephen Radney-MacFarland, Sean K Reynolds, and Mark Seifter

Cover Artist • Wayne Reynolds
Interior Artists • Abrar Ajmal, David Alvarez, Branko Bistrovic, Marius Bota, Eric Braddock, Anna Christenson, Donald Crank, Ivan Dixon, Vincent Dutrait, Jorge Fares, Lucas Graciano, Paul Guzenko, Mauricio Herrerra, Andrew Hou, Tim Kings-Lynne, Damien Mammoliti, Mark Molnar, Jim Nelson, Mary Jane Parjaron, Paolo Puggioni, Maichol Quinto, Denman Rooke, Mike Sass, Bryan Sola, Craig J Spearing, Sandara Tang, and Thomas Wievegg

Creative Director • James Jacobs
Editor-in-Chief • F. Wesley Schneider
Managing Editor • James L. Sutter
Senior Developer • Rob McCreary
Developers • John Compton, Adam Daigle, Mark Moreland, Jessica Price, Patrick Renie, and Owen K.C. Stephens
Associate Editors • Judy Bauer and Christopher Carey
Editors • Joe Homes and Ryan Macklin
Managing Art Director • Sarah E. Robinson
Senior Art Director • Andrew Vallas
Art Director • Sonja Morris
Graphic Designers • Emily Crowell and Ben Mouch

Publisher • Erik Mona
Paizo CEO • Lisa Stevens
Chief Operations Officer • Jeffrey Alvarez
Director of Sales • Pierce Watters
Sales Associate • Cosmo Eisele
Marketing Director • Jenny Bendel
Finance Manager • Christopher Self
Staff Accountant • Ashley Gillaspie
Chief Technical Officer • Vic Wertz
Software Development Manager • Cort Odekirk
Senior Software Developer • Gary Teter
Campaign Coordinator • Mike Brock
Project Manager • Jessica Price
Licensing Coordinator • Michael Kenway

Customer Service Team • Erik Keith, Sharaya Kemp, Katina Mathieson, and Sara Marie Teter
Warehouse Team • Will Chase, Mika Hawkins, Heather Payne, Jeff Strand, and Kevin Underwood
Website Team • Christopher Anthony, Liz Courts, Lissa Guillet, and Chris Lambertz

This book is dedicated to Gary Gygax and Dave Arneson.

Based on the original roleplaying game rules designed by Gary Gygax and Dave Arneson and inspired by the third edition of the game designed by Monte Cook, Jonathan Tweet, Skip Williams, Richard Baker, and Peter Adkison.

This game would not be possible without the passion and dedication of the thousands of gamers who helped playtest and develop it. Thank you for all of your time and effort.

First printing February 2015.
Printed in China.

Paizo Inc.
7120 185th Ave NE, Ste 120
Redmond, WA 98052-0577
paizo.com

Table of Contents

Embark on a Grand Adventure!

You're holding an introduction to a world of adventure and creativity unlike any other form of entertainment: tabletop roleplaying games. Maybe you picked up this book because you wonder how roleplaying games (also known as RPGs) work and want a walkthrough that didn't involve studying a large tome of rules. Or maybe you've been invited to play with some friends, and want to arrive better prepared. Maybe you played the *Pathfinder Roleplaying Game Beginner Box* and want the full experience that the Pathfinder rules have to offer, or have been playing for some time and would like a friendly reference.

Regardless, we're here to help. In this book, you'll find a friendly and straightforward guide to making your own character and becoming confident in the basics of the Pathfinder Roleplaying Game.

What Is the Pathfinder Roleplaying Game?

In the Pathfinder Roleplaying Game, you portray a heroic character who teams up with other heroes in an epic tale of adventure and intrigue, full of dangerous quests and legendary rewards. In a typical game session, the **Game Master** (or **GM** for short) and the **players** create a story together in which the players act as the story's main characters, known as **player characters** (or **PCs**). The GM plays the parts of villains, allies, bystanders, and even the environment itself, all while creating goals for the player characters to reach and challenges for them to overcome. Over time, the characters grow in power, gain new abilities, and find fantastic treasures, useful tools, and other loot to help them on their quest.

Everyone playing the game rolls dice at various times to determine whether characters' actions succeed or fail, as well as what impact those results have in the moment. This creates elements of chance in the story you're playing, and some of the best moments of roleplaying games come from overcoming odds in the story with a little luck and clever use of the rules.

The Pathfinder Roleplaying Game is a fantasy game, where magic is real and elves, dwarves, and more roam the world. Most characters fall into traditional fantasy roles like wizards and barbarians, and encounter classic monsters like orcs and dragons. As a player in the game, you create such a character and interact with the world. This book walks you through creating a character so you can participate in the game, and then teaches you how to do things with your character—including exploring, fighting monsters, and interactions with other characters. It also provides some tips for getting the most out of both your character and your gaming sessions.

Who This Book Is For

Over the years that we at Paizo have been playing RPGs, we've noticed that many new players learn how to play with the help of a patient Game Master or fellow players. These teachers guide new players through character creation, show them which dice to roll in different situations, and walk them through the basics of combat and other encounters.

We know that not everyone has one of those people sitting by their side at the gaming table. Some groups are composed entirely of new players. Some players have limited time and can't walk a newcomer through the game. And even seasoned players might want to play a class they've never tried before, only to realize there's an entire set of unfamiliar rules they now have to learn.

Unfortunately, we can't ship great GMs and expert players with every copy of the *Pathfinder RPG Core Rulebook*. Instead, we've made this book as both a guide for new players and a handy teaching reference for experienced roleplayers.

This book will teach you the following:

- The basic terminology and concepts used by the Pathfinder Roleplaying Game.
- How to create player characters and advance them from level 1 to level 20.
- The basics of combat, from moving around the battlefield and engaging with foes to more advanced tricks like combat maneuvers and tactical analysis.
- The foundations of roleplaying, from meeting archmages and queens to solving mysteries and bargaining with dragons.

You'll also get an introduction to the Pathfinder Society organized play program—a worldwide fantasy roleplaying campaign that inducts you into an elite league of explorers, archaeologists, and adventurers. Pathfinders, as members of the Society are called, are dedicated to discovering and chronicling the greatest mysteries and wonders of an ancient world beset by magic and evil, exploring dark alleys and political intrigue and traveling to far-flung and exotic locales on Golarion, the world of the Pathfinder Roleplaying Game.

What This Book Isn't

This book is a guide to playing the Pathfinder Roleplaying Game, but it isn't a substitute for the *Pathfinder RPG Core Rulebook*. Many rules and concepts in the Pathfinder RPG have more nuances, situational applications, and unusual circumstances than can be fully explained in just a sentence or two. In those cases, this book will direct you to a page in the *Core Rulebook* where you can find a detailed explanation of that concept or possibility. You can also read the same material in the **Pathfinder Reference Document** (also known as the **PRD**) at **paizo.com/prd**, a free online rules resource provided by Paizo.

This book also isn't intended to give experienced players advanced insights or cunning new strategies for optimizing their characters. The various guides in this book will show you how to make a character that is effective and fun to play, but they are intended for new or inexperienced players as well as for those unaccustomed to playing that type of character. Players looking for more advanced tactics and advice should look on our messageboards at **paizo.com**, where players, GMs, and Pathfinder creators all share tips.

Materials You'll Need to Play

In addition to this book and access to a copy of the *Core Rulebook* or the Pathfinder Reference Document, you should have the following things handy:

- A copy of a character sheet to use when making your character. You can download and print copies of the character sheet and other useful materials for free at **paizo.com/pathfinderRPG/resources**.
- A pencil for filling out your character sheet and updating it as you play.
- A set of roleplaying dice (see page 8).
- People to play with.

Getting the Most out of This Book

You can use the *Strategy Guide* as a cover-to-cover guide to learning to play the game, as a handy reference to remind yourself of the basic game mechanics, and as a source of inspiration for advancing your character or creating new ones!

Important Terms (page 7)

Take a moment to read through these terms. Most terms are defined when they are introduced, but there are a few that are so crucial to describing how the Pathfinder RPG works that you should be aware of them before you start making your character or reading about how to play the game.

Character Concept Quiz (pages 10–13)

This short quiz helps you figure out what sort of character you might like to play—whether your style best fits the mighty berserker, the wily illusionist, the skulking thief, and so on. Each of the quiz answers lead to a theme (explained in the next section).

Character Themes (pages 14–27)

The *Strategy Guide* provides 26 character themes for you to choose from. A **theme** is a set of inspirations for making a particular type of character, such as an archer who takes out enemies from afar or a barbarian who smashes her way through obstacles and foes. Each theme falls under the larger umbrella of a class, which is a similarly structured but broader template for making a character. The quiz mentioned above helps you pick a theme, though you can also choose one by browsing through the descriptions. Once you've

found a theme you like, its description directs you to the appropriate class guide for making that sort of character.

If you're already familiar with the classes in the Pathfinder RPG (introduced in the Class Guides chapter) and want to create a character without using a theme, feel free to skip this section.

Races (pages 28–29)

In addition to a theme, your character also has a race. This describes what type of being your character is, such as a human, elf, or dwarf. Each race has a different set of advantages and disadvantages, which makes them favor some character concepts over others. Each theme description in the previous section lists suggested races that fit best with that theme, but you can choose any race you like—it's sometimes more fun to play an unexpected combination.

Instructions for Using the Class Guides (pages 30–39)

These instructions walk you through the use of the assorted class guides. Here you can learn what the different abilities and numbers in each class mean, and how to fill those details out on your character sheet.

Class Guides (pages 40–113)

Ready to make your character? If so, turn to the appropriate class guide and get started. Each of the 11 core classes from the Pathfinder RPG has a detailed walkthrough for making a beginning character, with suggestions for prioritizing your character's most important abilities and skills, descriptions of the powers he or she has when starting out, and information on that class's key rules and concepts. You'll also find a guide to advancing (or "leveling up") your character, as well as specific tips for your theme.

Other Character Details (pages 114–117)

This section helps you put the final touches on your character, such as figuring out what languages he or she knows, acquiring adventuring equipment, and noting down personal details.

Playing the Game (pages 118–153)

Once you've built your character and are ready for adventure, this section helps you learn how to play the game, introducing the basics of combat and narrative play and providing some insight into strategies that work for different sorts of characters against different types of foes. You'll also find tips for learning more advanced combat and roleplaying techniques, as well as basic gaming table etiquette and advice on how to keep sessions exciting and fun for everyone.

Introduction to Pathfinder Society Organized Play (pages 154–157)

The Pathfinder Society Organized Play program (**PFS**) hosts a massive, worldwide multiplayer campaign in which thousands of people assemble in local game stores, homes, game conventions, and other locations to participate in an ever-evolving adventure in the Pathfinder setting of Golarion. You can find Pathfinder Society games in your area by visiting **paizo.com/pathfindersociety**. Best of all, there's no experience required—newcomers are welcome!

Important Terms and Concepts

If you see a game term or concept referenced in the text and you don't understand what it means, check this section for a short explanation.

Players and the Game Master

In the Pathfinder Roleplaying Game, the **players** portray heroic characters who go on exciting and dangerous adventures. One participant called the **Game Master** (**GM** for short) works with the others to play out this story by portraying the characters the heroes meet, monsters they fight, and many other details that go into telling a compelling story.

As a **player**, you get to make all of the decisions for your character, such as what abilities the character learns and what equipment your character carries. You also have control over other parts of your character, such as personality, motivations, exactly what he or she says, and how the character responds to various challenges. You can have your character try to do just about anything you can imagine, and even if the rules don't describe exactly how to resolve your action, you and the GM can decide how (and whether) it might work.

As a **GM**, you don't focus on a single character, but rather describe and reveal the world to the players as their characters explore it. You lay the groundwork for the story that everyone plays together, meaning you play the antagonists the characters confront, as well as the characters' allies and any strangers they meet along the way. You also play the world itself, choosing plot elements, describing cultures the heroes meet, and even giving life to the landscape and weather. You are the host, the director, and the supporting actors all in one. You're also the arbiter of what is and isn't allowed in the game or setting—yours is the final word on how rules questions or disagreements are to be decided.

Even though the players and GM may be playing characters at odds with one another, you're all playing out the story cooperatively. Whenever a character attempts a stunt, makes an attack, or tries to resist a harmful effect, a player rolls one or more dice, and the player and GM use the randomly rolled result to determine if that action succeeds or fails. The GM challenges the players to overcome various obstacles, but shouldn't make the tasks impossible. Remember: if everyone has had a good time playing, and the players feel tested but triumphant at the end of an encounter, everyone wins!

Notable Concepts

A roleplaying game is generally set up as a **campaign** or **adventure**—a series of game **sessions** (usually four or so hours that you spend together playing the game) that combine into a larger story. In each session, players pick up where the last session left off, decide what to do next, and then deal with both the results of their decisions and whatever surprises the GM may throw at them.

The Pathfinder RPG has some similarities to both board games (especially in the elements of chance introduced into the game by dice rolls) and video games (in that players play a character in a story), but Pathfinder is different from either in that it provides players with far more freedom. You can attempt to go anywhere and do pretty much anything in this game—even if the game doesn't provide specific rules for your attempt, it has a variety of general rules that can be adapted to whatever you're describing.

When the heroes get into a fight with others, that's known as an **encounter**. These combats are often played out physically at the table upon a **map** made up of a grid in which each square represents a 5-foot-by-5-foot space. On this map, metal or plastic figurines (known as **miniatures**) or cardboard **pawns** represent the various characters' positions and the current state of action.

Key Terms

Below are some terms that are used throughout this book, with their abbreviations noted in parentheses. Those with asterisks (*) are discussed in further detail in the Playing the Game chapter.

Player Character (PC): This is a character directly controlled by one of the players—typically a hero of the story you're playing.

Nonplayer Character (NPC): This is a character played by the Game Master (not one of the other players), such as a city guard or innkeeper, or even a monster such as a goblin.

Level: This number indicates how experienced a character is. Characters start at 1st level, and by adventuring can rise as high as 20th level over time. When a character gains a level, he or she receives new abilities and enhancements. See Leveling Up on page 36.

Dice (d4, d6, d8, d10, d12, d20, and d%): When the lowercase letter d is followed by a number, it refers to a die with that many sides. For example, a d6 is a six-sided die, and a d20 is a 20-sided die. Sometimes you roll multiple dice and add them together; in these cases, the number of dice goes in front of the "d" and the type of die goes after it. For example, 4d6 means "roll four six-sided dice and add them together." See Roleplaying Dice on page 8 for more on this.

Modifier*: This is a number added to a die roll or a number on your character sheet. For example, your attack roll might have a modifier of +5, meaning that when you make an attack, you add 5 to the number you roll on the d20 die to get your result (thus, a 12 on the die would count as a 17, and so on). A **bonus** is a modifier that is +0 or higher; a **penalty** is one that's −1 or lower.

Base Attack Bonus (BAB)*: This number is a modifier added to your attack rolls. A higher number means you're better at combat.

Difficulty Class (DC)*: When you roll a die to attempt a challenging action, this is the number your total (including any modifiers) must match or exceed to succeed at that action. Climbing a slippery wall, dropping prone to avoid dragon breath, and gaining a suspicious guard's trust all have their own DCs that are determined by the GM. The higher the DC, the more difficult the challenge.

Armor Class (AC)*: This number represents how difficult a character is to hit with weapons and some spells, and works much like a Difficulty Class for attacks. The higher the AC, the harder it is to hit that character. An average unarmored person has an AC of 10. Armor and various abilities can increase this number.

Hit Points (hp)*: This number represents how much physical harm your character can endure. Successful attacks against your character reduce this amount. When a character's hit point total becomes less than 0, he or she falls unconscious, and may even die.

Saving Throw*: This is a type of roll used to resist certain harmful events, like overcoming a poisonous bite, dodging out of the way of an explosion, or resisting a mind-controlling spell. This is sometimes just referred to as a **save**.

Roleplaying Dice

Whenever you're attempting a bold action, like swinging your sword at a goblin, delicately disabling a trap, or intimidating a group of brigands, you're going to roll one or more dice and use the result to determine what happens next in the story. That means you'll need a set of roleplaying dice in order to play the Pathfinder RPG.

You'll find the following in a standard set of roleplaying dice.

- **d20**: A 20-sided die. This is the die used for determining everything from whether you manage to strike an enemy with your weapon to how well you convince a stranger to trust you, how quickly you jump out of the way of an avalanche, and so on.
- **d12, d10, d8, d6, d4**: These dice are used in different combinations (depending on your class, weapon, and other factors) to determine the damage you do in combat, your character's number of hit points, the duration and results of spells and other effects, and more. Depending on the sort of character you're playing and what abilities he or she has, you might need more than one of a given die type. Many players benefit from having four d6s, and some benefit from having at least two d8s and two d4s. (Note that d4s can have their numbers on the sides or the points—read whichever number is right-side up.)
- **d%**: This 10-sided die (instead of 1, 2, 3, and so on, its sides are 10, 20, 30, etc.) is sometimes used in conjunction with a d10 to determine a number between 1 and 100. This is used more often by GMs than by players.

Parts of a Character

Your character is a combination of story elements you make up (such as personality) and a number of mechanical elements that describe how good the character is at particular tasks and challenges. The following are the broad ideas and rules pieces that you'll come up with as you make and play your character.

- **Concept**: To start with, you need a general concept of the sort of character you want to play. This tells you not only what sort of role you want in the story, but also which rules and options you should focus on for that character. In this book, we provide a number of general concepts called themes (starting on page 14), each of which gives you an idea of what that character does and guides you through choosing various options.
- **Class**: Your class is a set of rules that determine your character's approach to combat and other activities. Is she a spellcaster or a frontline fighter? Does she strike from the shadows or try to convince enemies to become friends? If you choose a theme, it will specify which class to play and which options to start with. For more on classes, see the Class Guides chapter starting on page 30.
- **Race**: Your character's race will play into his or her backstory and rules, giving him or her bonuses to different abilities and skills. For more on races, see the Races chapter starting on page 28.
- **Ability Scores**: Ability scores represent your character's raw talent in a particular category. Every skill check, attack roll, and saving throw—virtually every roll in the game, really—is based off of one of these ability scores. See Ability Scores on the next page.
- **Skills**: Skills describe your character's talent, experience, or education in non-combat challenges (though they may also factor into combat) ranging from persuasiveness to crafting ability to balance. See page 34 for more on skills.

- **Feats**: Feats are powers you can choose that enhance skills and abilities, give you new options in combat, and otherwise help shape your character's flavor. See page 34 for more on feats.
- **Other Information**: Other important aspects of your character that you'll want to determine and fill in on your character sheet include things like your movement speed (how many map squares a character can move during a combat turn), your Armor Class, your equipment, and more. See page 114 for these details.

Ability Scores

Characters in the Pathfinder RPG have six main attributes (known as **ability scores**) that influence pretty much everything they do in the world, as well as how they react when others try to harm or interact with them. The six abilities are as follows.

- **Strength**: This covers muscle and physical power. Strength is key for those who engage in hand-to-hand (or **melee**) combat.
- **Dexterity**: This covers agility, reflexes, and balance. Dexterity is key for ranged combat, dodging attacks, sneaking, and various acrobatic actions. It also influences who goes first in a battle.
- **Constitution**: This covers health and stamina. This ability determines a character's hit points and ability to resist certain effects like poison, making it an important score for everyone.
- **Intelligence**: This covers learned knowledge and deduction. Skills, languages, and some other mental elements are influenced by Intelligence. Some spellcasting abilities are based on Intelligence.
- **Wisdom**: This covers intuition, perception, and willpower. Wisdom is key to resisting many mental effects and avoiding ambushes. Some spellcasting abilities are based on Wisdom.
- **Charisma**: This covers strength of will, personal magnetism, ability to lead, and appearance. Charisma is key for interpersonal actions like making friends, bluffing, and even intimidating other characters. Some spellcasting abilities are based on Charisma.

The average ability score is 10 or 11. Having a score of 9 or 8 in an ability means that your character is slightly hampered in that area. An ability with a score of 12 or 13 means your character has a bit of an edge when that ability comes into play. Scores of 14 and higher mean your character is especially proficient or gifted in a given ability. A character's race (dwarf, elf, gnome, etc.) will apply bonuses and penalties to different ability scores.

Once you've come up with your character concept and made your initial character decisions, you'll determine your ability scores. Two common methods for doing so are rolling for random scores and assigning scores from a set list of numbers. Your GM will tell you which method to use when creating your character.

Rolling Randomly: Some people like to randomly roll their ability scores because it adds uncertainty to the character-making process. Roll 4d6, discard the single lowest die, add the remaining three dice together, and write the total on a piece of scratch paper or the margin of your character sheet. Do this six times, and assign each of those numbers to your abilities in whatever order you choose.

Assigning Scores: Some GMs prefer for everyone to start on a level playing field, and have all of the players use the same set of numbers in their ability scores: 15, 14, 13, 12, 10, and 8. If you use this method, here's a guide:

- Which ability is your character best at? Assign 15 to that.
- Which one is your character second best at? Assign 14 to that.
- Which is your character's biggest problem? Assign 8 to that.
- Which ability is just average? Assign 10 to that.
- Assign 13 to whichever of the two remaining abilities your character is better at, and 12 to the other.

There are several other methods your GM might have you use for filling in ability scores. See page 15 of the *Core Rulebook* for more.

Leveling Up Your Character

As your character proceeds through the adventure, she will gain experience, letting her learn new skills and become more powerful. This is known as **leveling up**. Some GMs determine when it's time for characters to go to the next level by giving out **experience points (XP)** for success in combat and other challenges; when a character reaches a particular XP threshold, he or she gains a level. Other GMs base level advancement on where the characters are in the story, often letting characters level up after completing a section of the adventure or overcoming a significant narrative challenge. The class guides for your character class describe all the elements of your character that change when you level up.

Useful Materials

As mentioned before, though this book is loaded with advice about how to create a character, get started in roleplaying, and learn tactics for overcoming challenges effectively, you'll need access to the *Core Rulebook* or the Pathfinder Reference Document (PRD) at **paizo.com/prd**. If you play often, it's worth investing in your own copy of the *Core Rulebook* so you can tag important pages and look up rules on your character's spells or powers during other players' turns so you don't hold up the action.

Similarly, while a roleplaying group can share dice, it's more convenient if you have your own. You'll want a standard set of roleplaying dice. If you're playing a spellcaster, you may want to pick up some additional d6s, since a lot of magical effects (like the damage from a *fireball* spell or the healing power from a cleric's channel energy) are calculated based on multiple d6 rolls.

Many GMs have a collection of miniatures and can provide players with something to use to represent their character, but you might want a miniature of your own. You can buy prepainted plastic miniatures (such as those in the Pathfinder Battles line), or, if you're feeling artistic, buy an unpainted metal or resin miniature and paint it yourself. Cardboard pawns are another option, such as those in the *Pathfinder RPG Beginner Box* or the Pathfinder Pawns line.

The GM needs several other tools, which are covered in more detail on page 8 of the *Core Rulebook*.

Ready to start making your character?
Turn the page to take the theme selection quiz, or go to page 14 to browse character themes.

CHARACTER THEMES

There are hundreds of options for player characters in the Pathfinder Roleplaying Game, providing virtually limitless combinations of features that determine their talents in combat and conversation, as well as a myriad of other situations that come up while roleplaying. To help you narrow down what sort of hero you might enjoy playing, the *Strategy Guide* offers 26 **themes**—iconic fantasy character types that cover different takes on mighty warriors, guardians of nature, masters of arcane magic, devout champions of the gods, and so on.

The list of themes starts on page 14. You can take the quiz below to find a theme or two that you'd like, or browse the list and choose one whose description or art inspires you. Once you've chosen a theme, you're well on your way to making your character!

Note: Character themes are unique to this book. As you start to read other Pathfinder RPG books, they will mention classes, races, and individual character aspects that come from your theme rather than referencing a theme directly.

THEME SELECTION QUIZ

Below are some questions about your character's style and approach to solving problems. The answers you pick either send you to another question or suggest a theme for your character. If a theme recommendation doesn't sound like the right fit for you, feel free to start the quiz over or browse the list of themes until you find something that excites you.

1. WHEN A FIGHT BEGINS, I...

A. Draw my weapon and dive into combat! *Go to question 2.*

B. Rally my allies and direct them to attack our enemies. *Go to question 3.*

C. Move quickly from enemy to enemy, striking several times before dodging out of reach. *Go to question 4.*

D. Cast powerful spells to smite the opposition. *Go to question 5.*

E. Sigh heavily about how my friends keep getting us all into trouble. *Go to question 6.*

2. WHAT KEEPS ME ALIVE IN COMBAT IS MY...

A. Armor. Lots and lots of armor! *Go to question 7.*

B. Endurance. I'm just too tough to die. *See the **Berserker** (page 16) or **Smasher** (page 24) themes.*

C. Speed. I'm so fast that nobody can touch me. *Go to question 4.*

D. Power. I hit so hard that nobody can hit me back. *Go to question 8.*

E. Magic. I have so many protective spells that other characters are envious. *Go to question 9.*

3. THE BEST TYPE OF ALLY IS...

A. One who will join me in standing toe-to-toe with the enemy in battle. *Go to question 2.*

B. One I summon with magic. *Go to question 10.*

C. My loyal animal sidekick. *Go to question 11.*

D. One who willingly charges ahead while I fight from a distance. *Go to question 12.*

E. One who won't get in my way while I demonstrate my awesomeness. *See the **Crusader** theme (page 18).*

4. I WIN FIGHTS BY...

A. Using a bow to shoot enemies from afar. *See the **Archer** theme (page 15).*

B. Performing all sorts of tricky maneuvers to trip, disable, and throw my opponents. *See the **Maneuver Specialist** theme (page 22).*

C. Striking foes quickly and dodging their assaults with ease. *Go to question 13.*

D. Waiting for the perfect opportunity—like the enemy forgetting I'm there—then stabbing my foe in a weak spot. *See the **Shadow** (page 23) or **Thief** (page 25) themes.*

5. MY SPELLCASTING STYLE IS DESCRIBED AS...

A. Destructive. Explosions, meteors, and giant telekinetic hammers all sound good to me. *See the* **Fire-Blooded** *(page 19) or* **Fury** *(page 20) themes.*

B. Supportive. I like to make my allies more powerful. *See the* **Troubadour** *theme (page 27).*

C. Defensive. I keep myself and others from being hurt, and heal us when we are. *See the* **Healer** *(page 20) or* **Stargazer** *(page 25) themes.*

D. Deceptive. Tricking my enemies is fun! *See the* **Illusionist** *(page 21) or* **Trickster** *(page 26) themes.*

E. Broad. I have a perfectly suited spell for every occasion! *See the* **Traditional Mage** *(page 26) theme.*

6. HOW WOULD YOU GET PAST A CASTLE'S GUARDS WITHOUT FIGHTING?

A. I'd go to an unguarded side of the castle and use my magic to blast a hole in the wall. *See the* **Fire-Blooded** *(page 19) or* **Fury** *(page 20) themes.*

B. I'd disguise my party so that the guards would just let us pass. *See the* **Illusionist** *(page 21) or* **Trickster** *(page 26) themes.*

C. I'd sneak into the castle through a tower window, unlock a door, and let down the drawbridge. *See the* **Shadow** *(page 23) or* **Thief** *(page 25) themes.*

D. I'd use my magic to predict when the guards will be distracted, and sneak past them when that time arrives. *See the* **Traditional Mage** *(page 26) or* **Stargazer** *(page 25) themes.*

E. I'd use clever wordplay to charm or confuse the guards into letting us pass. *See the* **Thief** *(page 25),* **Trickster** *(page 26), or* **Troubadour** *(page 27) themes.*

F. I'd summon a creature to draw the guards away from the door, giving us the opportunity to walk in unnoticed. *See the* **Angel-Born** *(page 14) or* **Conjurer** *(page 17) themes.*

7. I'M NOT JUST A SHINY SUIT OF ARMOR, I'M A...

A. Highly skilled warrior who uses a mighty shield! *See the* **Shield Fighter** *theme (page 24).*

B. Master of mounted combat who can run down my enemies! *See the* **Knight** *theme (page 21).*

C. Holy warrior who channels the power of my divine patron! *See the* **Battle Priest** *(page 16) or* **Crusader** *(page 18) themes.*

D. Monstrosity in battle! This armor is more like a sneeze guard that keeps the blood of my enemies from staining my clothes... *See the* **Brute** *theme (page 17).*

8. HOW DID YOU BECOME SO MIGHTY?

A. I perform an intense training regimen every day, making me strong enough to wield my huge weapon. *See the* **Brute** *theme (page 17).*

B. When I get really angry, sometimes I go a little crazy... *See the* **Berserker** *theme (page 16).*

C. Wielding two weapons at once makes me twice as deadly. *See the* **Dual-Weapon Warrior** *theme (page 19).*

D. I channel the power of nature, transform into an animal, and maul those who oppose me. *See the* **Nature Warrior** *theme (page 23).*

E. I lose myself in the moment and break everything in sight. Sometimes that includes furniture. Sometimes that includes villains. Sometimes I use furniture to break the villains. *See the* **Smasher** *theme (page 24).*

9. IF I HAD TO CHOOSE JUST ONE SPELL TO CAST BEFORE ENGAGING THE ENEMY, I WOULD...

A. Cast a blessing granted to me by my deity that enhances my natural strength and fortitude. *See the* **Battle Priest** *theme (page 16).*

B. Transform into a being of pure, elemental fire and burn those foes who stand before me. *See the* **Nature Warrior** *theme (page 23).*

C. Shield myself with arcane armor while growing claws that I can use to tear into the enemy. *See the* **Dragon-Child** *theme (page 18).*

10. WHEN I'M IN NEED OF AN ARMY, I USE MAGIC TO SUMMON...

A. Angels and celestial animals drawn down from the heavens to do battle with evil. *See the **Angel-Born** theme (page 14).*

B. Anything I desire! I command demons, celestials, beasts, monsters, elementals—whatever the situation calls *for! See the **Conjurer** theme (page 17).*

C. Animals, carnivorous plants, and other creatures of nature. *See the **Animal Friend** theme (page 15).*

D. Anything that serves as a distraction to buy me time while I cast my favorite spells. *Go to question 5.*

11. WHEN FIGHTING, MY ANIMAL COMPANION SERVES AS...

A. My loyal steed. I charge into combat on its back! *See the **Knight** theme (page 21).*

B. A capable combatant that keeps my foes off of me while I shoot them from afar. *See the **Archer** theme (page 15).*

C. A brave brawler, made more formidable by my powerful spells. *See the **Animal Friend** theme (page 15).*

12. I AM MOST EFFECTIVE WHEN SUPPORTING MY ALLIES WITH...

A. Inspiring words and songs that guide their attacks. *See the **Troubadour** theme (page 27).*

B. Healing magic that wipes away their wounds and allows them to press on. *See the **Healer** theme (page 20).*

C. Magic that shields them from harm, guides their strikes, and predicts our victory. *See the **Stargazer** theme (page 25).*

D. Arcane trickery that befuddles our enemies (and makes us look great by comparison). *See the **Illusionist** (page 21) or **Trickster** (page 26) themes.*

13. MY FAVORITE WEAPON IS...

A. A hefty weapon that smashes through my enemies' armor and bones! *See the **Brute** (page 17) and **Smasher** (page 24) themes.*

B. Two weapons! *See the **Dual-Weapon Warrior** theme (page 19).*

C. Something simple like a staff—or else just my fists, feet, elbows, and knees! *See the **Maneuver Specialist** (page 22) or **Martial Warrior** (page 22) themes.*

D. I don't need weapons—my magical bloodline grants me the power to attack with claws and teeth. *See the **Dragon-Child** theme (page 18).*

Now that you have a suggested theme, find its description in the list of themes beginning on the next page. Each theme description has a sidebar noting which class it belongs to; if you're satisfied with your theme, turn to the page listed and start creating your character!

If you already have some familiarity with the Pathfinder RPG core classes and aren't interested in using a theme, turn to page 40 and browse the class guides to start creating your character.

LIST OF THEMES

The 26 character themes listed in this book each reflect a **class**—a set of heroic abilities that cover a broad range of character concepts, from holy warriors to arcane scholars to focused martial artists to champions of nature. Each class in the Pathfinder Roleplaying Game has numerous customizable options that lead to all sorts of interesting and exciting characters, and the themes presented here focus on specific ways of using that class. This makes creating your character faster and simpler. Themes also provide guidance for when your character gains more power and abilities; see Leveling Up on page 36 for more information. Each theme has its own icon that will be used throughout this book.

Angel-Born · Animal Friend · Archer · Battle Priest · Berserker · Brute · Conjurer · Crusader · Dragon-Child · Dual-Weapon Warrior · Fire-Blooded · Fury · Healer

Illusionist · Knight · Maneuver Specialist · Martial Warrior · Nature Warrior · Shadow · Shield Fighter · Smasher · Stargazer · Thief · Traditional Mage · Trickster · Troubadour

These themes cover various ways of looking at the 11 classes from the *Pathfinder RPG Core Rulebook*, but they aren't the only ways to play those classes. Once you become comfortable with making characters and playing the Pathfinder RPG, set these themes aside and experiment with bringing your own concepts to life. After you've picked a theme, turn to the page listed in the bottom of that theme's sidebar to read about its class.

Additionally, all characters in the Pathfinder RPG belong to a **race**, each representing a vast set of people and cultures in the Pathfinder campaign setting. The seven races from the *Core Rulebook* are dwarves, elves, gnomes, half-elves, half-orcs, halflings, and humans. You will find out more about these when you read the Races section on pages 28–29. What's important to know right now is that each race has different advantages and detriments (known as "racial traits") that make it better suited for some classes and themes over others—notably by having bonuses to particular ability scores (see page 9) or having some other inherent talent. Each theme entry offers advice on picking a race that meshes well with it. You can choose a race based on optimal game rules, or for personal or story reasons that have nothing to do with rules. If you feel overwhelmed by this choice, picking the first race that your theme mentions is a good default.

ANGEL-BORN

"Those belong to the town guard," the woman said, pointing her staff at Jessen's cart full of stolen weapons. "I'm afraid I can't let you take them."

"Oh really?" Jessen sneered. "And you're going to stop me, are you? You and what army?"

The woman smiled sweetly and snapped her fingers. A host of winged creatures shimmered into being behind her, their eyes hard.

"This one."

The hint of celestial blood running through an angel-born sorcerer's veins gives her otherworldly power to call upon the forces of heaven in times of need. She distracts her foes with enchantment magic and slays them with her small host of celestial allies. Should an enemy spellcaster attempt to summon his own magical minions, the angel-born banishes them as quickly as they arrive. With natural charm and magical compulsion, she can convince her foes to reveal secrets, surrender, or even join her side. Some of her spells also enhance her fellows' ability to fight.

Picking a Race: Gnomes and halflings can make for great angel-born because of their Charisma bonuses—a key attribute for angel-born. Humans, half-elves, and half-orcs can also be good choices thanks to their flexible bonus which can be used to enhance the angel-born's Charisma.

- Summons and fights with celestial allies
- Uses innate magical power to cast spells
- Can learn to call more powerful allies to her side

Go to page 96 for the **sorcerer** class.

14

ANIMAL FRIEND

Masin lay facedown in the mud, clutching at the arrow in his thigh as the bandits moved warily forward. "You've got heart, outsider," their leader said. "I'll give you that much. But heart will only get you so far in this world. The rest is steel and brains, and what you've got in the former you lack in the latter. Or didn't the townies tell you how stupid it was to come into my woods alone?"

Masin's mumbled reply was lost to the sound of the storm.

"What's that?" The leader edged closer. "Speak up!"

Suddenly, a blood-curdling howl split the night, stopping the bandits in their tracks.

Masin raised his head. "I said, 'Who says I'm alone?'"

An animal friend focuses his energy on training and augmenting his animal companion, a loyal creature that grows more powerful as he does. When a massive tiger or wolf is bounding about the battlefield, it's easy for enemies to overlook the animal friend himself, and the animal friend is free to cast combat spells, weave additional enhancement spells for his friend, or even transform into a powerful beast and join in the carnage.

Picking a Race: Dwarves, humans, half-elves, and half-orcs all make good animal friends because they can have a bonus to Wisdom, an important attribute to animal friends. Gnomes have a close connection to nature, and their racial traits fit well with the theme. In addition, because gnomes and halflings are smaller-sized creatures, people of both races can use many animal companions as mounts.

- Fights with powerful animal ally
- Casts spells that draw upon the power of nature
- Can learn to take on animal form

Go to page 58 for the **druid** class.

ARCHER

"Just keep bringing me arrows," the stranger said. "I'll take it from there."

"You can't possibly kill them all!" The mayor ran pudgy hands through his remaining hair. "There are dozens of orcs out there! They'll be over the wall before you can get off a second shot!"

In response, the archer spun, drew, and let fly. The arrow arced away out of sight—and was met with a distant, guttural scream.

"Arrows," she said. "Lots of them. Now."

An archer is a peerless master of ranged combat, typically focusing on the bow. Unlike more traditional bowmen, the archer gains a number of nature-oriented abilities that make her a formidable hero who can confound enemies, escape retaliation, and track down the most difficult prey. In addition, the archer recruits a faithful animal companion that watches her back and engages her quarry, buying her just enough time to loose the last shaft. Where the archer shines the most is in combating one or more "favored enemies"—broad categories of creatures that the archer has sworn to defeat. The archer also knows a smattering of nature-based spellcasting.

Picking a Race: Archery is based on Dexterity, so elves make excellent archers as they have a Dexterity bonus. Half-elves and half-orcs also make great archers, particularly because they have excellent vision that allows them to spot enemies even when it's dim or dark.

- Takes out enemies from afar with ranged weapons
- Fights with faithful animal ally
- Can learn to fire a veritable storm of arrows

Go to page 84 for the **ranger** class.

BATTLE PRIEST

"Hold the line!" the sergeant bellowed—and then trailed off into a gurgle as a skeleton's arrow caught him in the throat.

"We're done for!" Kalar shouted. "There's no hope!"

The walking dead pressed forward, rusted spears glinting—and then suddenly blasted apart, ancient bones exploding in a spray of light.

From behind them, a woman emerged, bloody but radiant. She wiped her sword on a skeleton's tabard and smiled at Kalar. "There's always hope," she said, "as long as you have faith."

A battle priest empowers herself with magic to strengthen her prowess, making her a capable combatant—especially against evil and the undead. The battle priest's spells also allow her to heal her comrades and summon creatures from other planes of existence to the battlefield to fight as allies.

Picking a Race: Humans can make excellent battle priests as their natural versatility can be used to enhance their combat abilities. Half-orcs are also very potent as battle priests; their orc ferocity allows them to stay standing when an attack would cause others to fall unconscious, giving time for one last attack or one critical healing spell. Dwarves are also effective as battle priests, due to their stout nature.

- Channels divine power in battle
- Uses spells to become a stalwart front-line fighter
- Can heal wounds and learn to raise the dead

Go to page 52 for the **cleric** class.

BERSERKER

The berserker screamed and lashed out again and again, his axe hewing through limbs like a scythe through wheat. His own blood ran down his chest, mingling with that of others and staining his dirty furs a hideous crimson.

From his position behind the crumbling monument, Tyn fired an arrow, then ducked back down and looked to Cara. "Gods, look at him go! Do you think he'll ever stop?"

The paladin nodded solemnly. "When they're all dead," she said. "Or he is."

A berserker gains the ability to enter a terrifying rage that lends him superhuman might, resilience, and willpower at the cost of self-preservation. While enraged, he's able to surprise his foes with unpredictable attacks, quick reflexes, and excellent mobility. The berserker learns how to slay several creatures with a single swing of the sword, and even when pushed to the point at which other warriors would have to admit defeat, he is able to rouse his anger to continue the fight against all odds. Nobody hits harder or can take as much punishment.

Picking a Race: Half-orcs are classic berserkers as their inherent ferocity pairs well with the berserker's great endurance. Dwarves are incomparably durable and their natural resistance to magic combines with the magical resistance that berserkers have.

- Invokes the power of rage to slay foes
- Resistant to opponents' magic
- Can learn to shrug off wounds that would kill other heroes

Go to page 40 for the **barbarian** class.

BRUTE

Jumai watched as the challenger hefted his huge hammer. The man was big, no question about it. But even so, that hammer was ridiculous.

"Compensating for something?" he shouted. Jumai raised his rapier and gave it a twirl. "Seriously, man, have a little common sense. Can you even parry with that thing?"

In response, the big man turned and swung his hammer at one of the arena's support beams. It burst apart in a shower of splinters, making the stands above tilt dangerously. The audience screamed.

He turned back to Jumai and smiled. "What do you mean, 'parry'?"

Combining an education in combat theory with extensive training under acclaimed weapon masters, the brute wields a massive weapon with power and finesse. This specialized training makes the brute more accurate when attacking, able to deal more damage when attacks connect, and able to defend against physical assaults more effectively—though who needs to focus on defense when no enemy survives long enough to fight back? As the brute grows in power, he can take an assortment of new abilities and options that make him even more fearsome in a number of different ways.

Picking a Race: Humans, half-elves, and half-orcs can have above-average Strength, which improves attacks with their mighty weapons. This theme also greatly benefits from the dwarves' general resistances and their bonus to Constitution.

▶ Wields impressive weapons that deal significant damage

▶ Is fearless in battle due to strong defense

▶ Can choose to specialize in one group of weapons

Go to page 66 for the **fighter** class.

CONJURER

Larig gaped as Rasim's monster tore into the goblins, sending them fleeing in terror.

"You just summoned a demon!" he croaked.

"Devil, actually," Rasim replied. "So?"

"So?!" Larig's eyes bulged. "But they're evil!"

"Again: so?"

"But... but you're associating with monstrosities! What about your soul?"

Rasim smiled. "Ah, but Larig—I already associate with you..."

The conjurer shines by summoning a variety of creatures from other planes of existence—the heavens, hells, elemental planes such as fire or earth, and so on. He uses these temporary allies as weapons, defenders, and servants. Furthermore, he can augment the fighting capabilities of his allies with magic to make them act faster, strike harder, and resist attacks. As spellcasters who learn their magic from in-depth study, conjurers tend to be more knowledgable about a variety of subjects than those whose talent comes from strength or force of personality.

Picking a Race: Humans make excellent conjurers for their natural flexibility helps them learn must-have techniques for making the most of summoning spells. Elves are also a potent choice, as they have a natural boost to their magic, and their penalty to Constitution is less of a hindrance when enemies must first overwhelm a conjured army to harm a conjurer.

▶ Summons and enhances allies

▶ Casts spells to protect self and augment friends

▶ Can learn to call upon incredibly powerful creatures

Go to page 106 for the **wizard** class.

CRUSADER

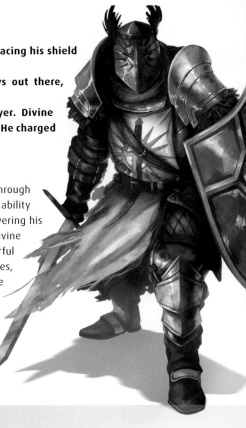

The crusader stood silently, armored form made tiny by distance, bracing his shield against the wave of onrushing demons.

"We have to get him to retreat," Thurmud hissed. "If he stays out there, he's history!"

As the first demons reached him, the crusader shouted a prayer. Divine power poured forth from his blade, scattering demons left and right. He charged in after it, scales and skin shredding beneath his onslaught.

"Or not," Thurmud admitted.

A crusader gains several powerful offensive and defensive abilities, and through his unwavering leadership, he can share these with nearby allies. His core ability simultaneously shields him from an evil creatures' attacks while empowering his own assaults. What sets him apart from other divine warriors is his divine bond with his weapon, which he can bless to temporarily gain powerful enchantments. Though the crusader is most effective against evil creatures, with his heavy armor and a sharp blade, he's well equipped to handle almost any threat.

Picking a Race: Crusaders benefit from the various flexible bonuses that humans have. The half-orc's natural intimidation and ferocity makes them suited to be crusaders, as does a half-elf's inherent resistance to enchantment spells—which some evil spellcasters enjoy using against their foes.

- Combines martial prowess with divine power
- Fights with magical bonded weapon
- Can smite the foes of his faith

Go to page 78 for the **paladin** class.

DRAGON-CHILD

"Get the caster!" the pirate captain shouted. "They're mean from a distance, but once you get up close, they cut apart like silk! That one ain't even got a proper weapon!"

To drive the point home, the captain charged toward Regar, ducking and dodging all the way. To his surprise, Regar stopped casting and merely stood there, not even moving as the pirate grabbed his arm. "Gotcha!"

"Indeed," Regar drawled, and held up a soft, manicured hand. As the pirate watched in horror, the fingers elongated, hardening into enormous claws. "Now let me show you what a *proper* weapon really is..."

Instead of lurking in the back casting spells, a dragon-child thrives on the front line. The claws he can grow make up for a lack of skill with weapons, and his magical enhancements more than compensate for his mediocre martial training. Given a moment to prepare, he can fight side by side with battle-hardened soldiers, all while keeping a reserve of powerful, destructive magic ready for other foes.

Picking a Race: Half-elves, half-orcs, and humans make some of the best dragon-children around because they can choose to boost Charisma or Strength—both important to these sorcerers—without sacrificing another ability in the way that other races do.

- Draconic heritage provides destructive magical power
- Fights ferociously with claws
- Can learn to breathe a deadly blast of energy

Go to page 96 for the **sorcerer** class.

DUAL-WEAPON WARRIOR

Bolof took his greataxe in both hands, eyeing the hydra warily. "Two against five," he said, waving the axe at the hydra's tangle of snapping, slavering jaws. "Not exactly fair odds."

"You're right," Danil said, and charged forward. His twin blades blurred, meeting steel-like scales with a crunch. In their wake, five heads plopped wetly to the cavern floor. He stepped back and sheathed his weapons.

"Ten on two is much more reasonable," he said. "Do you want to bring the torch now, or should we wait and kill it again?"

A dual-weapon warrior specializes in fighting with two weapons at once—a talent that offers his enemies as much pain as it does confusion. In addition to having exceptional melee talents and knowing numerous skills, the dual-weapon warrior develops critical techniques for dispatching particular types of enemies, navigating familiar terrain, and showing his allies clever tricks to tackle tough problems.

Picking a Race: Dwarves and half-orcs both have familiarity with unusual melee weapons that many foes aren't prepared to deal with. The half-elf's senses aid a dual-weapon warrior when he's hunting down enemies, and a human's overall versatility complements this theme's various abilities.

Wields two weapons for extra attacks

Is extra deadly against certain types of foes

Can learn to track and slay foes like

Go to page 84 for the **ranger** class.

FIRE-BLOODED

"Run!" the sorcerer yelled. "I'll hold them!" And before anyone could reply, she detonated a massive fireball at her feet, filling the entire corridor in flame. Monsters screamed as they were incinerated.

"I don't believe it," Jana whispered. "After all those snotty comments, she gave her life just so we could get away?"

"That would have been excessive," said a familiar voice as the smoke parted, revealing the sorcerer standing unscathed among the ashes of her foes.

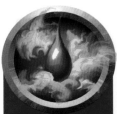

A fire-blooded sorcerer embraces the most destructive aspects of arcane magic, mercilessly throwing explosive spells into combat and slaying dozens of foes at once. She can change the types of damage her spells deal to best exploit her target's weaknesses—fire one moment, electricity the next. As she gains power, she develops resistance to these energies, allowing her to include herself in a spell's blast radius and walk out alive while those who foolishly surround her suffer her wrath.

Picking a Race: Gnomes' obsessive curiosity and intensity fit this theme well, and their racial traits complement the things these sorcerers need. Half-orcs have an appreciation for fire, and their ferocity lets them cast one last spell even when mortally wounded. Halflings also do well as fire-blooded because their small size and their Dexterity bonus mean they are able to dodge attacks while casting their spells.

Blasts foes with wild, destructive magic

Is unharmed by or resistant to certain energy types

Can learn to transform into a being of living fire

Go to page 96 for the **sorcerer** class.

FURY

"The land does not want you here," the woman intoned. "The sky does not want you. The river does not want you. They will not permit you to remain."

The merchant sneered. "And I suppose you speak for all of them, do you?"

"Sometimes," the woman admitted. As she spoke, long grasses reached up and grabbed the caravanners' feet. Above, storm clouds rumbled threateningly. "And sometimes, I let them speak for me..."

The fury embodies weather's natural destructive potential and the mystery that the wilderness has to offer. She incapacitates her foes by mixing clever spellcasting and evasive maneuvers. A fury's spells often hinder her foes' ability to respond effectively—whether by blinding, entangling, tripping, or crippling them. She can also summon packs of animals or elemental creatures to intercept tenacious enemies, and even more can bolster the fighting prowess of those she chooses to accompany.

Picking a Race: Half-elves and humans make powerful furies as they can use their versatility to benefit spellcasting by boosting their Wisdom—key to a fury's nature magic. Some players love playing elven furies because of elves' nature background, though an elf's racial traits don't complement what a fury needs. On the other hand, dwarves have racial traits that complement furies, though their subterranean origins aren't especially thematic.

- Commands elemental power against foes

- Turns the land itself against enemies

- Can learn to turn into a being of elemental might

Go to page 58 for the **druid** class.

HEALER

The healer sighed as he cut yet another arrow from Ostog's flesh, dropping it onto the quickly growing pile. "You know, Ostog, if you'd just wear some armor, I'd be able to use my magic for other things."

Ostog grunted. "Armor is for cowards."

"And people with some respect for their own mortality." The healer whispered a prayer and pressed his hands to the larger man's torn flesh, feeling it knit together beneath his fingers.

The big barbarian grinned. "Ostog the Unslain laughs at death."

"Of course, Ostog..."

The healer empowers his allies to fight at their very best through divine blessings that boost defenses—in a sense, preventative medicine that works alongside his true healing abilities. As he grows more powerful, the healer can restore health to dozens of targets at once, potentially taking his whole party from death's door to peak condition in a single moment. When the undead and other truly evil beings threaten the party, the healer can devastate them with the same holy abilities that he uses to help his friends.

Picking a Race: Nearly any race can do well as a healer. Humans, half-elves, and half-orcs can boost one of the two key healer abilities—Wisdom for spellcasting or Charisma for channeling divine energy. Gnomes and halflings also have an inherent boost to Charisma, so they have an natural inclination toward manifesting healing energy.

- Both heals and improves abilities of allies

- Uses divine magic for protection

- Can learn to heal nearly any wound and raise the dead

Go to page 52 for the **cleric** class.

ILLUSIONIST

The harpies descended in a screeching, cackling flock, talons outstretched and ready to rend. Below them, the adventurers cowered, caught completely off guard. Yet as the first harpy's claws touched flesh, the figures melted away like mist.

"Loose!" From the safety of the nearby rocks, a dozen arrows flew swift and sure, piercing feathered flesh and swatting harpies from the sky. Nocking another arrow, Tyrish turned to the illusionist. "Nice trick."

The spellcaster only smiled and touched the brim of his top hat.

The illusionist specializes in deception, tricking his adversaries into believing in that which isn't there and overlooking what is. Illusion magic is his strongest defense, for an enemy that attacks what isn't there has no chance of hitting. His phantasms and shadow magic are also his most versatile attack spells, for a clever illusionist is able to make an attack take the shape of the target's greatest fear.

Picking a Race: Gnomes make excellent illusionists as they have a natural gift that enhances their trickier magic. Half-elves and humans are also good choices as they can have above-average Intelligence—the cornerstone ability for illusionists—as well as increase their skill in bluffing, with and without magic.

- Uses trickery and illusion magic to confound foes

- Can cast a versatile set of spells

- Can learn to become invisible and hide allies in plain sight

Go to page 106 for the **wizard** class.

KNIGHT

Knight and steed formed an armored, glittering juggernaut as they fearlessly charged the devil. The knight whispered a prayer, and the tip of her lance glowed suddenly as bright as the sun as she collided with the fiend, driving it to the ground and scattering its minions in fear. She let go of the spear pinning the monstrosity in place and drew her sword, driving the rest of the devils before her in a panicked wave.

Eventually, she reined up and cantered back to her flabbergasted companions. "I apologize," she murmured. "It was most impolite of me not to save a few for you."

Charla was the first to laugh. "Something tells me we'll forgive you..."

The knight is a holy warrior borne into combat by a faithful mount that she can summon from the heavens. She is practiced in wearing strong armor so that she can shrug off the mightiest blows, and she's more than proficient in the weaponry that she uses to mete out justice. Even dark magic is of no concern to her as her faith steels her against evil spells and grants her a little magical talent that gives an extra edge in combat.

Picking a Race: Humans make excellent knights due to their racial traits that boost their skills, and human versatility allows them to train more quickly in mounted combat. It surprises some to find out that halflings and gnomes thrive as knights, for their small size means that their mounts are also smaller, so they can perform mounted combat maneuvers even in tight spaces.

- Rides a summoned celestial mount into battle

- Tough, armored front-line fighter

- Devastating when charging on a mount

Go to page 78 for the **paladin** class.

MANEUVER SPECIALIST

The hobgoblins advanced across the wall's narrow catwalk, grinning evilly.

"No weapons?" The lead hobgoblin gave a dark chuckle. "You're making this too easy for us."

"A true warrior is his own weapon," the human said softly. Before any of them could react, he shoved one hobgoblin over the parapet, slapped the sword from the second one's hand, and swept the feet out from under a third. The leader he grabbed around the neck and swung out over the drop, letting the terrified creature dangle.

"Perhaps now we can have a civil discussion," he whispered.

The maneuver specialist is a martial artist who specializes in disabling his opponents with combat maneuvers, stunning attacks, and a flurry of kicks. Most combatants risk retaliation when they attempt difficult maneuvers such as these, but the maneuver specialist is adept at slipping inside his target's reach and striking before the foe can respond. His techniques seem nearly magical, and by directing a mystical inner force called *ki*, he can execute even faster strikes, quicker dodges, and unmatched acrobatics.

Picking a Race: Half-orcs, humans, and half-elves can all attain exceptional Strength scores, which a maneuver specialist uses to wreak havoc. Dwarves can also make for good maneuver specialists as their boost in Constitution means they can last longer in a fight, and their Wisdom boost will benefit the maneuver specialist's ability to use *ki*.

- Is a skilled, agile unarmed and unarmored fighter
- Channels mystical inner force to fuel attacks
- Can learn to disarm, trip, and grapple foes

Go to page 72 for the **monk** class.

MARTIAL WARRIOR

The warrior spun, her staff a blur of motion. Bones cracked and wind rushed from lungs as the simple length of wood struck out again and again, drumming a frantic tattoo. Within moments, every one of her attackers was down and groaning. Not even breathing hard, she planted her staff on the ground and bowed to her new friends.

The rogue rolled her eyes at the wizard. "And you wanted to buy her a sword..."

The martial warrior wields unassuming weapons to deadly effect, typically favoring the humble quarterstaff. Such a hero, however, is also adept at using nearby objects to deal pain, turning chairs, ladders, and doors into lethal extensions of her martial arts mastery. She moves considerably fast on the battlefield, benefits from supernatural evasion, and can bypass almost any obstacle with a mix of agility, strength, and willpower.

Picking a Race: Half-orcs and humans both make excellent martial warriors as being able to have above-average Strength is what the theme needs. Half-elves are also strong choices as they can enhance their skill in acrobatic action.

- Turns any handy object into a deadly weapon
- Dodges attacks with speed and agility
- Can stun foes with a quick strike, leaving them vulnerable

Go to page 72 for the **monk** class.

NATURE WARRIOR

With a roar, the stranger transformed. Seams split and cloth ripped as arms and legs bulged. Fur sprouted across exposed skin as fingers turned to claws and jaws stretched into a fanged muzzle. In seconds, the man was gone, an enormous bear standing in his place.

The would-be thieves paused, looking back and forth between themselves and the bear. Then as one they turned and sprinted away.

The bear turned back to his companions.

Shaking his head, the old warrior sheathed his sword. "Well," he grumbled. "I guess that's *one* way to do it..."

The nature warrior is a powerful shapeshifter who is able to infiltrate enemy strongholds as a tiny animal or tear apart the opposition as an immense beast. Like the fury and animal friend themes, the nature warrior has the innate ability to channel the natural forces into spells—in his case, spells that embolden his ability to stand toe to toe with strong foes. He's also unhindered by natural obstructions, making him even deadlier when fighting in woodlands.

Picking a Race: Humans make excellent nature warriors as shapechanging makes up for many of the racial traits that other races have but humans don't. The half-orc's ferocity translates well when he shapeshifts, though half-orcs lose their natural ability to see in the dark. The stout natures and above-average Constitution that dwarves have makes them shine with this theme.

- Fights in a myriad of different animal forms
- Uses the terrain to best advantage
- Can cast powerful nature spells to give an edge in battle

Go to page 58 for the **druid** class.

SHADOW

"Isn't that just like a thief!" the priest snapped, barely managing to fend off the chimera's three snapping heads with his mace. "First sign of trouble, and they disappear, out the door like a—"

The twang of a crossbow cut him off. A bolt appeared in one of the chimera's monstrous eyes, followed by two daggers that tumbled end over end to lodge in the monster's other two throats. With a squeal, the beast collapsed.

"Well, never mind, then," the priest muttered.

"You're welcome," chimed a voice from the shadows.

The shadow specializes in flitting in and out of combat, striking enemies when they're distracted, disabled, or unaware of the shadow's presence. During those moments, her ability to harm foes increases greatly—her prowess with a knife to the back is as strong as a raging warrior swinging a greataxe. Along with her death-dealing talent, she has a wealth of skills that make her an excellent acrobat and a brilliant investigator.

Picking a Race: Halflings make formidable shadows, for their above-average Dexterity and small stature suit this theme, and their penalty to Strength doesn't get significantly in the way. Having enhanced agility and grace makes elves another solid choice. Humans, half-elves, and half-orcs are also good fits for this theme due to their flexibility.

- Stealthily strikes enemies for extra damage
- Boasts a large number of non-combat skills
- Can disarm traps and avoid danger

Go to page 90 for the **rogue** class.

SHIELD FIGHTER

"I'm just saying, that shield's a lot of weight to be lugging around constantly," Fabrio insisted. "It slows you down, makes you lumber like an armored aurochs. Now, maybe a buckler I could understand—that's a proper swordsman's weapon, it is—but that giant's dinner plate of yours is—"

He cut off as Rihan suddenly jerked the shield upward. Two dark-fletched arrows clanged harmlessly off its face. At the front of the line of troops, horns began to blow.

"...is a sound investment, and welcome in my wagon anytime," Fabrio finished weakly.

The shield fighter is a defense-oriented combatant who still packs a solid punch. Her armor keeps her standing when others would be beaten down, and her fierce strikes with sword or mace make less-armored foes suffer. She excels as a team player as she keeps adversaries busy while her cohorts at distance shoot bows or cast spells as those very enemies. As she grows more powerful, she masters a wide range of combat maneuvers, including learning how to fight with both sword and shield simultaneously, turning a defensive tool into a deadly weapon.

Picking a Race: Dwarves are ideal shield fighters, for they're hard to push out of the way, tough as nails, and resistant to magical assault. Half-orcs are also potent choices for this theme as their ferocity keeps them standing long enough to receive emergency healing and dive back into the fray. Most of the other races can make this theme work as well.

- Heavily armored, hard-hitting fighter
- Customizes style of fighting for extra effectiveness
- Can learn to use shield for offense and defense

Go to page 66 for the **fighter** class.

SMASHER

"It's a masterfully make lock," Sasha announced, seating herself cross-legged in front of the door. "Best get comfortable—we could be here for a little while."

"No time," Imani replied. "Move."

"What—" Sasha asked, and then she was scrambling aside as Imani ran at the door, armored shoulder leading. With a splintering crunch, the door flew from its hinges, landing several feet into the corridor beyond.

"So why exactly did you bring me along, again?" Sasha asked.

Sasha shrugged and stretched her neck. "Moral support."

The smasher enters a destructive rage that she directs at causing as much damage to enemies as to property. The powers she has while she rages allow her to bash down otherwise insurmountable obstacles. Faced with such a terror, most attackers choose to run, and with a wordless glare, she can convince the rest to join their comrades. As the smasher becomes more powerful, she can upend huge foes, snap bridges, and even break through walls.

Picking a Race: Half-orcs are a great choice for this theme, both in terms of story and because of their complementary racial traits. Humans and half-elves can also invest heavily in Strength to be effective smashers. Dwarven resilience and other racial traits help to make a well-rounded smasher. And although they're not effective in the role, gnomes and halflings would make very amusing and unexpected smashers.

- Turns her rage into raw strength
- Takes on enemies and obstacles with equal ease
- Can break down doors, smash faces, and snap weapons

Go to page 40 for the **barbarian** class.

STARGAZER

"The stars?" Herados coughed blood onto stones already slick with it. "Lady Luck stopped smiling on us when we first ran afoul of the bugbears, girl. No star signs or distant twinklings are going to save us now."

Emriana shook her head. "Oh, Herados... do you even know what the stars *are*?"

Herados looked confused. "I dunno—lights, I guess? Maybe jewels?"

Emriana walked out from behind the outcropping and raised her arms to the sky. In response, a column of flame shot down, engulfing the monsters.

"The stars, my friend, are *fire*..."

The stargazer uses divinations to predict threats she might face, prepare her spells as needed, and then employ that magic to deadly effect. Her powers can modify her allies' luck or inspire them to greatness, as though fate itself were on their side. When directing her attention to the opposition, she is adept at damaging and debilitating enemies, whether by magically commanding them to freeze in place or smiting them with her holy power.

Picking a Race: Those who have above-average Wisdom—humans, half-elves, half-orcs, and dwarves—make good candidates for stargazers as their magic is based primarily on being wise and one with their deities. Human flexibility also helps with increasing different facets of a stargazer's spellcasting. Half-elves have good abilities overall, and their ability to focus on a specific skill can hone their knowledge of religion, spellcraft, or diplomatic relations.

- Calls the wrath of heaven down on foes
- Alters chance and fate to favor allies
- Can learn to ask her deity for assistance

Go to page 52 for the **cleric** class.

THIEF

The knight looked the newcomer over dubiously. "Are you sure about this, Ariako? I didn't sign on with you in order to associate with thieves."

"Thieves?" The stranger smiled and shook his head. "From what your boss tells me, you want me to help you break into the private residence of a wizard—a lawful if morally repugnant citizen of the kingdom—then help you bypass his security system while you elude or outright slaughter his hired defenders."

He smirked. "All adventurers are thieves, my friend. Some of us are just more honest about our trade."

The thief is a master of a dark trade—trained in stealth, subterfuge, sabotage, and various social situations. He's very qualified to handle traps and locks, and his expertise in a wealth of other skills makes him a brilliant problem solver. He's no slouch in combat either, as the thief is accomplished at taking advantage of a foe's weaknesses to strike the most vulnerable places on the body.

Picking a Race: Halflings are natural thieves, as this theme makes excellent use of their enhanced Dexterity, natural grace and perception, and small size. Half-elves are also excellent thieves as they can use their innate skill focus to be better at their favorite talents. For thieves that make a habit of venturing into tombs and dungeons, the dwarven talent for spotting underground hazards and pick out valuable treasure come in handy. The other races can also make good thieves.

- Delivers precision strikes to debilitate foes
- Neutralizes locks and traps
- Can sneak into and out of dangerous places unseen

Go to page 90 for the **rogue** class.

TRADITIONAL MAGE

"What about armor?" the dwarf asked. "Got a spell for that, young missy?"

"Actually, yes."

"And can you fly then, too? And read my mind?"

"Those as well."

"And what about drinking a whole keg of dwarven ale in a single evening?"

The mage frowned. "Of course not. Why do you ask?"

The dwarf grinned and raised his mug. "Just making sure you need me around after all."

A traditional mage's strength is versatility—knowing as many spells as she cares to learn and employing them with pinpoint precision. As a universalist spellcaster, she can theoretically learn every spell ever penned. By collecting a wide variety of spells, the traditional mage acts as a magical troubleshooter who can overcome a tough encounters with a single incantation of just the right spell.

Picking a Race: Elves can make for excellent traditional mages, for their racial traits enhance magical aptitude overall, not just in one particular field of magic. Gnomes are a naturally curious race, which means that they fit the theme perfectly by their very nature alone. Humans and half-elves are also great traditional mages because they can have enhanced Intelligence and boost magic-oriented skills.

- Has a spell for nearly every occasion

- Wields knowledge and expertise in and out of battle

- Good at using a wide variety of magic items

Go to page 106 for the **wizard** class.

TRICKSTER

"I assure you, my lord, the opposition has no way of penetrating our defenses." The slaver smiled, piggish eyes almost disappearing above greasy cheeks. "Those who resent our business may rabble-rouse all they like, but money speaks louder than words, and a hundred mercenaries stand between us and the abolitionist cretins. You're completely safe in this fortress."

"It's kind of you to be so concerned with my safety, dear Crestin." As the newcomer spoke, his facial features seemed to shift, melting from those of Lord Gareth into a feminine visage the slaver knew all too well. "But I'm far more concerned with yours..."

A trickster, as the name suggests, is an expert at appearing to be something she's not and hiding in plain sight—and eventually learns how to disguise all of her allies, as well. Where others might needlessly waste resources on endless fighting, this hero glibly tricks the opposition into standing aside, muttering an apology, and even surrendering any guarded treasure. When forced into battle, the trickster uses magical performances to bolster her allies's acts of heroism in order to win the day.

Picking a Race: Halflings and gnomes both have an appreciation for trickery, and their racial traits complement the theme, whether it's the halfling's acrobatic prowess or the gnome's inherent talent with illusions. As humans and half-elves both have versatile skill sets that allow them to improvise in a wide variety of situations, they make good tricksters.

- Expert at disguise, infiltration, escape, and persuasion

- Boosts allies' natural talents

- Confounds foes with spells that befuddle the mind

Go to page 46 for the **bard** class.

TROUBADOUR

"This is no time for music!" Crage roared as a drow arrow grazed his arm. "Get out that fancy sword and fight!"

"Who says I'm not fighting?" Emilene replied as she drew her bow across the fiddle's strings. As the first, pure note rang out, Crage felt a sudden flood of warmth surge through his body. Suddenly the fear was gone, replaced by a confidence he hadn't felt since leaving the city guard. With a shout of delight, he plunged into the fray, his sword as light as a feather pen, tracing lines of red wherever he struck. In moments, all the drow were down.

He turned to Emilene. "How did you do that?"

Emilene smiled. "You fight your way. I'll fight mine."

With a virtuoso flourish or inspiring word, the troubadour motivates her allies, granting numerous boons to allies without necessarily joining the fray herself. She can also cast useful spells to fascinate, blind, and command her adversaries. Her natural charm wins the hearts of friend and foe alike. The troubadour is a jack-of-all-trades—no matter the task, she has some trick or talent to contribute.

Picking a Race: Half-elves make excellent troubadours, especially since they have the ability to boost their skills at musical performance. Halflings and gnomes both have high Charisma scores and are naturally outgoing, so they fit the theme very well. Humans and half-orcs can be quite capable in this role, particularly if they have above-average Charisma scores. Elven talents for magic also make them reasonable choices for troubadours.

- Weaves together magic and music

- Is a master of situations both in and out of combat

- Can boost the attacks and skills of allies

Go to page 46 for the **bard** class.

RACES

If you've picked a theme (or decided to create a character by directly picking a class from the following pages), it's time to choose your character's **race**—the type of creature your character is, such as a graceful elf, a clever human, or an indomitable dwarf. Your character's race not only grants traits that have rules effects, but also provides lots of material for developing your character's personality and backstory.

Read through the race entries below and choose one that is a good fit for the type of character you want to play. When choosing a race, use the guidance provided in the theme you've chosen. Each class guide has an Ability Scores section that talks about which ability scores (see page 9) are most important for that type of hero. Races that have bonuses on key ability scores may better fit a theme than those that don't. After you've selected a race, make note of your chosen race's features (such as ability score bonuses), and add them to your character sheet when you begin filling it out.

Racial Traits: Each race entry below tells you the page number of the *Pathfinder RPG Core Rulebook* on which you can learn more about that race. The traits listed for each race are explained in detail on that page of the *Core Rulebook*, and are listed here for quick reference and to give you a sense of what that race's pros and cons are. As you fill out your character sheet (see page 30 for more information about using the class guides to do this), add the race's ability score modifiers to your character's scores, and record the other racial traits in the Special Abilities section of your character sheet. Some racial traits also give bonuses on certain skills, which you write down the Skills area of the character sheet.

Character Size: Every character has a **size**, which influences some attributes and situations. Most of the races listed here are of average size (known as "Medium"), but two races—gnomes and halflings—are "Small." Information about what character size means in terms of the rules is listed in the racial traits section for each race in the *Core Rulebook*.

DWARVES

Dwarves (*Core Rulebook* 21) are naturally tough, stoic, and stubborn. Their sturdy builds provide exceptional stability; it's hard to physically move a dwarf. Their ongoing conflicts with goblins and giants grant them combat bonuses against these creatures. Dwarves also have keen eyes for metal goods and inconsistencies in stonework as well as a knack for using hammers and picks. They're naturally resistant to magic and poison.

Ability Scores: +2 Constitution, +2 Wisdom, –2 Charisma.
Saving Throws: +2 vs. poison, spells, and spell-like abilities.
Skill Modifiers: +2 Appraise (for metal and gemstones), +2 Perception (to notice unusual stonework).
Other Racial Traits: Darkvision, defensive training, hatred, slow and steady, stability, stonecunning, weapon familiarity.

ELVES

Elves (*Core Rulebook* 22) are exceptionally nimble and have keen minds, but their thin frames make them fragile compared to other races. They see well in dim light, and their keen ears miss little. They're immune to magical sleep effects and can shrug off most other enchantments. Elves' magic is very powerful, and their long life spans give them time to master various traditional weapons like swords and bows.

Ability Scores: +2 Dexterity, +2 Intelligence, –2 Constitution.
Saving Throws: +2 vs. enchantment spells and effects.
Skill Modifiers: +2 Perception, +2 Spellcraft (to identify magic items).
Other Racial Traits: Elven immunities, elven magic, low-light vision, weapon familiarity.

GNOMES

Gnomes (*Core Rulebook* 23) are hardy and outgoing, but they're smaller, slower, and weaker than other races. They have natural magical abilities and a knack for seeing through illusions, and their senses allow them to see in darkness. Each gnome has an obsession that makes him an expert in a profession or craft. Gnomes also bear a hatred for giants and kobolds, and gain combat bonuses against these creatures.

Ability Scores: +2 Constitution, +2 Charisma, –2 Strength.
Saving Throws: +2 vs. illusion spells and spell-like abilities.
Skill Modifiers: +2 Craft or Profession (any one), +2 Perception.
Other Racial Traits: Defensive training, gnome magic, hatred, low-light vision, slow speed, Small, weapon familiarity.

HALF-ELVES

Half-elves (*Core Rulebook* 24) are highly adaptable and may be strong, intelligent, wise, or outgoing depending on their respective backgrounds. Their mixed ancestry sometimes leads to social isolation, but that very heritage also gives them numerous benefits. Their elven side grants excellent vision and hearing, and they have some of their elven parent's immunities. From their human side, half-elves inherit a knack for learning new skills and an eagerness for trying out new things.

Ability Scores: +2 to any one ability score.
Saving Throws: No bonuses.
Skill Modifiers: +2 Perception.
Other Racial Traits: Adaptability, elf blood, elven immunities, low-light vision, multitalented.

HALF-ORCS

Half-orcs (*Core Rulebook* 25) have great strength, ferocity, and an intimidating demeanor, and even the ability to see in complete darkness thanks to their orc heritage. On the other hand, their human blood gives them versatility—they're equally quick, inspiring, or tough. Half-orcs are often ostracized outright by both parents, but they can overcome these stigmas. Half-orcs favor heavy, two-handed weapons just as orcs do.

Ability Scores: +2 to any one ability score.
Saving Throws: No bonuses.
Skill Modifiers: +2 Intimidate.
Other Racial Traits: Darkvision, orc blood, orc ferocity, weapon familiarity.

HALFLINGS

Halflings (*Core Rulebook* 26) are short, but their size grants them excellent agility at the cost of strength. Though they have a shallow stride, they move nimbly and stealthily. Halflings not only have considerable presence and personal magnetism; they're also naturally lucky and brave, and willing to stand up to even the most fearsome foes. Halflings generally train with the sling from a young age, making all of them proficient in the weapon.

Ability Scores: +2 Dexterity, +2 Charisma, –2 Strength.
Saving Throws: +1 on Fortitude, Reflex, and Will saves; +2 vs. fear.
Skill Modifiers: +2 Acrobatics, Climb, and Perception.
Other Racial Traits: Slow speed, Small, weapon familiarity.

HUMANS

Humans (*Core Rulebook* 27) can excel at practically any tasks they set their minds to. Although a particular human might be remarkably strong, cunning, agile, or observant, humans as a whole have few abilities besides their adaptability that make them stand out. But they do learn very quickly, picking up skills faster than other races, and they're adept at learning special feats and tricks.

Ability Scores: +2 to any one ability score.
Saving Throws: No bonuses.
Skill Modifiers: None.
Other Racial Traits: Bonus feat, skilled.

CLASS GUIDES

With the choices of theme and race made, it's time to sit down and define your character's powers! The theme you chose points to one of the 11 class guides found later in this section. The next few pages show you how to read the class guide for your selected class, how to use it to make choices, and where to write those choices down on your character sheet.

This section describes different aspects of your character—some of which have already been briefly discussed, like your race and ability scores—and indicates where in the class guide or in the *Pathfinder RPG Core Rulebook* to find further information about those aspects specific to your character's class. You will probably want to flip back and forth between this section, your class's guide, and the *Core Rulebook* as you fill out your character sheet.

 Need a character sheet? Download a copy for free at **paizo.com/pathfinderRPG/resources**.

WHAT'S IN A CLASS GUIDE

The first few pages of each class guide provide instructions on how to make a 1st-level character of that class, including suggestions for initial character options. The rest of the section walks you through what to choose when your character gains levels. At higher levels, these guides provide fewer details and suggestions—by then, you'll be more of an expert on who your character is than anyone else could be, and you'll have gained more familiarity with the options in the *Pathfinder RPG Core Rulebook*.

Character Sheet: The sections below explain how to transfer information from your class guide to your character sheet. Each section begins with a letter keyed to the character sheet guide on pages 38–39 to help you find the appropriate spot. Leave the boxes and lines on your character sheet blank until you have something to write there.

Quick Stats

The left sidebar on your class guide's first page contains basic information that applies to all characters of your class.

(A) Alignment: Your character's alignment is a guideline broadly describing his ethical and moral code. It has two components: one indicating where your character sits on the spectrum between law and chaos, and the second indicating where he sits on the spectrum between good and evil.

	Lawful: Values order and respects authority	**Neutral**: Balances law and individuality	**Chaotic**: Individualistic and free-spirited
Good: Helps without requiring rewards	**Lawful Good (LG)**: Obeys laws, keeps vows, protects those in need	**Neutral Good (NG)**: Balances own needs against the greater good	**Chaotic Good (CG)**: Follows own conscience and fights to free others
Neutral: Avoids risks without personal gain	**Lawful Neutral (LN)**: Holds to code of behavior even if it harms others	**Neutral (N)**: Prizes balance or is indifferent to morality	**Chaotic Neutral (CN)**: Individualistic, impulsive, or rebellious
Evil: Harms others for pleasure or gain	**Lawful Evil (LE)**: Sees laws as tools to exploit for own desires	**Neutral Evil (NE)**: Puts personal gain above all else	**Chaotic Evil (CE)**: Wants to see the world burn; may be unstable

Write your choice in the Alignment line on your character sheet using the two-letter abbreviation: lawful (L), neutral (N), or chaotic (C), followed by good (G), neutral (N), or evil (E).

(F) Base Attack Bonus: Your **base attack bonus** (**BAB**) represents how good you are at hitting things when you attack. Fill in the Base Attack Bonus box with the number your class guide tells you to use.

(C) Hit Points and Hit Dice: Your **hit points** (**hp**) indicate how much damage you can take before falling unconscious or dying (see page 137). Your maximum number of hit points is based on your class, level, and Constitution modifier (see Ability Scores on page 31). Write your hit points in the Total box on the HP section of your character sheet. Your **Hit Die** is the type of die you roll each time you level up to determine how many additional hit points you get. At 1st level, instead of rolling your Hit Die, you automatically gain the maximum value (thus, if your Hit Die is a d8, you start with 8 hit points). Your **Hit Dice** total equals the number of times you've rolled your Hit Die plus 1; generally, this is the same as your level. Certain feats or effects may depend on how many Hit Dice you have.

(E) **Saving Throws**: Saving throws represent your character's physical and mental resilience. **Fortitude (Fort)** saves let you resist poisons and diseases, and use your Constitution modifier (see below). **Reflex (Ref)** saves help you avoid area attacks like explosions or disasters like avalanches, and use your Dexterity modifier. **Will (Will)** saves help you overcome mental attacks like hypnotism, and use your Wisdom modifier. Your base save bonuses are determined by your class—see the Saving Throws section in the left sidebar on the first page of your class guide.

Fill in the Base Save column on your character sheet using the base save bonuses listed in your class guide. The Ability Modifier column refers to that saving throw's associated ability modifier: Constitution for Fortitude, Dexterity for Reflex, and Wisdom for Will. For the Misc Modifiers column, add together any special racial traits or class abilities (like halflings' racial bonus on all saves). Add up the numbers in each row and put that number in the Total box for each type of saving throw. If you have any situational bonuses or penalties on saving throws (like a fighter's bonus on Will saves versus fear effects), write them in the large box to the right of the saving throws so you remember to use them when needed. You can read more about saving throws on page 121.

Ability Scores

(B) Your ability scores (see page 9) represent your character's inherent capabilities in areas like physical strength, mental acuity, agility, and charm. Use the Ability Score section in your class guide to help you choose which abilities you should prioritize when assigning your scores. Choose carefully, since most of your character's capabilities—from making and dodging attacks to casting spells—are based on these scores.

Once you've determined your ability scores and modified them according to your character's race (see pages 28–29), write your final ability scores in the squares in the upper left part of your character sheet.

Strength (Str)	Muscle and physical power. Determines how hard you hit, how much damage you can do, and how good you are at physical tasks like swimming and climbing.
Dexterity (Dex)	Agility, reflexes, balance, and manual dexterity. Determines how hard it is for others to hit you, how good you are at shooting things, and your skill at many different tasks.
Constitution (Con)	Health and stamina, resistance to poison, and general physical resilience. Determines how many hit points you have, and thus how much damage you can take before dying.
Intelligence (Int)	Mental computing power, learning capacity, and ability to reason. Determines how much you know, how many skill points you get, and how many languages you speak.
Wisdom (Wis)	Willpower, common sense, awareness, and intuition. Determines your resistance to certain types of spells and other effects, and your ability to sense danger.
Charisma (Cha)	Personal magnetism, personality, influence, and ability to lead. Determines your ability to convince others, and how good you are at various social skills.

(B) **Ability Score Modifiers**: In addition to your ability scores, you'll have a **modifier** based on each score. Use the table below to determine the modifiers for your ability scores, then record them on your character sheet. Some elements (like how many spells you can cast) depend on an ability score, while others (like bonuses to skills) depend on an ability score modifier. Be careful to check which one you need to use when calculating each different part of your character!

Score	Modifier		Score	Modifier
1	–5		12–13	+1
2–3	–4		14–15	+2
4–5	–3		16–17	+3
6–7	–2		18–19	+4
8–9	–1		20–21	+5
10–11	+0		22+	etc...

 TIP Know Your Modifier: You'll use ability modifiers more often than your actual ability scores; you'll add your modifier to skills checks, saving throws, and a variety of other situations.

MANAGING HIT POINTS

When you take damage during play, subtract that amount from your total and write the amount in the Wounds/Current hp box.

The class guides provide descriptions of different spells, feats, and other powers so you don't need to look them up every time. Often, that information can't be summarized in a single sentence, so the text includes a reference to a page in the *Core Rulebook*. When you see such a reference after an ability, spell, or feat, look it up to understand how to use it.

DAMAGE REDUCTION

Damage reduction (**DR**) is an ability that some characters get from magic or class abilities. It reduces the amount of damage you take from weapons. If you have DR, write it in the DR box. See pages 561–562 of the *Core Rulebook* for more.

AID ANOTHER

Sometimes you can help an ally succeed at a skill check. Roll the check as if you were attempting it. If you get a 10 or higher, your ally can add 2 to her check (*Core Rulebook* 86).

TAKING 10 OR 20

If you're not in immediate danger, you might have the option to "take 10" or "take 20," which represents taking extra time to guarantee a roll of either 10 (success at most mundane tasks) or 20 (success at almost any task) (*Core Rulebook* 86).

Skills

(H) **Skills** are capabilities you can improve with training—knowing ancient languages, disguising yourself and your allies, and so on—and are a key component of who your character is. Throughout the game, you'll be asked to attempt **skill checks** to determine whether your character succeeds at tasks based on that skill.

When you gain a new level, you'll also gain a certain number of **skill ranks** you can assign. The number of skill ranks you have in any one skill can never exceed your character level, but you can keep investing in the same skills as you level up. The number of skill ranks you get at every level is listed in the Skills section of your class guide.

Each class has a list of **class skills**, which represents the skills at which characters of that class are particularly adept at. The first time you put a rank into a class skill, you get an extra +3 bonus to that skill. Your class skills are listed in the Skills section of your class guide, along with suggestions for which skills you should put ranks into when you begin creating your character.

You can use some skills **untrained**—meaning that even if you haven't put any ranks into them, you can attempt a check and add the appropriate ability modifier. When a skill has an asterisk after its name on the character sheet, it can only be used if **trained**—you can't even try to use it unless you put at least 1 rank in it.

For each skill you choose, write "1" in the Ranks column on your character sheet. Write "3" in the Misc. Mod. column for any class skills that you put a rank into. Since each skill is based on a different ability, you also get to add one of your ability modifiers to each skill check. Your character sheet tells you which ability each skill is based on; write the appropriate modifier in the Ability Mod. column for each skill. If you have a skill modifier from your class or race, such as an elf's bonus on Perception checks, add that to the Misc. Mod. column for that skill.

Weapon and Armor Proficiencies

This section of the guide tells you what types of weapons and armor that class can use, and gives suggestions for specific weapons and armor to start with. Armor comes in three main types: light, medium, and heavy (*Core Rulebook* 149). Weapons fall into multiple classes describing how they're used—melee or ranged—and what sort of training is needed to use them: simple, martial, or exotic (*Core Rulebook* 140).

If you're not using the weapons and armor named in the Suggested Starting Gear section for your class, adjust your total gold remaining to account for spending more or less.

The character sheet doesn't have a section for proficiencies, but you can note them down in the Special Abilities section of your character sheet.

Feats

(J) **Feats** are special tricks you know or talents for doing certain things better than others can. Most characters get one feat at 1st level, but human characters and certain classes get an extra feat. The number of feats you get at 1st level is listed in the Feats section of your class guide. Some feats have **prerequisites**, which are certain conditions you must meet to take the feat (for example, a Charisma score of at least 13 or a base attack bonus of +4 or higher).

Write your feats in the Feats section on the back of your character sheet. If a feat gives you an option that alters your rolls or statistics when you use it, note that next to the feat name so you don't have to look it up. For example, if you have the Power Attack feat (*Core Rulebook* 131), you might want to write "Can choose −1 on melee attack rolls for +2 on damage rolls" next to it for convenience.

Class Features

Each class has special powers and characteristics that distinguish it from other classes. For example, the sorcerer and wizard are both arcane spellcasters, but the sorcerer's bloodline bestows various unique powers upon her, while the wizard has an arcane bond with a creature or item. Your class guide outlines the special features of your class in the Class Features section.

(J) Record these class features in the Special Abilities section of your character sheet. Some class features may simply enhance skills or attacks, in which case you should

FAVORED CLASS BONUSES

Each class guide also contains a reminder to choose one of two options for whenever you attain a level in your character's favored class. Your character's favored class is generally the one you choose at 1st level. Each time you gain a new level in that class, you can choose to gain either 1 extra hit point or 1 extra skill rank. If you're playing a character that doesn't get many skill ranks at each level, you might want to compensate by selecting the skill rank. On the other hand, that extra hit point could make all the difference in a battle. Don't forget this bonus when you level up (see page 36)!

record those bonuses next to the features that they modify. Even though you're writing the effects of these features elsewhere, you should still note them in the Special Abilities section and add a brief description of what they do, so you remember where the benefits came from.

Spellcasting

(K) The various spellcasting classes use magic differently, and you can choose how to best utilize this section to track your spells. Regardless of your method, be sure fill out some of the information described below. For more information on spells, see pages 35, 138, and 139.

The Spells per Day column indicates the number of spells you can cast or prepare per day for each spell level, determined by your class. Check to see whether you get bonus spells (*Core Rulebook* 17) to write in the Bonus Spells column. The sum of these numbers indicates the total spells per day of each spell level you can cast.

Bards and sorcerers should write their spells known at each spell level in the Spells Known column. Other spellcasters can ignore this column.

The Spell Save DC column determines the saving throw target number for opponents to resist your spells. For each spell level, that number is 10 + the level of the spell + your spellcasting ability score modifier (Intelligence for wizards; Wisdom for clerics, druids, and rangers; and Charisma for bards, paladins, and sorcerers). See Saving Throws on page 31 for more information, or read page 121 of the Playing the Game section.

If you're a cleric, write your domains and 1st-level domain powers in the Domains/Specialty School section of your character sheet—see page 53 for more on domains. If you're a wizard, write your school specialization and 1st-level school power in this section—see page 107 for more on specialty schools. Sorcerers should write their bloodline (see page 97) in this section.

Suggested Starting Gear

(I) Suggested Starting Gear: Each class guide contains suggestions for gear to purchase at 1st level. Information on normal equipment can be found in the Equipment chapter of the *Core Rulebook* beginning on page 140. The gear bundles listed in the Suggested Starting Gear section of the class guide list equipment for each of the class themes. These bundles assume that your character started with the average amount of **gold pieces** (or **gp** for short) indicated on the Starting Wealth table (*Core Rulebook* 140). The cost of each gear bundle has been rounded to the nearest gold piece. In addition, you receive a free set of clothing worth up to 10 gp (*Core Rulebook* 159).

The total weight for each bundle is listed for both Small and Medium characters. Add up the weight of all your gear and compare the total to your carrying capacity (*Core Rulebook* 171). If your character's gear is reducing your speed, you can drop or stow items (such as bedrolls and food) in perilous situations. Fill in your gear choices and the weight of each item in the Gear section on the back of your character sheet. If you have armor or a shield, fill in its information in the AC Items section.

SPECIAL ABILITIES

Many creatures and classes have special abilities that work like spells. See page 221 of the *Core Rulebook* for details.

SELECTING SKILLS, FEATS, AND SPELLS

As you create your character, you have a number of choices to make regarding your character's skills, feats, and spells (if your character is a spellcaster). The following section is here to help you make sense of the descriptions of these options in the *Core Rulebook* so you can make the choice that's right for your character.

Reading a Skill

Skills represent some of the most basic abilities your character possesses. At every level, you receive a number of skill ranks to invest in skills that are important to your character, but to decide which ones are critical, you need to understand what each skill can accomplish. The Skills chapter of the *Core Rulebook* begins on page 86.

Name and Description: This section gives you a basic understanding of what the skill is all about. The description also specifies the ability score that is tied to that skill and whether or not wearing armor affects your use of that skill. If a skill's description doesn't fit the concept of your character, you can probably move on to the next skill.

Check: This section describes how you use the skill and what you can accomplish by making a successful skill check.

Action: This describes the sort of action you need to take to use the skill. Each round of play you have only a limited number of actions you can take. For more information on action types, see page 124 after you have finished creating your character.

Try Again: Some skills allow you to retry the check if you fail at your first attempt. If a skill allows you to try again, that fact is noted here.

Special: If the skill has any special rules associated with it, they are noted here.

Reading a Feat

Feats modify your character in a wide variety of ways, often giving you bonuses on certain actions or checks, or giving you special actions that only you can perform. Since the number of feats that you possess is limited, it's important to make sure you pick those that support your character concept whenever you get a new one. Feat descriptions contain the following information. The Feats chapter of the *Core Rulebook* begins on page 112.

Name and Description: These give you a basic understanding of what the feat is all about. Some feats have descriptors after them such as "(Combat)" or "(Metamagic)." While any character can take such feats, some classes give bonus feats that must be used to select feats with a specific descriptor.

Prerequisites: Some feats require that you meet certain criteria before you can take them. These prerequisites are listed here. Note that you can apply all the bonuses from gaining a level to your character before you select your feats, which might allow you to qualify for a feat at that time instead of waiting until a later level. For more on leveling up, see page 36.

Benefit: This tells you what bonuses the feat gives you. For many feats, this is a bonus to a particular ability, skill, saving throw, or attack roll. You should note this bonus in the appropriate area when you take the feat. For example, if you take the Iron Will feat, you gain a +2 bonus on Will saving throws. You should add this bonus to your Misc Modifier column and total it into your Will save when you take this feat.

Other feats grant you the ability to perform a special action, such as Spring Attack. While you don't have to spell out everything these feats can do on your character sheet, you should remember to make use of them during play, and possibly even write down their page numbers for easy reference.

Normal: This section describes how the rules work for a character who doesn't have the feat in question. It's usually just included for comparison purposes.

Special: If the feat has any special rules associated with it, they're noted here.

Reading a Spell

If your character class can cast spells, your class guide has a section on spellcasting that tells you how your spellcasting ability works and recommends spell choices at various levels. It doesn't tell you the full rules for spells, though—these rules can be found in the Spells chapter of the *Core Rulebook* (beginning on page 224). A spell's entry there contains a number of pieces of important information to help you understand how it works in the game, and follows the format below.

Name: This is what the spell is called. Note that some spells have alternate versions that are either more or less powerful. These are usually noted with the Lesser or Greater prefix, but they are listed alphabetically in the spell descriptions by the spell name.

Statistics: Each spell contains a number of important statistics that tell you how the spell is used in the game. These include its school, level, range, duration, and more (numbers 2–10 in the diagram below). Note that some spells are modifications of other existing spells, working the same way except as noted in the new description. In such cases, the new spell shares the statistics of the existing spell unless noted otherwise.

Description: Beyond the statistics of the spell, this tells you what the spell actually does when you cast it. If the spell targets your foes, it also tells you what happens if they resist its effects.

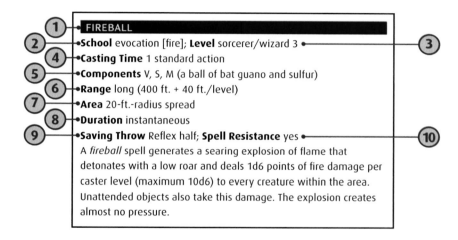

FIREBALL

School evocation [fire]; **Level** sorcerer/wizard 3
Casting Time 1 standard action
Components V, S, M (a ball of bat guano and sulfur)
Range long (400 ft. + 40 ft./level)
Area 20-ft.-radius spread
Duration instantaneous
Saving Throw Reflex half; **Spell Resistance** yes
A *fireball* spell generates a searing explosion of flame that detonates with a low roar and deals 1d6 points of fire damage per caster level (maximum 10d6) to every creature within the area. Unattended objects also take this damage. The explosion creates almost no pressure.

(1) The spell's **name** goes at the top.

(2) This is the spell's **school**, which is important for wizards (who can choose a school of magic as part of their training) and some monsters (for example, undead are immune to enchantment spells), and has other rules effects. (*Core Rulebook* 209)

(3) The spell's **level** tells you which classes can get that spell and the spell level for each of those classes. A spell can have different spell levels for different classes—for example, *hold person* is a 2nd-level cleric spell but a 3rd-level sorcerer/wizard spell. (*Core Rulebook* 212)

(4) The **casting time** is the kind of action casting the spell is. Casting most combat spells is a standard action, but some take longer. (*Core Rulebook* 213)

(5) This entry tells you what kind of **components** (magic words, gestures, or weird ingredients) the spell uses. (*Core Rulebook* 212)

(6) The spell's **range** may be a specific distance (like "touch" or "30 feet"), or it might change with your caster level ("short" or "long"). (*Core Rulebook* 213)

(7) The spell's **area** is listed here. (*Core Rulebook* 214)

(8) The spell's **duration** is how long the spell lasts. (*Core Rulebook* 215)

(9) If the spell allows a **saving throw** to resist it, the kind of saving throw and the effect of a successful save are listed here. If no saving throw is allowed, this section says "none." The DC of the saving throw is 10 + the spell's spell level for the class you're using to cast it + your spellcasting ability modifier. (*Core Rulebook* 216).

(10) Some creatures have an ability called **spell resistance** that gives them an extra chance to not be affected by a spell. This line tells you whether the spell resistance ability can work against the spell or not. (*Core Rulebook* 217)

CASTING SPELLS FROM SCROLLS

A scroll contains the written form of a spell. You can cast a spell once from a scroll; as it's activated, the writing vanishes. To cast a spell from a scroll, you must have that spell on the spell list for your class (wizards can't cast cleric spells, for example). If the spell is of a higher level than you can currently cast, you run the risk of the spell failing. See page 490 of the *Core Rulebook* for more details about casting spells from scrolls.

SPELL LEVEL AND CHARACTER LEVEL

You'll note that there are references to "spell level" in spells. This isn't the same as your character level! The spell level refers to a level from 1st to 9th that reflects how powerful a spell is. As your spellcaster gains levels, she will have access to spells of higher spell levels. See your class guide for details.

BONUS SPELLS

Spellcasting characters are able to gain access to additional spells based on how high their primary spellcasting ability score is (such as Intelligence for wizards). Each class has specific details. For more on the rule in general, see Table 1–3 on page 17 of the *Core Rulebook*.

LEVELING UP

The Leveling Up section of each class guide explains the abilities your character gets at 2nd level and higher. Some of these abilities are enhancements to earlier abilities, and others are entirely new.

For each new level your character attains, the Level Up bar for that level in your class guide provides details on all the things that change.

Things That Change at Every Level: Regardless of your class, some aspects of your character change every time you level up.

- At every level, you will gain new hit points to increase your total.
- At every level, you will gain new skill ranks to spend on skills.
- At some levels, your base attack bonus will increase. For some classes, this happens at every level
- At some levels, one or more of your base saving throw bonuses increase (Fortitude, Reflex, or Will).

Each of these changes is shown in the bar along the top of the section for that level—all you need to do is add the number in each box to its respective score.

For example, let's say you're playing a 1st-level barbarian with 12 total hit points and a Constitution score of 15, meaning that your Constitution modifier is +2 (see page 31 for more on ability score modifiers). Your GM has just told you that your character has reached 2nd level. Turn to that level's Level Up bar, which looks like this.

The hp box in your 2nd Level section says "1d12 + Con." Suppose you roll a d12 and get an 8. Next, you add your Constitution modifier (+2), for a total of 10. Finally, you add that total to your earlier hit point total of 12—you now have a total of 22 hit points.

Not every saving throw bonus increases at each level, but often at least one of them increases.

You get a set number of skill ranks based on your class, and add your Intelligence modifier to that number to get your total new skill ranks for that level. You must assign all of the skill ranks when leveling up; you can't bank skill points to spend at future levels, but you will get new ones at each level.

Many classes have a special feature that increases at each level, such as a barbarian's total rounds of rage or the number of spells in a wizard's spellbook. Such features are included in your class's Level Up bar.

2nd Level

	HP	SKILL RANKS	BAB	FORT	REF	WILL	RAGE
	1d12 + Con	4 + Int	+1	+1	—	—	+2 rounds

Your hit points increase by 1d12 + your Constitution modifier. Unlike at 1st level, you must roll for these hit points.

You gain a number of skill ranks equal to 4 + your Intelligence modifier. If you're human, don't forget the bonus skill rank per level.

Your base attack bonus and Fortitude save bonus each go up by 1.

Rage Power: At every even level you choose a rage power, which gives you an extra ability or boost whenever you're raging. Most are passive bonuses—they're always working, without needing to be activated, but a few are activated with an action (such as a standard action). Some can be used only once per rage, making you mightier when you really need it.

Consider taking the no escape rage power, which lets you chase down a fleeing enemy and still make a full attack on your next turn.

Consider taking the knockback rage power, which allows you to bull rush an enemy across the battlefield once per round.

Uncanny Dodge: This ability prevents you from being flat-footed, meaning you're not as vulnerable when an enemy surprises you.

In addition to the increases listed in your Level Up bar, most classes get other new powers each time they level up—new feats, spells, powers for animal companions, and so on. These differ for each class, and are described below the Level Up bar. In many cases, when you have choices (such as a new feat or class feature), this section gives you suggestions about those options.

When there are good choices for feats, spells, or other powers appropriate for your theme, your theme's icon appears under the class feature, along with theme-specific advice on your options.

The Level Up bars look a bit different for each class, since the classes grows in different ways. For example, some classes have class-specific powers that increase at every level or every other level, like the amount of healing energy a cleric can channel or the number of spells in a wizard's spellbook. If your class has such a feature, these increases are shown under a red heading in the upper-right corner of the Level Up bar for each level.

Spells

As spellcasting characters gain levels, they can cast more spells per day, and cast more powerful spells. If your character class is primarily a spellcasting one—the bard, cleric, druid, sorcerer, or wizard—the basics of how you cast spells is explained with the rest of the information you need to know at 1st level. If your class doesn't gain spells until later levels (namely the paladin or ranger), you'll learn about how to prepare and cast spells in the Level Up bar for the level at which you first gain the ability to cast spells.

At each new level, the Level Up section informs you whether you can now cast spells of a new spell level, and also reminds you of increases to the number of lower-level spells you can cast per day. If your character learns additional spells when leveling up, be sure to add those spells to the list on your character sheet.

CHOOSING SPELLS
If your character is a spellcaster, your choice of spells is one of the key aspects defining who he is. You may want to choose spells that follow a particular theme to emphasize your character's nature or personality, but know that you may encounter creatures that are immune to certain types of spells or situations that require versatility. Consider choosing a few spells that differ from your typical selections.

ATTACKS AND WEAPONS

The class guides don't have specific sections showing you how to calculate your weapon attack bonuses, as weapon choice is individual and most classes have many weapons options available. Weapon attack bonus and damage are influenced by multiple factors, like your class, your character's ability scores, and which weapon you've chosen. Other factors like feats and class abilities can also affect attacks and damage, so it's helpful to write any modifiers that come from these sources down on your character sheet ahead of time, to let you clearly see your options and make combat easier. For more on combat, see pages 120–143 of this book and the Combat chapter starting on page 178 of the *Core Rulebook*.

Weapon Attack Bonuses

Your attack bonus with a particular weapon is determined as follows.

> **Attack bonus** = your base attack bonus + your Strength or Dexterity modifier (depending on the weapon and attack) + any other bonuses or penalties

When you attack with a particular weapon, roll a d20 and add your weapon's attack bonus as determined above to find out whether your attack is successful.

Many factors affect attack bonuses, such as weapon quality, effects of spell, and certain feats. You may also get bonuses or take penalties based on your size. If you're using a ranged weapon, you add your Dexterity modifier instead of your Strength, and you may take penalties based on your distance from the target (see Range on page 144 of the *Core Rulebook*). Make sure to write down your attack bonus for each weapon you plan to use regularly.

Weapon Damage

When your attack hits your enemy, you determine how much damage your foe takes by rolling other dice. Find out which die to use by looking up your weapon on page 142 of the *Core Rulebook*. Much of the time, your weapon's damage is based on this formula.

> **Damage dealt** = damage die or dice + your Strength modifier + any other bonuses or penalties

Make sure to write down your damage die or dice for each weapon you plan to use regularly. Just as with attack bonuses, many factors can grant you damage bonuses, like using magic weapons, having various feats, or being affected by certain spells.

YOUR CHARACTER SHEET

Your character sheet helps you calculate and remember everything you need to know to play your character in both combat and noncombat situations. The information that goes on your sheet is found elsewhere in this section, in your class guide, and in Additional Details on page 114.

 (A) Character Details: This section contains personal story information about your character, like her name, homeland, and deity, as well as some rules-focused details like class, race, and size category.

 (B) Abilities: Write your character's ability scores and modifiers here, as well as temporary modifiers applied during play.

 (C) Hit Points and Initiative: Record your character's total hit points, and keep track of any damage she's taken here. This is also where you record your character's initiative bonus and damage reduction (if applicable).

 (D) Armor Class: Write down your character's Armor Class (including touch and flat-footed AC) and any temporary modifiers applied during play in this section.

 (E) Saving Throws: Record your character's bonuses to saving throws in this section, along with any temporary adjustments.

 (F) Attacks: Note down both your character's base attack bonus and the attack bonuses with each of her weapons in this section. Her Combat Maneuver Bonus and Defense (CMB and CMD) and Spell Resistance (SR) are found here as well.

 (G) Speed: Record your character's base speed, and speed under special circumstances—swimming, wearing armor, and so on.

 (H) Skills and Languages: Your character's bonuses to skills are recorded here, as are the languages she speaks.

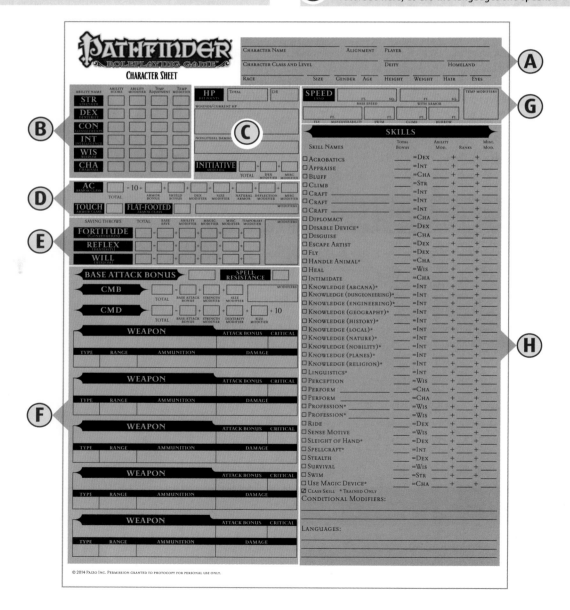

© 2014 Paizo Inc. Permission granted to photocopy for personal use only.

Gear: Keep track of your character's money and the weight of the possessions she's carrying here. Note the non-weapon gear she has in the Gear section, as well as any items that affect Armor Class in the AC Items section.

 Feats and Special Abilities: Write down the feats you have chosen for your character in this section; include a short summary of each feat's effect. Any special abilities from your character's race or other sources should be noted in the Special Abilities section. If you're tracking your experience points, do so at the bottom of this section.

 Spells: This section helps you track which spells your character know, how many spells per day she can cast for each spell level, the Difficulty Class for saving throws against her spells, and other spellcasting details.

 The class guides introduce most of the basic concepts you'll need to create a 1st-level character, but they don't cover every detail on your character sheet. After you've gone through the 1st-level section of your class guide, turn to the Additional Details section on pages 114–117 for help with filling in the rest of your character's details.

PATHFINDER RPG CHARACTER SHEET

AC ITEMS

	BONUS	TYPE	CHECK PENALTY	SPELL FAILURE	WEIGHT	PROPERTIES

TOTALS

SPELLS

SPELLS KNOWN	SPELL SAVE DC	LEVEL	SPELLS PER DAY	BONUS SPELLS
		0		—
		1st		
		2nd		
		3rd		
		4th		
		5th		
		6th		
		7th		
		8th		
		9th		

CONDITIONAL MODIFIERS

DOMAINS/SPECIALTY SCHOOL

0 □□□□□□□□

1st □□□□□□□□

2nd □□□□□□□□

3rd □□□□□□□□

4th □□□□□□□□

5th □□□□□□□□

6th □□□□□□□□

7th □□□□□□□□

8th □□□□□□□□

9th □□□□□□□□

GEAR

ITEM	WT.

TOTAL WEIGHT

LIGHT LOAD		LIFT OVER HEAD	
MEDIUM LOAD		LIFT OFF GROUND	
HEAVY LOAD		DRAG OR PUSH	

MONEY

CP

SP

GP

PP

FEATS

SPECIAL ABILITIES

EXPERIENCE POINTS | NEXT LEVEL

BARBARIAN

Barbarians destroy enemies with their athletic skill, peerless endurance, and savage rage. Your barbarian might be a berserker who loses herself in battle frenzy, or a smasher who demolishes every obstacle in her path.

 **BERSERKER (PAGE 16)** **SMASHER (PAGE 24)**

ALIGNMENT

You can't have a lawful alignment.

HIT DIE

Your Hit Die is a d12 (the highest in the game)! At 1st level, you have 12 hit points plus your Constitution modifier.

BASE ATTACK BONUS +1

Your base attack bonus is +1, and it will increase at every level.

SAVING THROWS

Barbarians are known for their physical toughness.

FORTITUDE +2

Your Fortitude save bonus is +2 plus your Constitution modifier.

REFLEX +0

Your Reflex save bonus is +0 plus your Dexterity modifier.

WILL +0

Your Will save bonus is +0 plus your Wisdom modifier.

ABILITY SCORES

Barbarians need a high Strength score to deliver powerful swings in melee combat. A high Constitution score lets you use your rage ability (see next page) for longer and keeps you alive while you wreak havoc. Don't ignore Dexterity; a good Dexterity score improves your Armor Class and helps you act earlier in a fight.

SKILLS

Barbarians' physical toughness makes them ideal party members to lead the way against physical challenges, and their connection to their own primal nature gives them insight into the instincts that drive other wild creatures.

 **SKILL RANKS PER LEVEL**
4 + Intelligence modifier

Class Skills for Barbarians

Acrobatics
Climb
Craft
Handle Animal
Intimidate
Knowledge (nature)
Perception
Ride
Survival
Swim

- Having a high Strength score means you have natural athletic ability, so consider putting a rank into Climb or Swim to make the most of it.
- Social skills are vital because not every encounter involves a fight—consider channeling your barely leashed rage into the Intimidate skill.
- Put a rank into Perception so enemies have a harder time sneaking up on you.
- Barbarians make talented outdoorsmen, so consider putting a rank into Survival.

 Remember, if you put at least 1 rank into any of your class skills, you get a +3 bonus to your total for that skill to represent your class training. At 1st level, you can't put more than 1 rank in a particular skill. If you're human, you get an additional skill rank to spend at each level, including 1st level.

 TIP On your character sheet, make sure to put a check in the box to the left of each of the skills listed above to show that they're class skills.

WEAPON AND ARMOR PROFICIENCIES

Your combat training allows you to freely use most types of weapons and all but the heaviest armor.

Most barbarians favor one big, high-damage melee weapon (like a greatsword). The increased Strength you get while raging boosts your damage tremendously. If you like taking bigger risks for bigger rewards, try a weapon that does less base damage but delivers immensely powerful critical hits (see page 136).

You'll be hurtling into combat often, so spend some money on armor. Light studded leather or chain shirts will allow you more agility but give you less protection; medium armor such as a breastplate will slow you down, but the Armor Class increase might save your life.

FEATS

As a barbarian, you'll benefit most from feats that enhance your combat abilities, such as the ones below.

YOU GET ONE FEAT AT 1ST LEVEL
Two if you're human

Extra Rage	Get 6 additional rounds of rage every day. You can take this feat multiple times; its effects stack. This is useful if you expect multiple encounters per day. (*Core Rulebook* 124)
Power Attack	Want to eliminate an enemy with a single blow? Trade accuracy for power—take a –1 penalty on melee attack rolls to gain a +2 bonus on damage rolls. It's even more effective when you use a weapon with two hands! (*Core Rulebook* 131)
Step Up	Follow and slay archers and spellcasters who try to step outside of your reach. If an adjacent foe takes a 5-foot step, you can take a 5-foot step as an immediate action to remain adjacent to him. (*Core Rulebook* 135)
Toughness	Absorb powerful hits without flinching—add 3 to your total hit points, plus an additional 1 for every Hit Die you possess or gain beyond 3. (*Core Rulebook* 135)

CLASS FEATURES

Fast Movement: Add 10 to the base move speed for your race. This ability is automatic, so you don't have to activate it (*Core Rulebook* 31).

Rage: This is the central feature of the barbarian class—the ability to fly into a destructive, unstoppable rage (*Core Rulebook* 32). When you rage, you gain the following:

- *+4 Morale Bonus to Strength*: This bonus boosts your melee attacks' damage and helps you hit. It also helps with climbing, swimming, and bashing doors apart, so don't forget this utility when you're in a tight spot.
- *+4 Morale Bonus to Constitution (+2 hit points per Hit Die and +2 bonus on Fortitude saving throws)*: The extra hit points and bonus on Fortitude saves help you survive fights, but remember that they go away when your rage ends; they're a loan, and once you stop raging, you have to pay back all of those borrowed hit points, even if it kills you—literally! Keep an ally with healing abilities around in case you're gravely injured while raging.
- *+2 Morale Bonus on Will Saving Throws*: Your rage allows you to focus on your enemies and not be distracted by illusions, helping you take out tricky spellcasters and monsters who can cloud warriors' minds.
- *–2 Penalty to Armor Class*: Novice barbarians often make the mistake of raging at every opportunity. It might feel good to hit for gratuitous damage against puny foes, but the Armor Class penalty during rage might allow enemies to hit you more often.

You can rage a number of rounds per day equal to
4 + your Constitution modifier + 2 for every barbarian level after 1st level.

TIP While raging, you can't use Charisma-, Intelligence-, or Dexterity-based skills. After your rage ends, you become fatigued (*Core Rulebook* 567) for 2 × the number of rounds you spent in rage, which makes it harder to hit enemies and dodge attacks until you recover.

SUGGESTED STARTING GEAR

Barbarians start with 105 gp.

Berserker: Greatsword, morningstar, dagger, javelins (4), studded leather, backpack, bedroll, flint and steel, sunrod, trail rations (4 days), waterskin, whetstone; *Cost* 97 gp (8 gp left); *Weight* 60 lbs. (Medium) or 30 lbs. (Small).

Smasher: Greataxe, warhammer, dagger, javelins (4), scale mail, backpack, bedroll, flint and steel, sunrod, trail rations (4 days), waterskin, whetstone; *Cost* 96 gp (9 gp left); *Weight* 76 lbs. (Medium) or 38 lbs. (Small).

FAVORED CLASS BONUS

For each barbarian level you attain, gain:

+1 *to hp total*

Adding to your hit points helps you survive combat.

OR

+1 *skill rank*

Your skills reflect your wilderness mastery.

LEVELING UP

The next few pages explain the abilities you get at 2nd level and higher. Some of these abilities are just additions to your 1st-level abilities, and are noted in a Level Up bar: additional hit points and skill ranks, additional rage rounds per day, and increases to your base attack bonus, Fortitude save bonus, Reflex save bonus, and Will save bonus.

This information is also presented as Table 3–2: Barbarian on page 32 of the *Pathfinder RPG Core Rulebook*.

 BERSERKER (PAGE 16)   **SMASHER** (PAGE 24)

Many of the class features you gain as you level up are focused on your combat abilities, particularly your ability to rage. You should carefully evaluate your options when selecting a rage power or feat to make sure it fits with the other choices you have made for your character. This also applies to selecting among the available gear and magic items your character acquires as you go on adventures. If you find yourself with a powerful magic sword, consider picking up a feat that enhances your abilities while you're wielding it.

2nd Level

HP	SKILL RANKS	BAB	FORT	REF	WILL	RAGE
1d12 + Con	4 + Int	+1	+1	—	—	+2 rounds

Your hit points increase by 1d12 + your Constitution modifier. Unlike at 1st level, you must roll for these hit points.

You gain a number of skill ranks equal to 4 + your Intelligence modifier. If you're human, don't forget the bonus skill rank per level.

Your base attack bonus and Fortitude save bonus each go up by 1.

Rage Power: At every even level you choose a rage power, which gives you an extra ability or boost whenever you're raging. Most are passive bonuses—they're always working, without needing to be activated, but a few are activated with an action (such as a standard action). Some can be used only once per rage, making you mightier when you really need it.

> Consider taking the no escape rage power, which lets you chase down a fleeing enemy and still make a full attack on your next turn.

> Consider taking the knockback rage power, which allows you to bull rush an enemy across the battlefield once per round.

Uncanny Dodge: This ability prevents you from being flat-footed, meaning you're not as vulnerable when an enemy surprises you.

3rd Level

HP	SKILL RANKS	BAB	FORT	REF	WILL	RAGE
1d12 + Con	4 + Int	+1	—	+1	+1	+2 rounds

Feat: You gain another feat. You should consider some of the same choices you had at 1st level. In addition, you might consider Iron Will, which helps to protect you against confusion and domination effects that might otherwise turn your strength against the party.

> If you took Power Attack at 1st level, consider taking Cleave, a feat that lets you hit two foes with one attack.

> If you took Power Attack at 1st level, consider taking Improved Sunder, which allows you to shatter your foes' weapons and armor.

Trap Sense +1: This ability helps you dodge traps more easily. It's still probably not a good idea to trigger traps unless you have to.

4th Level

HP	SKILL RANKS	BAB	FORT	REF	WILL	RAGE
1d12 + Con	4 + Int	+1	+1	—	—	+2 rounds

Ability Score Increase: You gain a permanent +1 increase to one ability score of your choice. This should be added to an ability score that's important to you—like Strength or Constitution—especially if you have an odd number in either of them, as your modifier increases at even numbers.

Rage Power: You gain a rage power.

> Consider taking the animal fury rage power, which grants you a bite attack while you're raging.

> Consider taking the strength surge rage power, which allows you to perform a truly herculean feat of strength once per rage.

5th Level

	HP	SKILL RANKS	BAB	FORT	REF	WILL	RAGE
	1d12 + Con	4 + Int	+1	—	—	—	+2 rounds

Feat: You gain another feat. You should consider some of the same choices you had at earlier levels. In addition, consider taking advantage of your savage nature with Intimidating Prowess, which allows you to add your Strength modifier to your Intimidate checks. Given your high Strength score, this bonus should be impressive.

 If you took Cleave earlier and enjoy using it, consider taking Great Cleave. Great Cleave works just like Cleave, but there's no limit to the number of enemies you could hit in one swing—great if you're in a crowded area!

If you took the knockback rage power earlier, consider taking Improved Bull Rush, which makes you even better at pushing enemies into dangerous terrain.

Improved Uncanny Dodge: This ability prevents you from being flanked, except by rogues who are at least 4 levels higher than you.

6th Level

	HP	SKILL RANKS	BAB	FORT	REF	WILL	RAGE
	1d12 + Con	4 + Int	+1	+1	+1	+1	+2 rounds

Attack Bonus: Now that your base attack bonus is +6, you gain a second attack (at an attack bonus of +1) whenever you make a full attack (see page 122). From now on, any bonuses to your BAB apply to this attack as well.

Rage Power: You gain a rage power.

 Consider taking the roused anger rage power. This allows you to begin raging even if you're fatigued, though you become exhausted afterward (exhaustion imposes harsher penalties than fatigue). Because rage is so important to you, this ability grants you a valuable contingency in case you become fatigued or need to re-enter rage very quickly.

 Consider taking the intimidating glare rage power, which allows you to scare a nearby creature as a move action (a scared creature is less likely to hit you, and it's more vulnerable to your allies' spells).

Trap Sense +2: Your trap sense ability bonus increases by 1.

7th Level

	HP	SKILL RANKS	BAB	FORT	REF	WILL	RAGE
	1d12 + Con	4 + Int	+1	—	—	—	+2 rounds

Feat: You gain another feat. You should consider some of the same choices you had at earlier levels, but this is your first opportunity to pick some very powerful feats that have significant prerequisites.

 Consider taking the Lunge feat, which allows you to increase your reach while you make attacks on your turn. This is perfect for making a full attack when your enemy would otherwise be just a little too far away.

 If you enjoy using Improved Sunder, consider taking Greater Sunder, which allows you to sunder objects more easily and deal any excess damage to the item's wielder. If you like the idea of making one big attack each round, consider taking Vital Strike, which allows you to deal extra damage when you attack only once instead of multiple times.

Damage Reduction 1/—: This lets you shrug off attacks, ignoring 1 point of damage every time a physical weapon hits you.

8th Level

	HP	SKILL RANKS	BAB	FORT	REF	WILL	RAGE
	1d12 + Con	4 + Int	+1	+1	—	—	+2 rounds

Ability Score Increase: You gain a permanent +1 increase to an ability score.

Rage Power: You gain a rage power.

 Consider taking the unexpected strike rage power. This allows you to strike anyone who approaches you while you're raging, so you can hit a creature once on *its* turn and then keep up the offensive on *your* turn.

 If you've taken the intimidating glare rage power, consider taking the terrifying howl rage power. This lets you send any foes you've already intimidated into a panic, causing them to flee in terror.

9th Level

	HP	SKILL RANKS	BAB	FORT	REF	WILL	RAGE
	1d12 + Con	4 + Int	+1	—	+1	+1	+2 rounds

Feat: You gain another feat. You now qualify for Improved Critical, a powerful feat that doubles the critical threat range of your favorite weapon. By now you have likely landed some amazing critical hits, so you know how powerful this feat can be.

Trap Sense +3: Your trap sense ability bonus increases by 1.

10th Level

	HP	SKILL RANKS	BAB	FORT	REF	WILL	RAGE
	1d12 + Con	4 + Int	+1	+1	—	—	+2 rounds

Damage Reduction 2/—: Your damage reduction increases by 1.

Rage Power: You gain a rage power.

Consider taking the clear mind rage power, which allows you to reroll a single Will save during a rage. This might be all that saves you from being mind-controlled and turning on your allies.

Consider taking the unexpected strike rage power. There's no reason that the berserker should have all the fun.

11th Level

	HP	SKILL RANKS	BAB	FORT	REF	WILL	RAGE
	1d12 + Con	4 + Int	+1	—	—	—	+2 rounds

Feat: You gain another feat. If you selected Vital Strike earlier and enjoy using it, consider taking Improved Vital Strike, which increases the bonus damage even more. Also consider Critical Focus, which makes you better at confirming critical hits; Critical Focus is also a prerequisite for critical-boosting feats you might want to gain later.

Attack Bonus: Now that your base attack bonus is +11, you gain a third attack (at an attack bonus of +1) whenever you make a full attack (see page 122). From now on, any bonuses to your BAB apply to this attack as well.

Greater Rage: Your rage bonuses to Strength and Constitution both increase to +6, and your rage bonus on Will saves increases to +3.

12th Level

	HP	SKILL RANKS	BAB	FORT	REF	WILL	RAGE
	1d12 + Con	4 + Int	+1	+1	+1	+1	+2 rounds

Ability Score Increase: You gain a permanent +1 increase to an ability score of your choice.

Rage Power: You gain a rage power.

Consider taking the fearless rage rage power. This makes you immune to most types of fear-based effects while raging, making it that much harder to take you out of the fight.

Consider taking the mighty swing rage power, which lets you automatically confirm one critical threat while you're raging. This is especially useful for your third attack of the round, since you're less likely to confirm critical threats with that attack.

Trap Sense +4: Your trap sense ability bonus increases by 1.

13th Level

	HP	SKILL RANKS	BAB	FORT	REF	WILL	RAGE
	1d12 + Con	4 + Int	+1	—	—	—	+2 rounds

Feat: You gain another feat. If you selected Critical Focus at 11th level, consider taking Staggering Critical, which causes the victim of a critical hit to lose part of its action on its next turn.

Damage Reduction 3/—: Your damage reduction increases by 1.

14th Level

	HP	SKILL RANKS	BAB	FORT	REF	WILL	RAGE
	1d12 + Con	4 + Int	+1	+1	—	—	+2 rounds

Indomitable Will: This ability grants you a large bonus on Will saves against enchantment spells and effects.

Rage Power: You gain a rage power. By 14th level, you probably have many of the essential rage powers, so now is a good time to explore other options. The increased damage reduction rage power is a solid choice.

15th Level

	HP	SKILL RANKS	BAB	FORT	REF	WILL	RAGE
	1d12 + Con	4 + Int	+1	—	+1	+1	+2 rounds

Feat: You gain another feat. Many critical strike feats are now available to you.

Trap Sense +5: Your trap sense ability increases by 1.

16th Level

	HP	SKILL RANKS	BAB	FORT	REF	WILL	RAGE
	1d12 + Con	4 + Int	+1	+1	—	—	+2 rounds

Ability Score Increase: You gain a permanent +1 increase to an ability score of your choice.

Attack Bonus: You gain a fourth attack (at an attack bonus of +1) when making a full attack. Any bonus to BAB applies to this attack as well.

Damage Reduction 4/—: Your damage reduction increases by 1.

Rage Power: You gain a rage power.

17th Level

	HP	SKILL RANKS	BAB	FORT	REF	WILL	RAGE
	1d12 + Con	4 + Int	+1	—	—	—	+2 rounds

Feat: You gain another feat. If you already selected Improved Vital Strike and enjoy it, consider taking Greater Vital Strike, which increases the damage dealt by the single attack even more.

Tireless Rage: Using your rage ability no longer fatigues you. This means you can enter rage more than once in a combat (raging, ending the rage, then raging again), allowing you additional uses of your "once per rage" abilities.

18th Level

	HP	SKILL RANKS	BAB	FORT	REF	WILL	RAGE
	1d12 + Con	4 + Int	+1	+1	+1	+1	+2 rounds

Rage Power: You gain a rage power.

Trap Sense +6: Your trap sense ability increases by 1.

19th Level

	HP	SKILL RANKS	BAB	FORT	REF	WILL	RAGE
	1d12 + Con	4 + Int	+1	—	—	—	+2 rounds

Feat: You gain another feat.

Damage Reduction 5/—: Your damage reduction increases by 1.

20th Level

	HP	SKILL RANKS	BAB	FORT	REF	WILL	RAGE
	1d12 + Con	4 + Int	+1	+1	—	—	+2 rounds

Ability Score Increase: You gain a permanent +1 increase to an ability score of your choice.

Mighty Rage: Your rage bonuses to Strength and Constitution both increase to +8, and your rage bonus on Will saves increases to +4.

Rage Power: You gain a rage power.

BARD

Versatile deceivers, inspiring commanders, and beguiling enchanters, bards are adept at most tasks. Your bard could be a trickster who ferrets out secrets or a troubadour who dazzles enemies and inspires allies.

 TRICKSTER (PAGE 26) **TROUBADOUR (PAGE 27)**

ALIGNMENT

You can be of any alignment.

HIT DIE

Your Hit Die is a d8. At 1st level, you have 8 hit points plus your Constitution modifier.

BASE ATTACK BONUS +0

Your base attack bonus is +0, but it will increase at most levels. Versatility is your greatest strength, but you can hold your own in combat.

SAVING THROWS

Your wit isn't the only quick thing about you, and you have a strong mind that resists trickery.

FORTITUDE +0

Your Fortitude save bonus is +0 plus your Constitution modifier.

REFLEX +2

Your Reflex save bonus is +2 plus your Dexterity modifier.

WILL +2

Your Will save bonus is +2 plus your Wisdom modifier.

ABILITY SCORES

Bards use their high Charisma scores to charm others. A high Intelligence score is also valuable because it grants additional skill points, and skills are one of the bard's strongest features.

TIP A high score in any ability might help you fill a secondary role, but high Dexterity and Constitution scores will help keep you alive in battle.

SKILLS

Bards have the longest list of class skills in the game. What's more, your versatile performance class feature will give you even more skills; at later levels, you'll gain the ability to use your Perform skill modifier in place of two other skill check modifiers. Take time to look over the skill list and plan ahead to avoid investing too heavily in the skills you want to replace.

SKILL RANKS PER LEVEL
6 + Intelligence modifier

Class Skills for Bards

Acrobatics
Appraise
Bluff
Climb
Craft
Diplomacy
Disguise
Escape Artist
Intimidate
Knowledge (all categories)
Linguistics
Perception
Perform
Profession
Sense Motive
Sleight of Hand
Spellcraft
Stealth
Use Magic Device

- If you want to trick others and lie effectively, put a rank in Bluff.
- Put a rank in Diplomacy so you can easily befriend and persuade others.
- A rank in at least one Knowledge skill will help you recall facts that might save your allies time and effort.
- Having a rank in Perception arms you against enemies trying to sneak up on you and your allies.
- Put a rank in a Perform skill so you can make the most of your class abilities.

 Remember, if you put at least 1 rank into any of your class skills, you get a +3 bonus to your total for that skill to represent your class training. At 1st level, you can't put more than 1 rank in a particular skill. If you're human, you gain an additional skill rank to spend at each level, including 1st level.

WEAPON AND ARMOR PROFICIENCIES

You are proficient with all simple weapons and a good selection of martial weapons. The rapier and the longsword are both reliable and effective choices for a main weapon. Don't forget a ranged weapon; although you're no slouch in hand-to-hand combat, it's often wiser to fire a few arrows and let front-line warriors take the hits. You're proficient with light armor and shields, which are enough to protect you from the occasional attack, but not enough to save you if you charge ahead alone.

FEATS

A bard can progress in many different directions, so there's no one right feat to take. That said, consider choosing a feat that either boosts your combat abilities or increases your skill check modifiers.

YOU GET ONE FEAT AT 1ST LEVEL
Two if you're human

Alertness	Gain a +2 bonus to two skills that are important to a bard: Perception and Sense Motive. These bonuses have the potential to increase at higher levels. (*Core Rulebook* 117)
Combat Expertise	Take a –1 penalty on attack rolls and combat maneuver checks to gain a +1 bonus to Armor Class. This is a prerequisite for several other interesting feats. (*Core Rulebook* 119)
Extra Performance	Get an additional 6 rounds of bardic performance each day (see below). This feat helps you avoid running out of your daily allotment as you gain more types of performances and more reasons to use the class feature. (*Core Rulebook* 124)
Improved Initiative	Gain a +4 bonus on initiative checks. Because many of your abilities enhance your allies, being able to act before they do maximizes your effectiveness. (*Core Rulebook* 127)

Also check out Toughness (*Core Rulebook* 135), for a dead bard tells no tales. Spell Focus (enchantment) (*Core Rulebook* 134) makes your persuasive spells harder to resist. Dodge (*Core Rulebook* 122) increases your Armor Class, which is helpful because your spellcasting ability penalizes you if you wear medium or heavy armor.

CLASS FEATURES

Bardic Knowledge: This ability allows you to attempt Knowledge skill checks even if you don't have any ranks in them, and it grants an ever-increasing bonus on all of those checks (*Core Rulebook* 35).	

Bardic Performance: The ability to weave a powerful performance that can inspire allies and confound enemies is a core feature of the bard class. You can use bardic performance for a number of rounds per day equal to 4 + your Charisma modifier, and you gain an additional 2 rounds for every additional bard level you gain (see page 35 of the *Core Rulebook* for all the 1st-level components of bardic performance).

Spells: Bards are versatile arcane spellcasters who don't need to prepare spells ahead of time—a bard can cast any spell he knows at any time, assuming he hasn't used up his daily allotment of spells of that level. Pick four 0-level spells (cantrips) and two 1st-level spells to learn (see Table 3–4: Bard Spells Known on page 37 of the *Core Rulebook*). If you have a Charisma score of 12 or higher, you can cast an extra 1st-level spell; if it's 20 or higher, you can cast two additional 1st-level spells (see Table 1–3: Ability Modifiers and Bonus Spells on page 17 of the *Core Rulebook*). The Difficulty Class to resist the effects of your spells equals 10 + the spell's spell level + your Charisma modifier.

    0-Level Spells: Some strong options for any bard are *ghost sound*, *light*, and *prestidigitation*.

    1st-Level Spells: The bard is not an exceptional healer, but knowing *cure light wounds* can be a lifesaver.

	For 0-level spells, consider *detect magic*, *mage hand*, *message*, and *open/close*, all of which help you covertly learn about others, sneak around, and communicate. For 1st-level spells, consider *alarm*, *disguise self*, *expeditious retreat*, *feather fall*, *magic aura*, *sleep*, and *ventriloquism*.
	For 0-level spells, consider *summon instrument*, which ensures you always have a tool for your trade. For 1st-level spells, consider *charm person*, *grease*, *hideous laughter*, *hypnotism*, and *remove fear*.

 TIP Bardic performance has some straightforward uses (like inspire courage), and several subtle abilities that require a lighter touch (like fascinate). As you grow more comfortable playing your character, experiment with finding new, creative uses for this ability.

LEVELING UP

The next few pages explain the abilities you get at 2nd level and higher. Some of these abilities are just additions to your 1st-level abilities, and are noted in a Level Up bar: additional hit points and skill ranks, additional bardic performance rounds per day, and increases to your base attack bonus, Fortitude save bonus, Reflex save bonus, and Will save bonus.

The information about what you gain at each level is also presented as Table 3–2: Bard and Table 3–3: Bard Spells Known on pages 36–37 of the *Core Rulebook*.

 TRICKSTER (PAGE 26)   **TROUBADOUR** (PAGE 27)

As a bard, you're one of the more versatile characters in the game. As you gain levels, be on the lookout for class features, feats, and spells that complement the strengths of your fellow adventurers. You can also use your wide variety of abilities to mitigate any of the weaknesses of the group. For example, if one of your allies is frequently knocked unconscious by foes, adding a few cure spells (like *cure light wounds* or *cure moderate wounds*) to your list of spells known might allow you to keep them in the fight.

2nd Level

	HP	SKILL RANKS	BAB	FORT	REF	WILL	PERFORMANCE
	1d8 + Con	6 + Int	+1	—	+1	+1	+2 rounds

Your hit points increase by 1d8 + your Constitution modifier. Unlike at 1st level, you must roll for these hit points.

Your base attack bonus, Reflex save bonus, and Will save bonus go up by 1.

Versatile Performance: You gain the ability to use one of your Perform skill modifiers in place of your modifiers for two skills related to that Perform skill. If at least one of these related skills doesn't use Charisma, picking that Perform skill effectively turns it into a Charisma-based skill for you; for example, Perform (dance) lets you use its bonus for Acrobatics and Fly, both of which are Dexterity-based skills.

 Oratory, percussion, and dance are useful choices for you.

 Sing, dance, and wind are useful choices for you.

Well-Versed: You gain a +4 bonus on saving throws against the same sort of tricky magic that you use yourself. This is a big help when dealing with enemy bards and monsters with music-based attacks.

Spells: You gain another 1st-level spell known and another 0-level spell known, and can cast an additional 1st-level spell per day.

3rd Level

	HP	SKILL RANKS	BAB	FORT	REF	WILL	PERFORMANCE
	1d8 + Con	6 + Int	+1	+1	—	—	+2 rounds

Feat: You gain another feat. Consider some of the same feat choices you had at 1st level.

Inspire Competence +2: This use of bardic performance allows you to give an ally a +2 bonus on skill checks. This can help a skilled ally overcome a difficult challenge or keep an unskilled ally from holding everyone back.

Spells: You gain another 1st-level spell known and another 0-level spell known, and can cast an additional 1st-level spell per day.

4th Level

	HP	SKILL RANKS	BAB	FORT	REF	WILL	PERFORMANCE
	1d8 + Con	6 + Int	+1	—	+1	+1	+2 rounds

Ability Score Increase: You gain a permanent +1 increase to one ability score of your choice. This should be added to an ability score that's important to you—like Charisma—especially if you have an odd number in that score, as this will increase your ability modifier.

Spells: You gain two 2nd-level spells known, and can cast one 2nd-level spell per day. *Glitterdust, heroism, mirror image,* and *suggestion* are all excellent choices. If your Charisma score is 14 or higher, you can cast an additional 2nd-level spell per day.

 Consider *invisibility, minor image,* and *silence.*

Consider *enthrall, sound burst,* and *tongues.*

5th Level

	HP	SKILL RANKS	BAB	FORT	REF	WILL	PERFORMANCE
	1d8 + Con	6 + Int	—	—	—	—	+2 rounds

Feat: You gain another feat. If you already have Spell Focus (enchantment) and often cast enchantment spells, consider Greater Spell Focus (enchantment), which increases the Difficulty Classes of such spells by an additional 1.

Inspire Courage +2: Your inspire courage performance bonus increases by 1.

Lore Master: You can take 10 on any Knowledge check in which you have ranks by calculating the result as if you had rolled a 10 on the check (see the sidebar on page 32). Once per day, you can take 20 (*Core Rulebook* 86).

Spells: You gain another 2nd-level spell known, and can cast an additional 2nd-level spell and an additional 1st-level spell per day. You can exchange one spell of 1st level or lower that you know for a different spell of the same level. For example, if you know *detect secret doors* but haven't really been using it, you can unlearn it and learn *feather fall* instead.

6th Level

	HP	SKILL RANKS	BAB	FORT	REF	WILL	PERFORMANCE
	1d8 + Con	6 + Int	+1	+1	+1	+1	+2 rounds

Suggestion: You can now use bardic performance to implant a suggestion in a target's mind. This is best used outside of combat, as keeping a creature fascinated long enough to make this work is very difficult when there are deadly distractions.

Versatile Performance: Choose another Perform skill to benefit from this ability. Avoid picking a Perform skill that duplicates skills related to your 2nd-level versatile performance class feature. For example, comedy and string both have Bluff as a related skill, so picking string when you already have comedy would get you only one new related skill.

Spells: You gain another 2nd-level spell known, and can cast an additional 2nd-level spell per day.

7th Level

	HP	SKILL RANKS	BAB	FORT	REF	WILL	PERFORMANCE
	1d8 + Con	6 + Int	+1	—	—	—	+2 rounds

Feat: You gain another feat.

Bardic Performance: You can now begin a bardic performance as a move action instead of a standard action if you want, meaning you could begin performing and either make an attack or cast a spell in the same round.

Inspire Competence +3: Your inspire competence performance bonus increases by 1.

Spells: You gain two 3rd-level spells known and another 1st-level spell known; you can cast one 3rd-level spell per day. *Confusion*, *haste*, and *slow* are all excellent choices. If your Charisma score is 16 or higher, you can cast an additional 3rd-level spell per day.

 Consider *blink*, *deep slumber*, *displacement*, *glibness*, and *major image*.

 Consider *charm monster*, *good hope*, and *sculpt sound*.

8th Level

	HP	SKILL RANKS	BAB	FORT	REF	WILL	PERFORMANCE
	1d8 + Con	6 + Int	+1	—	+1	+1	+2 rounds

Ability Score Increase: You gain a permanent +1 increase to an ability score of your choice.

Attack Bonus: Now that your base attack bonus is +6, you gain a second attack (at an attack bonus of +1) whenever you make a full attack (see page 122). From now on, any bonuses to your BAB apply to this attack as well.

Dirge of Doom: You can now use bardic performance to scare your enemies, reducing their combat effectiveness. Creatures with the shaken condition (*Core Rulebook* 568) also take a penalty on saving throws, meaning you have a better chance to affect them with your spells.

Spells: You gain another 3rd-level spell known, and can cast an additional 3rd-level spell and an additional 2nd-level spell per day. You can change one spell of 2nd level or lower that you know for a different spell of the same level.

9th Level

	HP	SKILL RANKS	BAB	FORT	REF	WILL	PERFORMANCE
	1d8 + Con	6 + Int	—	+1	—	—	+2 rounds

Feat: You gain another feat.

Inspire Greatness: You can now use bardic performance to enhance one ally in combat. Starting at 12th level, you will affect more allies.

Spells: You gain another 3rd-level spell known, and can cast an additional 3rd-level spell and an additional 1st-level spell per day.

10th Level

	HP	SKILL RANKS	BAB	FORT	REF	WILL	PERFORMANCE
	1d8 + Con	6 + Int	+1	—	+1	+1	+2 rounds

Jack-of-All-Trades: This ability allows you to use any skill, even ones that require training but in which you don't have any ranks.

Versatile Performance: Choose another Perform skill to benefit from this ability; see the 6th-level section for advice.

Spells: You gain two 4th-level spells known and another 2nd-level spell known; you can cast one 4th-level spell per day. *Dimension door*, *hold monster*, and *freedom of movement* are all excellent choices. If your Charisma score is 18 or higher, you can cast an additional 4th-level spell per day.

 Consider *dominate person*, *greater invisibility*, *modify memory*, and *zone of silence*.

 Consider *break enchantment*, *cure critical wounds*, *rainbow pattern*, and *shadow conjuration*.

11th Level

	HP	SKILL RANKS	BAB	FORT	REF	WILL	PERFORMANCE
	1d8 + Con	6 + Int	+1	—	—	—	+2 rounds

Feat: You gain another feat.

Inspire Competence +4: Your inspire competence performance bonus increases by 1.

Inspire Courage +3: Your inspire courage performance bonus increases by 1.

Lore Master: You can take 20 on a Knowledge skill check one additional time per day.

Spells: You gain another 4th-level spell known and another 1st-level spell known; you can cast an additional 4th-level spell and an additional 3rd-level spell per day. You can exchange one spell of 3rd level or lower that you know for a different spell of the same level.

12th Level

	HP	SKILL RANKS	BAB	FORT	REF	WILL	PERFORMANCE
	1d8 + Con	6 + Int	+1	+1	+1	+1	+2 rounds

Ability Score Increase: You gain a permanent +1 increase to an ability score of your choice.

Soothing Performance: You gain the ability to heal your allies using bardic performance. Because it takes 4 rounds for the healing to take effect, it's a difficult ability to use in combat, but it's a great way to heal the party between encounters.

Spells: You gain another 4th-level spell known, and can cast an additional 4th-level spell and an additional 2nd-level spell per day.

13th Level

	HP	SKILL RANKS	BAB	FORT	REF	WILL	PERFORMANCE
	1d8 + Con	6 + Int	—	—	—	—	+2 rounds

Feat: You gain another feat.

Bardic Performance: You can now begin a bardic performance as a swift action instead of as a standard or move action, freeing up your other actions in the round for actions like attacking, moving, and casting spells.

Spells: You gain two 5th-level spells known and another 3rd-level spell known; you can cast one 5th-level spell per day. *Persistent image* and *song of discord* are versatile and effective spell choices. If your Charisma score is 20 or higher, you can cast an additional 5th-level spell per day.

 Consider *mind fog*, *mirage arcana*, *mislead*, *seeming*, and *shadow walk*.

 Consider *greater dispel magic*, *greater heroism*, *mass suggestion*, and *shadow evocation*.

14th Level

	HP	SKILL RANKS	BAB	FORT	REF	WILL	PERFORMANCE
	1d8 + Con	6 + Int	+1	—	+1	+1	+2 rounds

Frightening Tune: This is essentially an upgraded version of dirge of doom (from 8th level). It makes enemies frightened instead of just shaken—frightened enemies run away, buying you time and giving you an advantage against opponents who didn't run (*Core Rulebook 567*).

Versatile Performance: Choose an additional Perform skill to benefit from this ability.

Spells: You gain another 5th-level spell known and another 2nd-level spell known; you can cast an additional 5th-level spell and an additional 4th-level spell per day. You can change one spell of 4th level or lower that you know for a different spell of the same level.

15th Level

	HP	SKILL RANKS	BAB	FORT	REF	WILL	PERFORMANCE
	1d8 + Con	6 + Int	+1	+1	—	—	+2 rounds

Attack Bonus: Now that your base attack bonus is +11, you gain a third attack (at an attack bonus of +1) whenever you make a full attack (see page 122). From now on, any bonuses to your BAB apply to this attack as well.

Feat: You gain another feat.

Inspire Competence +5: Your inspire competence performance bonus increases by 1.

Inspire Heroics: Give an ally within 30 feet a +4 bonus on saving throws and Armor Class.

Spells: You gain another 5th-level spell known, and you can cast an additional 5th-level spell and an additional 3rd-level spell per day.

16th Level

	HP	SKILL RANKS	BAB	FORT	REF	WILL	PERFORMANCE
	1d8 + Con	6 + Int	+1	—	+1	+1	+2 rounds

Ability Score Increase: You gain a permanent +1 increase to an ability score of your choice.

Spells: You gain two 6th-level spells known and another 4th-level spell known; you can cast one 6th-level spell per day. *Eyebite* and *geas/quest* are both excellent choices, as they give you powerful attacks against many kinds of creatures. If your Charisma score is 22 or higher, you can cast an additional 6th-level spell per day.

 Consider *find the path*, *greater scrying*, *permanent image*, *project image*, and *veil*.

 Consider *animate objects*, *greater shout*, *heroes' feast*, *irresistible dance*, and *mass charm monster*.

17th Level

	HP	SKILL RANKS	BAB	FORT	REF	WILL	PERFORMANCE
	1d8 + Con	6 + Int	—	—	—	—	+2 rounds

Feat: You gain another feat.

Inspire Courage +4: Your inspire courage performance bonus increases by 1.

Lore Master: You can take 20 on a Knowledge check one additional time per day.

Spells: You gain another 6th-level spell known and another 3rd-level spell known; you can cast an additional 6th-level spell and an additional 5th-level spell per day. You can exchange one spell of 5th level or lower that you know for a different spell of the same level.

18th Level

	HP	SKILL RANKS	BAB	FORT	REF	WILL	PERFORMANCE
	1d8 + Con	6 + Int	+1	+1	+1	+1	+2 rounds

Mass Suggestion: Your suggestion bardic performance can now affect a large group of creatures.

Versatile Performance: Choose an additional Perform skill to benefit from this ability.

Spells: You gain another 6th-level spell known, and can cast an additional 6th-level spell and an additional 4th-level spell per day.

19th Level

	HP	SKILL RANKS	BAB	FORT	REF	WILL	PERFORMANCE
	1d8 + Con	6 + Int	+1	—	—	—	+2 rounds

Feat: You gain another feat.

Inspire Competence +6: Your inspire competence performance bonus increases by 1.

Spells: You gain another 5th-level spell known, and you can cast an additional 6th-level spell and an additional 5th-level spell per day.

20th Level

	HP	SKILL RANKS	BAB	FORT	REF	WILL	PERFORMANCE
	1d8 + Con	6 + Int	+1	—	+1	+1	+2 rounds

Ability Score Increase: You gain a permanent +1 increase to an ability score of your choice.

Deadly Performance: You can strike a creature dead with your performance.

Spells: You gain another 6th-level spell known and another 4th-level spell known; you can cast an additional 6th-level spell per day. You can exchange one spell of 5th level or lower that you know for a different spell of the same level.

CLERIC

Clerics are holy warriors and powerful spellcasters who devote themselves to the gods. Some excel at battle, others dispense healing magic, and still more serve their deities by way of mysticism and divination.

 BATTLE PRIEST (PAGE 16)   **HEALER (PAGE 20)**   **STARGAZER (PAGE 25)**

ALIGNMENT

Your alignment must be within one step of your deity's, along either the law/chaos axis or the good/evil axis.

HIT DIE

Your Hit Die is a d8. At 1st level, you have 8 hit points plus your Constitution modifier.

BASE ATTACK BONUS +0

Your base attack bonus is +0, but it will increase at most levels.

SAVING THROWS

It's important for a cleric to be wise, which also increases her willpower.

FORTITUDE +2

Your Fortitude save bonus is +2 plus your Constitution modifier.

REFLEX +0

Your Reflex save bonus is +0 plus your Dexterity modifier.

WILL +2

Your Will save bonus is +2 plus your Wisdom modifier.

ABILITY SCORES

All clerics benefit from a high Wisdom score, which empowers their spellcasting. Most have an above-average Charisma score, as that influences the power and frequency of the divine energy they can channel into others.

 TIP Don't neglect Strength and Constitution, especially if you plan to wade into battle.

 Battle Priest: After Wisdom, you need Strength and Constitution. While you shouldn't neglect your Charisma score, it doesn't have to be your secondary focus.

 Healer: Charisma is your most important ability after Wisdom. Choose Constitution over Strength so you can survive in battle.

 Stargazer: After Wisdom, a mix of Charisma and Constitution is optimal. You may want a relatively high Intelligence score as well, to enhance the number of Knowledge skills you have.

SKILLS

Clerics' high Wisdom scores make them adept at using Wisdom-based skills like Heal, but their magical healing quickly eclipses skill-based healing, and their limited number of skill ranks forces them to focus on just a few skills.

 **SKILL RANKS PER LEVEL**
2 + Intelligence modifier

Class Skills for Clerics

Appraise
Craft
Diplomacy
Heal
Knowledge (arcana, history, nobility, planes, religion)

Linguistics
Profession
Sense Motive
Spellcraft

- Put a rank in a Knowledge skill that appeals to you, or in the generally useful Knowledge (religion) and Knowledge (history).
- Take advantage of your high Wisdom by putting a rank into Sense Motive to discern when and why people are lying.
- If you have any skill ranks left over, consider Perception so you're more aware of your surroundings.

 Remember, if you put at least 1 rank into any of your class skills, you get a +3 bonus to your total for that skill to represent your class training. At 1st level, you can't put more than 1 rank in a particular skill. If you're human, you gain an additional skill rank to spend at each level, including 1st level.

WEAPON AND ARMOR PROFICIENCIES

You are proficient with all simple weapons, light armor, medium armor, and shields (except tower shields). You are also proficient with the favored weapon of your deity—see Table 3–6 on page 43 of the *Core Rulebook* for specifics.

 Invest in the best armor you can afford, even if it means buying a somewhat poorer melee weapon. A well-protected (and conscious) cleric is much better at keeping others in the party alive.

FEATS

If you plan to focus on combat, choose a feat that enhances your battle abilities (such as Toughness). If you would rather focus on casting, choose a spell feat instead.

 **YOU GET ONE FEAT AT 1ST LEVEL**
Two if you're human

Extra Channel	Get two extra uses of your channel energy ability (see below) per day. (*Core Rulebook* 123)
Scribe Scroll	Bring some specialized cleric spells along on every adventure without having to use up a spell slot. (*Core Rulebook* 132)
Selective Channeling	Choose which creatures to affect with channeled energy so you can avoid healing your foes during combat. (*Core Rulebook* 132)
Toughness	Add 3 to your total hit points, plus an additional 1 for every Hit Die you possess or gain beyond 3. (*Core Rulebook* 135)

CLASS FEATURES

Channel Energy: Every cleric can channel the power of her faith through her holy or unholy symbol of her deity into a wave of divine energy that affects all creatures in a 30-foot radius (centered on the cleric).

A good cleric (or cleric of a good deity) channels positive energy, which at the cleric's choice can either heal living creatures or harm undead creatures. An evil cleric (or cleric of an evil deity) channels negative energy, which can either harm living creatures or heal undead creatures. A neutral cleric who worships a neutral deity must choose whether she channels positive or negative energy. Once this choice is made, it can't be reversed.

The amount of damage healed or dealt is 1d6 points of damage, plus an additional 1d6 points for every 2 cleric levels beyond 1st. A successful Will save halves this damage (DC = 10 + 1/2 your level + your Charisma modifier).

Aura (Ex): A cleric of a chaotic, evil, good, or lawful deity has a particularly powerful aura corresponding to her deity's alignment (see the *detect evil* spell on page 266 of the *Core Rulebook* for details).

Domains: A cleric's choice of deity influences her alignment, her values, and how others see her. It also affects what magic she can perform, in part by allowing her access to collections of magical powers and spells known as **domains**. A cleric chooses two domains from among those belonging to her deity (*Core Rulebook* 43). She can select an alignment domain (Chaos, Evil, Good, or Law) only if her alignment matches that domain.

For each level of cleric spell a cleric can cast, she gains one bonus spell slot, which can be used each day to prepare one of her domain spells (but not any other cleric spell). If one of the cleric's domain spells is not on the cleric spell list, she can prepare that spell only in a domain spell slot.

 Consider the Glory, Law, or War domains to maximize your combat potential.

 The Healing domain is an obvious choice, but the Charm, Community, Good, and Protection domains maximize healing power while allowing you to work well with the team in other ways.

 The Luck, Nobility, and Rune domains maximize your mystic, leadership, or information-gathering powers. The main advantage of taking the Rune domain is gaining Scribe Scroll as a bonus feat.

SUGGESTED STARTING GEAR

Clerics start with 140 gp.

Battle Priest: Longsword (or favored weapon of your deity; adjust cost and weight accordingly), dagger, light crossbow with 20 bolts, scale mail, light wooden shield, backpack, bedroll, flint and steel, spell component pouch, sunrod, trail rations (4 days), waterskin, wooden holy symbol; *Cost* 121 gp (19 gp left); *Weight* 64 lbs. (Medium) or 33 lbs. (Small).

Healer: Quarterstaff, dagger, light crossbow with 20 bolts, studded leather, backpack, bedroll, flint and steel, healer's kit, spell component pouch, sunrod, trail rations (4 days), waterskin, wooden holy symbol; *Cost* 128 gp (12 gp left); *Weight* 50 lbs. (Medium) or 26 lbs. (Small).

Stargazer: Spear, dagger, light crossbow with 20 bolts, studded leather, backpack, bedroll, flint and steel, holy water (2 flasks), spell component pouch, sunrod, trail rations (4 days), waterskin, wooden holy symbol; *Cost* 130 gp (10 gp left); *Weight* 53 lbs. (Medium) or 28 lbs. (Small).

SPELLS AND ORISONS

Clerics cast **divine spells**—spells that are granted to them by their deities. Unlike wizards and sorcerers, who must draw from a limited number of known spells, clerics are able to access most of the cleric spell list when choosing which spells to prepare for the day, giving them great flexibility. As a 1st-level cleric, each day you can prepare three different **orisons** (0-level spells that you can cast as often as you want) and one 1st-level spell (which you can cast once per day) by praying or meditating for an hour. You can also prepare one of your two 1st-level domain spells when preparing your other spells. If your Wisdom score is 12 or higher, you can prepare additional spells per day (see Table 1–3 on page 17 of the *Core Rulebook*).

You can also turn your spells (with the exception of orisons and domain spells) into healing or damage, thanks to spontaneous casting (see below).

At later levels, you will gain the ability to prepare and cast more powerful spells. You can only prepare a spell if your Wisdom score is at least 10 + the level of that spell; for instance, you need a Wisdom score of 12 or higher to prepare 2nd-level cleric spells.

SPONTANEOUS CASTING

A good cleric (or a neutral cleric of a good deity) can channel stored spell energy from the spells she has prepared into healing spells that she has not prepared ahead of time. The cleric can "lose" any prepared spell that's not an orison or a domain spell to cast any cure spell of the same spell level or lower (a **cure spell** is any spell with "cure" in its name).

An evil cleric (or a neutral cleric of an evil deity) can't convert prepared spells to cure spells, but can instead convert them to **inflict spells** (any spell with "inflict" in its name).

A cleric who is neither good nor evil and whose deity is neither good nor evil can convert spells to cure spells if she chose to channel positive energy, or to inflict spells if she chose to channel negative energy.

 Never prepare *cure light wounds* or other cure spells if you're good-aligned. Instead, use spontaneous casting to turn other spells into cure spells when you need them.

FAVORED CLASS BONUS

For each cleric level you attain, gain:

+1 to hp total

Adding to your hit points helps battle priests survive combat.

OR

+1 *skill rank*

Additional skill ranks benefit healers and stargazers.

LEVELING UP

The next few pages explain the abilities you get at 2nd level and higher. Some of these abilities are just additions to your 1st-level abilities, and are noted in a Level Up bar: additional hit points and skill ranks, additional channel energy damage dice, and increases to your base attack bonus, Fortitude save bonus, Reflex save bonus, and Will save bonus.

The information about what you gain at each level is also presented as Table 3–5: Cleric on page 40 of the *Core Rulebook*.

  BATTLE PRIEST (PAGE 16) **HEALER (PAGE 20)** **STARGAZER (PAGE 25)**

As you advance in levels, you gain an increasingly large number of spells you can cast per day. Since you can change the spells you have prepared each morning, your biggest challenge is in ensuring that you have the right tools to help you and your group. A *lesser restoration* or *remove disease* spell can prove invaluable in the right situation.

2nd Level

HP	SKILL RANKS	BAB	FORT	REF	WILL	CHANNEL ENERGY
1d8 + Con	2 + Int	+1	+1	—	+1	—

Your hit points increase by 1d8 + your Constitution modifier. Unlike at 1st level, you must roll for these hit points.

You also gain a number of skill ranks equal to 2 + your Intelligence modifier. If you're human, don't forget the bonus skill rank per level.

Your base attack bonus, Fortitude save bonus, and Will save bonus each go up by 1.

Spells: You can prepare one additional 1st-level spell and one additional orison (0-level spell) per day.

3rd Level

	HP	SKILL RANKS	BAB	FORT	REF	WILL	CHANNEL ENERGY
	1d8 + Con	2 + Int	+1	—	+1	—	+1d6

Feat: You gain another feat. If you haven't taken Extra Channel or Selective Channeling yet, choose one of those feats. Combat Casting will make it easier to cast spells in the midst of battle.

Spells: You can prepare one 2nd-level spell per day, plus one of your 2nd-level domain spells. If your Wisdom score is 14 or higher, you can prepare an additional 2nd-level spell per day. Consider *lesser restoration* (which can restore ability damage) and *hold person* (which can be extremely useful for capturing prisoners or locking down a single foe).

 Consider *dominate person*, *greater invisibility*, *modify memory*, and *zone of silence*.

4th Level

	HP	SKILL RANKS	BAB	FORT	REF	WILL	CHANNEL ENERGY
	1d8 + Con	2 + Int	+1	+1	—	+1	—

Ability Score Increase: You gain a permanent +1 increase to one ability score of your choice. This should be added to an ability score that's important to you, like Wisdom. If your Wisdom is already very high, add to Charisma, Constitution, or Dexterity—especially if you have an odd number in one of them, as your modifier increases at even numbers.

Spells: You can prepare one additional 2nd-level spell and one additional 1st-level spell per day.

 Ex-Clerics: As a cleric, you gain your spellcasting power and other class features from your deity. If you repeatedly or severely act against the interests of your deity, she may withdraw her approval. This means you lose all spells and class features until you atone for your misdeeds (*Core Rulebook* 41).

5th Level

	HP	SKILL RANKS	BAB	FORT	REF	WILL	CHANNEL ENERGY
	1d8 + Con	2 + Int	—	—	—	—	+1d6

Feat: You gain another feat. Choose Extra Channel or Selective Channeling if you haven't taken them yet, or Brew Potion to supply your party members with healing potions so you don't need to convert as many spells into healing. If you summon creatures often, consider Spell Focus (conjuration), which is a prerequisite for a feat that will make your summoned allies stronger.

 Heavy Armor Proficiency is probably worthwhile, since it allows you to wade into battle in sturdier armor.

Spells: You can prepare one 3rd-level spell per day (two if your Wisdom score is 16 or higher), plus one of your 3rd-level domain spells. *Magic circle against chaos/evil/good/law* are useful for any and all clerics (note that those are four different spells).

 Prayer improves your allies' luck in combat, and you should always prepare it in hostile environments. *Animate dead* can create useful minions as flankers or as a diversion. *Searing light* is your go-to ranged spell.

 Spiritual weapon lets you disrupt spellcasters and knock out the foes that others have almost, but not quite, finished off.

 Locate object is an incredibly useful spell. You can, for instance, target an object that a monster is carrying as it flees, or give an item as a "gift" to secretly track a person under suspicion. *Speak with dead* is also remarkably helpful, though less often.

Spells and Alignment: Some spells have alignment descriptors—good, evil, chaotic, or lawful—in their descriptions. Clerics can't cast spells with an alignment opposed to their own or that of their deities. For example, a good cleric or a cleric who worships a good deity can't cast evil spells.

6th Level

	HP	SKILL RANKS	BAB	FORT	REF	WILL	CHANNEL ENERGY
	1d8 + Con	2 + Int	+1	+1	+1	+1	—

Spells: You can prepare one additional 3rd-level spell and one additional 2nd-level spell per day.

7th Level

	HP	SKILL RANKS	BAB	FORT	REF	WILL	CHANNEL ENERGY
	1d8 + Con	2 + Int	+1	—	—	—	+1d6

Feat: You gain another feat. Mobility and Augment Summoning are both good options, though the latter requires Spell Focus (conjuration) as a prerequisite. Clerics gain a really strong summoning spell at every spell level, so build on that strength.

Spells: You can prepare one 4th-level spell (two if your Wisdom score is 18 or higher) and one additional 1st-level spell per day, plus one of your 4th-level domain spells. *Air walk* has a long duration, and is a great utility spell for scouting and ambushes.

 Divine power is a staple for you in combat, and *freedom of movement* is excellent for both you and your friends. *Greater magic weapon* is entirely worthwhile as well.

 Freedom of movement is very useful when moving around a battlefield. *Dismissal* is a great way to get rid of extraplanar foes. *Neutralize poison* is helpful; consider scribing it on a scroll that you keep around for the times an ally fails a saving throw against poison.

 Lesser planar ally and *summon monster IV* are both potentially very useful. Focus on the spells that an outsider brings with it—you may find that the gp cost is cheaper than the price of scrolls to do the same thing. *Discern lies* is helpful for questioning shady characters, and *divination* is superb for gathering information.

8th Level

	HP	SKILL RANKS	BAB	FORT	REF	WILL	CHANNEL ENERGY
	1d8 + Con	2 + Int	+1	+1	—	+1	—

Ability Score Increase: You gain a permanent +1 increase to an ability score. Wisdom, Charisma, or Constitution are your best bets, in roughly that order. Always bump up an odd-numbered ability score to an even number, as your modifier increases at even numbers.

Attack Bonus: Now that your base attack bonus is at +6, you gain a second attack (at an attack bonus of +1) whenever you make a full attack (see page 122). From now on, any bonuses to your BAB apply to this attack as well.

Spells: You can prepare one additional 4th-level spell and one additional 3rd-level spell per day.

9th Level

	HP	SKILL RANKS	BAB	FORT	REF	WILL	CHANNEL ENERGY
	1d8 + Con	2 + Int	—	—	+1	—	+1d6

Feat: You gain another feat. Consider some of the options mentioned earlier that you haven't yet taken.

Spells: You can prepare one 5th-level spell (or two if your Wisdom score is 20 or higher) and one additional 2nd-level spell per day, plus one of your 5th-level domain spells. All clerics should consider *breath of life*, as it's a quick way to save an ally from death.

 Righteous might is a pure battle priest power-up; prepare it and use it well. *Wall of stone* has great battlefield utility—use it to split the opposition or protect your party's flank. *Summon monster V* calls powerful creatures to destroy your foes.

 Scrying is an excellent divination spell that you should use frequently. One of the best divination spells available to clerics, it lets you observe encounter areas or particular individuals remotely. Never be surprised by what lies behind a dungeon door!

10th Level

	HP	SKILL RANKS	BAB	FORT	REF	WILL	CHANNEL ENERGY
	1d8 + Con	2 + Int	+1	+1	—	+1	—

Spells: You can prepare one additional 5th-level spell and one additional 4th-level spell per day.

11th Level

	HP	SKILL RANKS	BAB	FORT	REF	WILL	CHANNEL ENERGY
	1d8 + Con	2 + Int	+1	—	—	—	+1d6

Feat: You gain another feat.

Spells: You can prepare one 6th-level spell (two if your Wisdom score is 22 or higher) and one additional 3rd-level spell per day, plus one of your 6th-level domain spells. *Antilife shell* combines really well with a party of archers or spellslingers. *Blade barrier* deals efficient damage, and *greater dispel magic* takes down opposing magical power quickly. *Wind walk* helps with overland travel for the whole group.

 The big gun for healers is—not surprisingly—the spell *heal*. Its reversed form, *harm,* is a strong option to drop on your enemies.

12th Level

	HP	SKILL RANKS	BAB	FORT	REF	WILL	CHANNEL ENERGY
	1d8 + Con	2 + Int	+1	+1	+1	+1	—

Ability Score Increase: You gain a permanent +1 increase to an ability score of your choice.

Spells: You can prepare one additional 6th-level spell and one additional 5th-level spell per day.

13th Level

	HP	SKILL RANKS	BAB	FORT	REF	WILL	CHANNEL ENERGY
	1d8 + Con	2 + Int	—	—	—	—	+1d6

Feat: You gain another feat.

Spells: You can prepare one 7th-level spell (two if your Wisdom score is 24 or higher) and one additional 4th-level spell per day, plus one of your 7th-level domain spells. Spells like *ethereal jaunt* help you scout areas without fear of being detected by foes. The spell *resurrection* will hopefully never be necessary, but note that it can be used on any character, not just allies.

 A spell like *refuge* can be your ticket out of a disastrous encounter, and it's extremely useful for scouts in your party.

 The long duration and ability to cast spells through *greater scrying* makes it worth using against difficult foes.

14th Level

	HP	SKILL RANKS	BAB	FORT	REF	WILL	CHANNEL ENERGY
	1d8 + Con	2 + Int	+1	+1	—	+1	—

Spells: You can prepare one additional 7th-level spell and one additional 6th-level spell per day.

15th Level

	HP	SKILL RANKS	BAB	FORT	REF	WILL	CHANNEL ENERGY
	1d8 + Con	2 + Int	+1	—	+1	—	+1d6

Attack Bonus: Now that your base attack bonus is +11, you gain a third attack (at an attack bonus of +1) whenever you make a full attack (see page 122). From now on, any bonuses to your BAB apply to this attack as well.

Feat: You gain another feat.

Spells: You can prepare one 8th-level spell (or two if your Wisdom score is 26 or higher) and one additional 5th-level spell per day, plus one of your 8th-level domain spells. *Discern location* is a great new spell for any cleric.

16th Level

	HP	SKILL RANKS	BAB	FORT	REF	WILL	CHANNEL ENERGY
	1d8 + Con	2 + Int	+1	+1	—	+1	—

Ability Score Increase: You gain a permanent +1 increase to an ability score of your choice.

Spells: You can prepare one additional 8th-level spell and one additional 7th-level spell per day.

17th Level

	HP	SKILL RANKS	BAB	FORT	REF	WILL	CHANNEL ENERGY
	1d8 + Con	2 + Int	—	—	—	—	+1d6

Feat: You gain another feat.

Spells: You can prepare one 9th-level spell (two if your Wisdom score is 28 or higher) and one additional 6th-level spell per day, plus one of your 9th-level domain spells. *Mass heal* can turn a rout into a fighting chance. *Miracle* is a wildly flexible and useful spell. *Summon monster IX* puts celestial or infernal creatures at your command. *Greater spell immunity* is the sort of spell that can turn the tide of battle—if you know your enemy, you can cast this at just the right time to avoid their best attack spells.

18th Level

	HP	SKILL RANKS	BAB	FORT	REF	WILL	CHANNEL ENERGY
	1d8 + Con	2 + Int	+1	+1	+1	+1	—

Spells: You can prepare one additional 9th-level spell and one additional 8th-level spell per day.

19th Level

	HP	SKILL RANKS	BAB	FORT	REF	WILL	CHANNEL ENERGY
	1d8 + Con	2 + Int	+1	—	—	—	+1d6

Feat: You gain another feat.

Spells: You can prepare one additional 9th-level spell and one additional 7th-level spell per day.

20th Level

	HP	SKILL RANKS	BAB	FORT	REF	WILL	CHANNEL ENERGY
	1d8 + Con	2 + Int	+1	+1	—	+1	—

Ability Score Increase: You gain a permanent +1 increase to an ability score of your choice.

Spells: You can prepare one additional 9th-level spell and one additional 8th-level spell per day.

DRUID

Druids are defenders of nature, wielders of elemental energies, and masterful shapeshifters. Your druid bonds closely with an animal companion, commands the forces of nature, or turns into a massive beast to maul enemies.

 ANIMAL FRIEND (PAGE 15)   **FURY** (PAGE 20)   **NATURE WARRIOR** (PAGE 23)

ABILITY SCORES

A druid must be in touch with nature to command its magic, so you'll want a high Wisdom score.

TIP Regardless of your theme, a decent **Constitution** and **Dexterity** will help keep you alive.

	Animal Friend: Developing relationships with wild animals and magical beasts calls for a high Charisma score to better influence them.
	Fury: The higher your Wisdom score is, the harder it will be for your opponents to resist or dodge the effects of your spells.
	Nature Warrior: You'll want a high Strength score to empower your melee attacks, and a decent Constitution to sustain you while you deliver them.

SKILLS

A druid is often the party member called upon to act as the party's guide, animal handler, and survival expert. Druids also gain a class feature at 1st level that acts like the Diplomacy skill for animals.

 **SKILL RANKS PER LEVEL**
4 + Intelligence modifier

Class Skills for Druids

Climb	Perception
Craft	Profession
Fly	Ride
Handle Animal	Spellcraft
Heal	Survival
Knowledge (geography, nature)	Swim

- Put a rank in Handle Animal so you can train creatures and give them commands.
- A rank in Knowledge (nature) will help you identify natural plants, animals, and hazards.
- Put a rank in Perception so you can spot your enemies before they can surprise you.
- Track creatures, survive in the wild, and avoid getting lost with a rank in Survival.

 Remember, if you put at least 1 rank into any of your class skills, you get a +3 bonus to your total for that skill to represent your class training. At 1st level, you can't put more than 1 rank in a particular skill. If you're human, you get an additional skill rank to spend at each level, including 1st level.

Side panel

ALIGNMENT
You must have at least one neutral component to your alignment.

HIT DIE
Your Hit Die is d8. At 1st level, you have 8 hit points plus your Constitution modifier.

BASE ATTACK BONUS +0
Your base attack bonus is +0, but it will increase at most levels. You receive plenty of spells that can make you as effective as a more combat-oriented class for short periods of time.

SAVING THROWS
A druid must be able to endure harsh conditions and have the willpower to persevere.

FORTITUDE +2
Your Fortitude save bonus is +2 plus your Constitution modifier.

REFLEX +0
Your Reflex save bonus is +0 plus your Dexterity modifier.

WILL +2
Your Will save bonus is +2 plus your Wisdom modifier.

WEAPON AND ARMOR PROFICIENCIES

You're proficient with a modest selection of simple and martial weapons (*Pathfinder RPG Core Rulebook* 49): the scimitar, scythe, and spear are all fairly powerful, and you also gain access to a spell called *shillelagh* that can make the club and the quarterstaff very effective. Don't forget to select a ranged weapon; although some themes are very capable on the front line, it's often wiser to fire a few sling bullets and let the fighter or the paladin take the hits.

You should spend some money on armor. You're proficient with light armor, medium armor, and shields, though you may not use metal armors.

FEATS

A druid can be built to fill almost any role, so there's no "right" feat to take. That said, consider choosing a feat that boosts your combat abilities or your spellcasting abilities.

YOU GET ONE FEAT AT 1ST LEVEL
Two if you are human

Combat Casting	Gain a +4 bonus on concentration checks when casting spells in the middle of combat. (*Core Rulebook* 119)
Dodge	Get a +1 dodge bonus to AC, even when using wild shape. (*Core Rulebook* 122)
Improved Initiative	Gain a +4 bonus on initiative checks. This can allow you to hit clustered enemies with an area spell before they can move. (*Core Rulebook* 127)
Spell Focus (conjuration, evocation, transmutation)	Strengthen your spells and make your enemies less likely to resist them. Spell focus (conjuration) is also a prerequisite for Augment Summoning, which is a great feat for many druids. (*Core Rulebook* 134)

CLASS FEATURES

Nature Bond: Gain either an animal companion or extra spells and abilities from one of the following cleric domains: Air, Animal, Earth, Fire, Plant, Water, or Weather.

A druid receives many potent spells that can augment animals and can cast spells on an animal companion that she otherwise would only be able to cast on herself, so after you cast a few spells, your animal companion might give the group's fighter a run for his money. Several good animal companions are the bear (a good all-around choice), big cat (a very powerful striker), crocodile (a strong combat choice that benefits from an additional movement mode), and wolf (a strong, fast companion that trips enemies to make them easier to hit).

A domain grants you excellent boons. You receive an additional spell slot each level, and many domain spells don't normally appear on a druid's spell list. Each domain also grants a pair of thematic abilities.

	Choose the animal companion nature bond.
	Choose a cleric domain. A good choice might be the Fire domain, as it grants you even more powerful combat options.
	Either choice is good. An animal companion can be your ally on the front lines, and a domain can help to shore up your spellcasting abilities.

Nature Sense: This ability is a one-time boost to your Knowledge (nature) and Survival skill checks.

Wild Empathy: This ability allows you to calm wild animals and magical beasts, just as Diplomacy can influence more intelligent creatures to be friendly.

SPELLS AND ORISONS

Druids cast **divine spells**—spells that are granted to them by nature. You spend an hour meditating each day to prepare one 1st-level spell from the druid spell list (*Core Rulebook* 229). You can cast this spell once that day. Each day you may prepare three different **orisons** (0-level spells that you can cast as often as you want). If your Wisdom score is 12 or higher, you can cast additional spells per day (see Table 1–3 on page 17 of the *Core Rulebook*).

If you chose the cleric domain option for your nature bond, you may also choose one 1st-level domain spell to prepare. You can choose different spells each day, granting you a great deal of flexibility. While the spells listed below are suggestions for what works well for each theme, you should experiment with a wide variety of spells and determine which of them work best for you.

You can only cast a spell if your Wisdom score is at least 10 + the level of the spell; for instance, you need a Wisdom score of 12 or higher to cast 2nd-level druid spells.

1st-Level Spells: You're not as good at healing as a cleric, but you're still one of the better healers around. Consider preparing *cure light wounds* at least once to help keep yourself and others alive.

 Consider *hide from animals, magic fang,* and *speak with animals.* These grant you the ability to deal with animals and to augment your animal companion.

 Consider *entangle, magic stone, obscuring mist,* and *produce flame,* which will give you a wide range of damaging and debilitating spells.

 Consider *faerie fire, longstrider,* and *shillelagh* to more easily target, reach, and damage your enemies. Until you gain the wild shape ability, *shillelagh* will likely be your favorite spell.

As you advance in level as a druid, there are many options to consider. You gain a number of spell slots, which should be carefully tailored to the terrain you expect to encounter each day. (For instance, taking *entangle* while underground won't do you much good, so you should probably choose a different spell that day.) In addition, once you reach 4th level, you gain the ability to turn into an animal with wildshape. To get the most out of this ability, you should familiarize yourself with the animals in the *Pathfinder RPG Bestiary* and its sequels. These books are usually used exclusively by the GM to determine the monsters you'll face, but as a druid, they determine the forms that you can assume and the abilities you can gain while using wildshape.

FAVORED CLASS BONUS

For each druid level you attain, gain:

+1 *to hp total*

Adding hit points helps nature warriors survive combat.

OR

+1 *skill rank*

Diversify your skill set.

⬆ LEVELING UP

The next few pages explain the abilities you get at 2nd level and higher. Some of these abilities are just additions to your 1st-level abilities, and are noted in a Level Up bar: additional hit points and skill ranks, and increases to your base attack bonus, Fortitude save bonus, Reflex save bonus, and Will save bonus.

This information is also presented as Table 3–7: Druid on page 50 of the *Core Rulebook*.

 ANIMAL FRIEND (PAGE 15)   **FURY (PAGE 20)**   **NATURE WARRIOR (PAGE 23)**

	Train and magically enhance your animal companion until it's the equal of any two-legged warrior.
	Call on the elements and the land itself to hinder and damage your foes.
	Combine magic and martial prowess to make yourself a paragon of nature's might.

2nd Level

HP	SKILL RANKS	BAB	FORT	REF	WILL
1d8 + Con	4 + Int	+1	+1	—	+1

Your hit points increase by 1d8 + your Constitution modifier. Unlike at 1st level, you must roll for these hit points.

You also gain a number of skill ranks equal to 4 + your Intelligence modifier. If you're human, don't forget the bonus skill rank per level.

Your base attack bonus, Fortitude save bonus, and Will save bonus each go up by 1.

Nature Bond (animal companion): Your animal companion gains a Hit Die (and hit points), +1 base attack bonus (BAB), +1 Will, a skill rank, and a feat. As you increase in level, the animal companion's Hit Dice, BAB, saves, skills, feats, Natural Armor Bonus, and Strength and Dexterity bonuses increase, as well as the number of bonus tricks it gains. See Table 3–8: Animal Companion Base Statistics on page 52 of the *Core Rulebook*, and Animal Choices on pages 53–54 of the *Core Rulebook*.

Woodland Stride: You can now walk easily through much of the difficult terrain you find in the wilderness, which both improves your movement speed and gives you a tactical edge when fighting others in the wilderness.

Spells: You can prepare one additional orison and 1st-level spell per day.

3rd Level

HP	SKILL RANKS	BAB	FORT	REF	WILL
1d8 + Con	4 + Int	+1	—	+1	—

Feat: You gain another feat. You should consider some of the same choices you had at 1st level.

 You now also qualify for Power Attack, which allows you to deal more damage, especially with weapons you wield with two hands.

Nature Bond (animal companion): Your animal companion gains evasion. Instead of taking half the normal amount of damage from a spell or effect that deals damage on a successful save, your animal companion takes no damage.

Trackless Step: You never leave tracks for others to follow (though you can choose to leave a trail if desired).

Spells: You can prepare one 2nd-level spell per day (two if your Wisdom score is 14 or higher). Consider *barkskin*, which grants a long-lasting boost to armor class.

 Consider *bull's strength* or *reduce animal*; you can use the former to strengthen your animal companion and the latter to allow your companion to follow you into tight spots in the dungeon.

 Consider *flaming sphere*, *gust of wind*, *heat metal*, *owl's wisdom*, or *resist energy*. These spells either deal energy damage, help you resist energy damage, or improve your spells' saving throw DCs.

 Consider *bull's strength* or *flame blade*. You can use either to augment your melee attacks.

4th Level

	HP	SKILL RANKS	BAB	FORT	REF	WILL
	1d8 + Con	4 + Int	+1	+1	—	+1

Ability Score Increase: You gain a permanent +1 increase to one ability score of your choice. This should be added to an ability score that's important to you—like Wisdom—especially if you have an odd number in the score, as your modifier increases at even numbers.

Nature Bond (animal companion): Your animal companion gains a permanent +1 increase to one ability score of your choice.
Nature Bond (domain): If you selected the Animal domain, you gain an animal companion (though it's weaker than a typical druid animal companion gained through nature bond).

Resist Nature's Lure: You gain a +4 bonus on saving throws against the effects of fey and plants.

Wild Shape 1/Day: You gain the versatile ability to transform into a Small or Medium animal, often gaining better mobility, ability score modifiers, and natural attacks. You will gain the ability to become bigger or smaller animals as you gain levels, and will be able to take the forms of other types of creatures. Talk with your GM and look through the *Pathfinder RPG Bestiary* to find a few animal forms that you would like to use, and record their special abilities so you'll have them at hand when you use this ability.

Spells: You can prepare one additional 2nd-level spell and one additional 1st-level spell per day.

5th Level

	HP	SKILL RANKS	BAB	FORT	REF	WILL
	1d8 + Con	4 + Int	—	—	—	—

Feat: You gain another feat. If you plan on frequently utilizing your wild shape ability, consider Natural Spell, which allows you to cast spells even if you're a bird or a bear.

Spells: You can prepare one 3rd-level spell per day (two if your Wisdom score is 16 or higher).

	Consider preparing *greater magic fang* to boost either your or your animal companion's attacks.
	Consider preparing *greater magic fang* to boost either your or your animal companion's attacks.
	Consider preparing *call lightning*, *sleet storm*, or *spike growth*.

6th Level

	HP	SKILL RANKS	BAB	FORT	REF	WILL
	1d8 + Con	4 + Int	+1	+1	+1	+1

Nature Bond (animal companion): Your animal companion gains a +4 morale bonus on saving throws against enchantment spells and effects.
Nature Bond (domain): Most domains available to a druid grant an additional ability at this level.

Wild Shape 2/Day: You gain an additional use of wild shape, and you can now transform into Large and Tiny animals and Small elementals.

Spells: You can prepare one additional 3rd-level and one additional 2nd-level spell per day.

7th Level

	HP	SKILL RANKS	BAB	FORT	REF	WILL
	1d8 + Con	4 + Int	+1	—	—	—

Feat: You gain another feat. If you enjoy taking the form of fast-moving creatures with one powerful attack, consider Mobility. If you already have that feat, Spring Attack is a good choice that will improve your hit-and-run capabilities.

Nature Bond (animal companion): Some animal companions—especially those that started as Medium creatures—become much more powerful at 7th level.

Spells: You can prepare one 4th-level spell (two if your Wisdom score is 18 or higher) and one additional 1st-level spell per day. Consider *freedom of movement*, as it completely negates a wide range of debilitating effects for a long period of time, or *dispel magic*, a versatile spell that can shut down your enemies' plans in a multitude of ways.

	Consider *air walk* to allow your animal companion to chase after aerial foes.
	Consider *flame strike* or *ice storm* to rain down punishment over a large area.

8th Level

	HP	SKILL RANKS	BAB	FORT	REF	WILL
	1d8 + Con	4 + Int	+1	+1	—	+1

Ability Score Increase: You gain a permanent +1 increase to an ability score of your choice.

Attack Bonus: Now that your base attack bonus is +6, you gain a second attack (at an attack bonus of +1) whenever you make a full attack (see page 122). From now on, any bonuses to your BAB apply to this attack as well.

Nature Bond (domain): If you chose the Weather domain, you gain the ability to call down multiple lightning strikes at once.

Wild Shape 3/Day: You gain an additional use of wild shape, and your list of possible forms expands.

Spells: You can prepare one additional 4th-level spell and one additional 3rd-level spell per day.

9th Level

	HP	SKILL RANKS	BAB	FORT	REF	WILL
	1d8 + Con	4 + Int	—	—	+1	—

Feat: You gain another feat.

Nature Bond (animal companion): Your animal companion gains the multiattack ability, which either grants it the Multiattack feat or allows it to attack one additional time each round. In addition, your animal companion gains a permanent +1 increase to one ability score of your choice.

Venom Immunity: You're now immune to all poisons, sparing you from one of the most common sources of ability damage.

Spells: You can prepare one 5th-level spell (two if your Wisdom score is 20 or higher) and an additional 2nd-level spell per day. If you're not already preparing healing spells stronger than *cure light wounds*, strongly consider using at least one spell slot to prepare a 4th-level or higher "cure" spell; *cure light wounds* is no longer strong enough for emergency healing at this level.

 Consider *animal growth* to make your animal companion Huge.

 Consider *call lightning storm* or *wall of fire* to gain even more firepower.

 Consider *death ward* or *stoneskin* to protect you against physical damage and many negative energy effects.

 In addition to Common and whatever languages a druid may gain due to her Intelligence score or Linguistics ranks, all druids speak Druidic, a secret language forbidden to non-druids.

10th Level

	HP	SKILL RANKS	BAB	FORT	REF	WILL
	1d8 + Con	4 + Int	+1	+1	—	+1

Wild Shape 4/Day: You gain an additional use of wild shape, and your list of possible forms expands.

Spells: You can prepare one additional 5th-level spell and one additional 4th-level spell per day.

11th Level

	HP	SKILL RANKS	BAB	FORT	REF	WILL
	1d8 + Con	4 + Int	+1	—	—	—

Feat: You gain another feat.

Spells: You can prepare one 6th-level spell (two if your Wisdom score is 22 or higher) and one additional 3rd-level spell per day. Consider *spell staff*, a druid-only spell that allows you to store one spell for later use, almost as though you had an extra spell slot. Even a nature warrior can make good use of this spell between encounters. You could also consider *greater dispel magic* in order to remove your enemies' magical defenses or banish a debilitating effect.

 Consider *liveoak* to acquire a long-lasting, mobile tree ally in addition to your animal companion.

 Consider *antilife shell* and *fire seeds* to keep your enemies at bay and gain several types of explosive attacks.

12th Level

	HP	SKILL RANKS	BAB	FORT	REF	WILL
	1d8 + Con	4 + Int	+1	+1	+1	+1

Ability Score Increase: You gain a permanent +1 increase to an ability score of your choice.

Wild Shape 5/Day: You gain an additional use of wild shape, and you can now turn into almost any Huge or smaller animal, plant, or elemental.

Spells: You can prepare one additional 6th-level spell and one additional 5th-level spell per day.

13th Level

	HP	SKILL RANKS	BAB	FORT	REF	WILL
	1d8 + Con	4 + Int	—	—	—	—

Feat: You gain another feat.

A Thousand Faces: You can now take the form of any humanoid, as per the spell *alter self*.

Spells: You can prepare one 7th-level spell (two if your Wisdom score is 24 or higher) and one additional 4th-level spell per day. Consider *heal*, as it restores many hit points and removes most negative conditions. *Changestaff* is a nice way to get a long-lasting ally for any type of druid.

 Consider *creeping doom*, *fire storm*, or *sunbeam* to expand your repertoire of spells that harass and damage many creatures at once.

14th Level

	HP	SKILL RANKS	BAB	FORT	REF	WILL
	1d8 + Con	4 + Int	+1	+1	—	+1

Nature Bond (animal companion): Your animal companion gains a permanent +1 increase to one ability score of your choice.

Wild Shape 6/Day: You gain an additional use of wild shape.

Spells: You can prepare one additional 7th-level and one additional 6th-level spell per day.

15th Level

	HP	SKILL RANKS	BAB	FORT	REF	WILL
	1d8 + Con	4 + Int	+1	—	+1	—

Attack Bonus: Now that your base attack bonus is +11, you get a third attack (at an attack bonus of +1) whenever you make a full attack (see page 122). From now on, any bonuses to your BAB apply to this attack as well.

Feat: You gain another feat.

Nature Bond (animal companion): Your animal companion gains improved evasion. Not only does it take no damage on most successful Reflex saves, it only takes half the normal amount of damage even if it fails the saving throw.

Timeless Body: You're now virtually immune to aging.

Spells: You can prepare one 8th-level spell (two if your Wisdom score is 26 or higher) and one additional 5th-level spell per day. Consider *reverse gravity*, as it can slow down foes or debilitate them while you take care of more important matters.

 Consider *animal shapes* so your entire party can sneak around as animals.

 Consider *finger of death*, *earthquake*, *sunburst*, or *whirlwind* so nothing can stand against your elemental might.

 Consider *word of recall* as an emergency escape contingency in case you get in over your head.

16th Level

	HP	SKILL RANKS	BAB	FORT	REF	WILL
	1d8 + Con	4 + Int	+1	+1	—	+1

Ability Score Increase: You gain a permanent +1 increase to an ability score of your choice.

Wild Shape 7/Day: You gain an additional use of wild shape.

Spells: You can prepare one additional 8th-level spell and one additional 7th-level spell per day.

17th Level

	HP	SKILL RANKS	BAB	FORT	REF	WILL
	1d8 + Con	4 + Int	—	—	—	—

Feat: You gain another feat.

Spells: You can prepare one 9th-level spell (two if your Wisdom score is 28 or higher) and one additional 6th-level spell per day. Among these are several powerful ally-summoning spells such as *shambler* (which is most potent when combined with electricity spells) and *elemental swarm*.

	Consider *foresight* and *shapechange*, which grant you long-lasting defensive benefits and a huge set of polymorph options, respectively.
	Consider *foresight* and *shapechange*, which grant you long-lasting defensive benefits and a huge set of polymorph options, respectively.
	Consider *storm of vengeance*, which can strike down entire armies at once.

18th Level

	HP	SKILL RANKS	BAB	FORT	REF	WILL
	1d8 + Con	4 + Int	+1	+1	+1	+1

Wild Shape 8/Day: You gain an additional use of wild shape.

Spells: You can prepare one additional 9th-level and one additional 8th-level spell per day.

19th Level

	HP	SKILL RANKS	BAB	FORT	REF	WILL
	1d8 + Con	4 + Int	+1	—	—	—

Feat: You gain another feat.

Spells: You can prepare one additional 9th-level and one additional 7th-level spell per day.

20th Level

	HP	SKILL RANKS	BAB	FORT	REF	WILL
	1d8 + Con	4 + Int	+1	+1	—	+1

Ability Score Increase: You gain a permanent +1 increase to an ability score of your choice.

Nature Bond (animal companion): Your animal companion gains a permanent +1 increase to one ability score of your choice.

Wild Shape (at will): You can now use wild shape as often as you want.

Spells: You can prepare one additional 9th-level spell and one additional 8th-level spell per day.

FIGHTER

Tough and powerful warriors, fighters shrug off enemy attacks and lay their foes low. Your fighter might be a brute brandishing a two-handed weapon or a shield fighter who can survive even the worst punishment.

 BRUTE (PAGE 17)   **SHIELD FIGHTER** (PAGE 24)

ABILITY SCORES

Most fighters specialize in melee combat with just enough ranged weapon skill to threaten distant or flying foes. You'll want a high Strength score to deal more damage and a high Constitution score to stay alive.

 TIP Your defense and ranged abilities are based on Dexterity, so you'll want a solid Dexterity score.

Brute: Because two-handed weapon combat relies on dealing maximum damage, throw everything you can into Strength. Whatever is left over should go into Constitution.

Shield Fighter: Your best ability score should be Strength, but your more well-rounded approach to combat means you can afford a good score in Constitution or Dexterity. Constitution gives you better survivability, while Dexterity helps your Armor Class and ranged attacks.

SKILLS

Fighters are versatile warriors who can fill a lot of different combat roles, but their limited number of skill ranks means they must be choosy about which skills they learn to make the most of advantages like their high Strength.

 SKILL RANKS PER LEVEL *2 + Intelligence modifier*

Class Skills for Fighters
Climb
Craft
Handle Animal
Intimidate
Knowledge (dungeoneering, engineering)
Profession
Ride
Survival
Swim

- With your high Strength score, you have natural athletic ability, so consider putting a rank into Climb or Swim.
- If you have high Charisma, put a rank into Intimidate to use your physical presence to influence minion monsters, guards, and lesser foes.
- If you want to be knowledgeable about dungeon dangers, put a rank into Knowledge (dungeoneering).
- If you plan to fight from horseback, put a rank into Ride to help ensure control of your mount.

 Remember, if you put at least 1 rank into any of your class skills, you get a +3 bonus to your total for that skill to represent your class training. At 1st level, you can't put more than 1 rank in a particular skill. If you're human, you get an additional skill rank to spend at each level, including 1st level.

WEAPON AND ARMOR PROFICIENCIES

Your combat training means you can freely use most kinds of weapons and armor.

Wear the heaviest armor you can afford—at 1st level, that's probably scale mail or chainmail. Heavy armor will slow down your movement (see Speed, *Pathfinder RPG Core Rulebook* 150), but you'll need the extra protection. As soon as you can afford it, get banded mail, half-plate, or full plate.

Choose a big melee weapon (such as a greatsword or battleaxe) to deal a lot of damage, or a one-handed weapon (such as a longsword or warhammer) if you plan to use a shield. Save a few gold pieces by using a heavy wooden shield rather than steel.

FEATS

As a fighter, you'll benefit from choosing feats that enhance your combat abilities, such as the ones below. Like every character, you get a feat at 1st level, but fighters also get bonus feats (one at first level, and one at every even level). These bonus feats must be selected from those listed as combat feats (they say "(Combat)" after the feat name in the *Core Rulebook*).

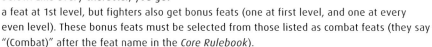

YOU GET TWO FEATS AT 1ST LEVEL
Three if you're human

Weapon Focus		Gain a +1 bonus on attacks made with your main weapon. This is a great feat for both themes. (*Core Rulebook* 136)
	Power Attack	Want to eliminate a foe with a single blow? Trade accuracy for power—take a –1 penalty on melee attack rolls to gain a +2 bonus on damage rolls. (*Core Rulebook* 131)
	Cleave	Make an attack using your full attack bonus. If that attack succeeds, use your full attack bonus to strike an additional adjacent foe. You'll need to have Power Attack to take this feat. (*Core Rulebook* 119)
	Shield Focus	With Shield Focus, you can improve your Armor Class to survive long enough to slay your foes. (*Core Rulebook* 133)
	Improved Initiative	React faster to combat. Improved Initiative gives you a +4 bonus on initiative checks. (*Core Rulebook* 127)

TIP **Feat chains** are series of feats that build on each other, such as Mobility/Dodge/Spring Attack; the last feats in such chains are often quite powerful, and your abundance of available feats allows you to work through the chain more quickly than characters of other classes.

SUGGESTED STARTING GEAR
Fighters start with 175 gp.

Brute: Greatsword, battleaxe, dagger, light crossbow with 20 bolts, throwing axe, backpack, bedroll, flint and steel, sunrod, trail rations (4 days), waterskin, whetstone; Cost 165 gp (10 gp left); Weight 70 lbs. (Medium) or 36 lbs. (Small).

Shield Fighter: Longsword, flail, dagger, javelins (4), chain shirt, heavy wooden shield, backpack, bedroll, flint and steel, sunrod, trail rations (4 days), waterskin, whetstone; Cost 144 gp (31 gp left); Weight 69 lbs. (Medium) or 35 lbs. (Small). Option: Exchange the longsword for a bastard sword to do more damage by spending an extra 20 gp and gaining 2 more pounds of weight (1 more pound for Small characters).

FAVORED CLASS BONUS
For each fighter level you attain, gain:
+1 to hp total: Adding to your hit points helps you survive combat.
OR
+1 skill rank Diversify your skill set.

LEVELING UP

The next few pages explain the abilities you get at 2nd level and higher. Some of these abilities are just additions to your 1st-level abilities, and are noted in a Level Up bar: additional hit points and skill ranks, and increases to your base attack bonus, Fortitude save bonus, Reflex save bonus, and Will save bonus.

The information about what you gain at each level is also presented as Table 3–9: Fighter on page 56 of the *Core Rulebook*.

 BRUTE
(PAGE 17)

 SHIELD FIGHTER
(PAGE 24)

As a fighter, you should pay close attention to the weapons and armor available to you as you advance in level. Choosing your abilities (such as weapon training) carefully and tailoring your selections to the magic weapons you've found while adventuring will give you an edge in combat and ensure that your feats and class features don't go to waste.

2nd Level

	HP	SKILL RANKS	BAB	FORT	REF	WILL
	1d10 + Con	2 + Int	+1	+1	—	—

Your hit points increase by 1d10 + your Constitution modifier. Unlike at 1st level, you must roll for these hit points.

You also gain a number of skill ranks equal to 2 + your Intelligence modifier. If you're human, don't forget the bonus skill rank per level.

Your base attack bonus and Fortitude save bonus each go up by 1.

Bonus Feat: You gain a combat feat. Consider one of those suggested at 1st level.

 Consider the Cleave feat if you don't already have it, or Quick Draw (to draw your weapon as a free action) if you do.

 If your Dexterity is 15 or higher, consider Two-Weapon Fighting, which allows you to attack with both your weapon and your shield on your turn. If not, consider Combat Reflexes (if you're tired of enemies running past you), Quick Draw (to draw your weapon as a free action), or Step Up (to follow a moving opponent).

Bravery +1: This ability gives you a +1 bonus on saves against fear.

3rd Level

	HP	SKILL RANKS	BAB	FORT	REF	WILL
	1d10 + Con	2 + Int	+1	—	+1	+1

Feat: You gain another feat. You could choose a combat feat, or improve some other aspect of your character, such as boosting one of your weaker saving throws (with Iron Will or Lightning Reflexes), adding to one or more skills (with feats like Athletic or Skill Focus), increasing your hit points (with Toughness), or improving your maneuverability (with Nimble Moves and Acrobatic Steps).

 Consider the Great Cleave feat if you often fight many opponents at once, or Step Up to pursue a moving target. Great Cleave works just like Cleave, but there's no limit to the number of enemies you could hit in one swing—great if you're crowded in!

 If you have Two-Weapon Fighting, consider Improved Shield Bash—it lets you keep the shield's Armor Class bonus when you attack. If not, consider Combat Reflexes or a feat suggested earlier for your theme.

Armor Training 1: You become more maneuverable while wearing armor. Reduce your armor's armor check penalty by 1 (to a minimum of 0) and increase its maximum Dexterity bonus by 1. Medium armor no longer slows your movement.

4th Level

	HP	SKILL RANKS	BAB	FORT	REF	WILL
	1d10 + Con	2 + Int	+1	+1	—	—

Ability Score Increase: You gain a permanent +1 increase to one ability score of your choice. This should be added to an ability score that's important to you—like Strength or Constitution—especially if you have an odd number in either of them, as your modifier increases at even numbers.

Bonus Feat: Choose Weapon Specialization with your main weapon. This increases your damage with that weapon by +2 and allows you take even better feats at higher levels.

5th Level

HP	SKILL RANKS	BAB	FORT	REF	WILL
1d10 + Con	2 + Int	+1	—	—	—

Feat: You gain another feat.

Weapon Training 1: Find your melee weapon in the list of weapon groups (*Core Rulebook* 56) and select that weapon group. This ability gives you a +1 bonus on attack and damage rolls when using any weapon in that group, as well as on combat maneuver checks (see page 132) while using any weapon in that group and to Combat Maneuver Defense (see page 115) against weapons of that group.

 Many of the feats available to fighters involve improving your skills with a particular weapon or a particular facet of combat (such as critical hits). While it might be tempting to try to be good at everything, choosing a focus can help you become an unstoppable force in battle.

6th Level

HP	SKILL RANKS	BAB	FORT	REF	WILL
1d10 + Con	2 + Int	+1	+1	+1	+1

Attack Bonus: Now that your base attack bonus is +6, you gain a second attack (at an attack bonus of +1) whenever you make a full attack (see page 122). From now on, any bonuses to your BAB apply to this attack as well.

Bonus Feat: You gain a combat feat. If your Dexterity is at least 13, consider Dodge to increase your Armor Class. Dodge also unlocks other useful feats like Mobility and Spring Attack.

 Consider Improved Bull Rush (which allows you to push opponents) or Improved Overrun (which lets you move through opponents).

 If you're often making shield bash attacks, consider Double Slice (which allows you to add your full Strength bonus on those attacks), Improved Two-Weapon Fighting (which gives you a second attack with your off-hand weapon), or Shield Slam (which allows you to push opponents with a shield bash). Otherwise, look over the feats recommended for lower levels.

Bravery +2: Your bravery bonus against fear attacks increases by 1.

7th Level

HP	SKILL RANKS	BAB	FORT	REF	WILL
1d10 + Con	2 + Int	+1	—	—	—

Feat: You gain another feat.

Armor Training 2: Your armor training ability improves, reducing your armor's armor check penalty by 1 (to a minimum of 0) and increasing its maximum Dexterity bonus by 1. Heavy armor no longer slows your movement.

8th Level

HP	SKILL RANKS	BAB	FORT	REF	WILL
1d10 + Con	2 + Int	+1	+1	—	—

Ability Score Increase: You gain a permanent +1 increase to an ability score of your choice.

Bonus Feat: You gain a combat feat. Greater Weapon Focus increases your attack bonus with your main weapon and is required if you want Greater Weapon Specialization at 12th level.

 If you're having an easy time hitting but want to deal more damage, consider Improved Critical to increase how often you threaten a critical hit.

 If you prefer to boost defense instead of offense, consider Greater Shield Focus to increase your Armor Class by an additional 1 when using a shield.

9th Level

HP	SKILL RANKS	BAB	FORT	REF	WILL
1d10 + Con	2 + Int	+1	—	+1	+1

Feat: You gain another feat. Consider Critical Focus, especially if your weapon's critical threat range is 19–20 or 18–20.

Weapon Training 2: The bonus for the weapon group you chose at 5th level increases by 1. You also get to pick a second weapon group and gain a +1 bonus for that group as well; consider choosing whatever group your ranged weapon belongs to, or choose the close weapon group if you're using a shield.

10th Level

	HP	SKILL RANKS	BAB	FORT	REF	WILL
	1d10 + Con	2 + Int	+1	+1	—	—

Bonus Feat: You gain a combat feat. Spellbreaker is a useful feat for killing enemy spellcasters. Otherwise, consider Weapon Focus or Weapon Specialization with a ranged or backup weapon.

 Consider the Lunge feat to give yourself more reach and mobility in battle (as you don't have to move as far to get opponents into range of your weapon). Dazzling Display lets you show off an impressive weapon maneuver to give multiple enemies a fear-based −2 penalty on attacks, saves, and checks. This also unlocks Shatter Defenses for later, which lets you slip past enemies or attack them without their Dexterity bonus to AC.

 Consider Greater Weapon Focus or Greater Shield Focus—whichever one you didn't choose at 8th level.

Bravery +3: Your bravery bonus against fear attacks increases by 1.

11th Level

	HP	SKILL RANKS	BAB	FORT	REF	WILL
	1d10 + Con	2 + Int	+1	—	—	—

Attack Bonus: Now that your base attack bonus is +11, you get a third attack (at an attack bonus of +1) whenever you make a full attack (see page 122). From now on, any bonuses to your BAB apply to this attack as well. If you have Vital Strike, using that feat is even more effective with a third attack to give up.

Feat: You gain another feat. Consider increasing your damage output with Improved Vital Strike (which is a better version of Vital Strike), debilitating your opponents with a critical feat (such as Bleeding Critical or Sickening Critical), or making progress on a feat chain (like Dodge/ Mobility/Spring Attack or Power Attack/Bull Rush/Greater Bull Rush).

Armor Training 3: Your armor training ability improves, reducing your armor's armor check penalty by 1 (to a minimum of 0) and increasing its maximum Dexterity bonus by 1.

 If you make shield bash attacks, Shield Master negates your two-weapon fighting penalties with the shield, and lets you add your shield's defensive enhancement bonus on your attack roll.

12th Level

	HP	SKILL RANKS	BAB	FORT	REF	WILL
	1d10 + Con	2 + Int	+1	+1	+1	+1

Ability Score Increase: You gain a permanent +1 increase to an ability score of your choice.

Bonus Feat: You gain a combat feat. Consider selecting Greater Weapon Specialization to increase your favorite weapon's damage by an additional +2. Consider selecting Penetrating Strike if you want to be more effective at fighting monsters with damage reduction. If you have a critical feat, consider selecting a second one, as that will unlock Critical Mastery once you reach 14th level.

13th Level

	HP	SKILL RANKS	BAB	FORT	REF	WILL
	1d10 + Con	2 + Int	+1	—	—	—

Feat: You gain another feat. Staggering Critical is a great option for slowing down deadly opponents.

Weapon Training 3: The bonuses for all your current weapon groups increase by 1. You get to pick a third weapon group and get a +1 bonus for that group as well. Consider choosing a backup melee weapon with a different damage type (bludgeoning, piercing, or slashing) than your main melee weapon.

14th Level

	HP	SKILL RANKS	BAB	FORT	REF	WILL
	1d10 + Con	2 + Int	+1	+1	—	—

Bonus Feat: You gain a combat feat. If you have at least two critical feats, consider Critical Mastery, which lets you apply two critical effects per critical hit.

Bravery +4: Your bravery bonus against fear attacks increases by 1.

15th Level

	HP	SKILL RANKS	BAB	FORT	REF	WILL
	1d10 + Con	2 + Int	+1	—	+1	+1

Feat: You gain another feat. Consider Blinding Critical, as fighting a blinded opponent gives you a significant advantage.

Armor Training 4: Your armor training ability improves, reducing your armor's armor check penalty by 1 (to a minimum of 0) and increasing its maximum Dexterity bonus by 1.

16th Level

	HP	SKILL RANKS	BAB	FORT	REF	WILL
	1d10 + Con	2 + Int	+1	+1	—	—

Ability Score Increase: You gain a permanent +1 increase to an ability score of your choice.

Attack Bonus: Now that your base attack bonus is at +16, you gain a fourth attack (at an attack bonus of +1) whenever you make a full attack (see page 122). From now on, any bonuses to your BAB apply to this attack as well.

Bonus Feat: You gain a combat feat. If you have Penetrating Strike, consider upgrading to Greater Penetrating Strike to bypass even more enemy damage reduction.

17th Level

	HP	SKILL RANKS	BAB	FORT	REF	WILL
	1d10 + Con	2 + Int	+1	—	—	—

Feat: You gain another feat. Stunning Critical is a powerful choice and available for the first time at this level.

Weapon Training 4: The bonuses for all your current weapon groups increase by 1. You get to pick a fourth weapon group and get a +1 bonus for that group. By this point, you have probably already selected groups for your favorite weapons, so feel free to pick something unusual.

18th Level

	HP	SKILL RANKS	BAB	FORT	REF	WILL
	1d10 + Con	2 + Int	+1	+1	+1	+1

Bonus Feat: You gain a combat feat.

Bravery +5: Your bravery bonus against fear attacks increases by 1.

19th Level

	HP	SKILL RANKS	BAB	FORT	REF	WILL
	1d10 + Con	2 + Int	+1	—	—	—

Feat: You gain another feat.

Armor Mastery: You gain DR 5/— (see Damage Resistance on page 127) whenever you're wearing armor or using a shield.

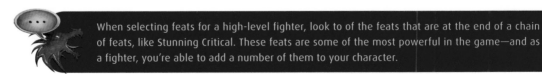

When selecting feats for a high-level fighter, look to of the feats that are at the end of a chain of feats, like Stunning Critical. These feats are some of the most powerful in the game—and as a fighter, you're able to add a number of them to your character.

20th Level

	HP	SKILL RANKS	BAB	FORT	REF	WILL
	1d10 + Con	2 + Int	+1	+1	—	—

Ability Score Increase: You gain a permanent +1 to an ability score of your choice.

Bonus Feat: You gain a combat feat. If you don't have Improved Critical with your main weapon, consider selecting it now, as your weapon mastery ability relies on threatening critical hits.

Weapon Mastery: Choose your main weapon for this ability, which automatically confirms critical hits, increases the critical hit damage multiplier by 1, and prevents you from being disarmed of that weapon.

MONK

Monks are highly trained martial artists and peerless acrobats. The monk class's huge variety of abilities allows you to play an unarmed warrior or a fast-striking master of simple yet deadly weapons.

 MANEUVER SPECIALIST (PAGE 22)   **MARTIAL WARRIOR** (PAGE 22)

ALIGNMENT

You must have a lawful alignment.

HIT DIE

Your hit die is d8. At 1st level, you have 8 hit points plus your Constitution modifier.

BASE ATTACK BONUS +0

Your base attack bonus is +0, but it will increase at most levels. Flurry of blows makes your attacks even more effective.

SAVING THROWS

Monks go through intense physical and mental training.

FORTITUDE +2

Your Fortitude save bonus is +2 plus your Constitution modifier.

REFLEX +2

Your Reflex save bonus is +2 plus your Dexterity modifier.

WILL +2

Your Will save bonus is +2 plus your Wisdom modifier.

ABILITY SCORES

Monks balance many ability scores, often prioritizing Strength to hit harder and Wisdom to evade attacks and gain more ki. Dexterity is important because monks don't wear armor, as is Constitution in case you're hit.

 TIP Don't worry as much about Intelligence and Charisma, though you may want an Intelligence score of at least 13, which allows you to qualify for powerful feats.

SKILLS

Monks' rigorous physical and mental training helps them excel in skills that require strength as well as those benefiting from a keen mind. Your party is likely to turn to you for insight into others' motivations and for help in defeating enemies.

 **SKILL RANKS PER LEVEL**
4 + Intelligence modifier

Class Skills for Monks

Acrobatics	Perform
Climb	Profession
Craft	Ride
Escape Artist	Sense Motive
Intimidate	Stealth
Knowledge (history, religion)	Swim
Perception	

- Put a rank into Acrobatics so you can easily move around obstacles and enemies.
- Put a rank in Climb or Swim to leverage your high Strength score and help you move even more efficiently.
- Put a rank into Perception so you can spot your enemies before they can surprise you.
- Take advantage of your high Wisdom score by putting a rank into Sense Motive to see through others' attempts to lie.

 Remember, if you put at least 1 rank into any of your class skills, you get a +3 bonus to your total for that skill to represent your class training. At 1st level, you can't put more than 1 rank in a particular skill. If you're human, you gain an additional skill rank to spend at each level, including 1st level.

WEAPON AND ARMOR PROFICIENCIES

You are proficient with a modest selection of simple, martial, and exotic weapons, many of which you can use with the flurry of blows class ability. You'll benefit from having a weapon or two that deal different types of damage than your unarmed strikes, so grab a kama or siangham. Don't forget a ranged weapon; although you're usually fighting on the front lines, circumstances might make it hard to reach your enemies.

Don't worry about armor or shields; you can't use them effectively, and they interfere with many of your class abilities.

FEATS

Monks gain extra feats quite often. In addition to the feat every character gets at 1st level, monks gain an extra feat at 1st level as well as a bonus feat every 4 levels. As you gain levels, new feats become available.

YOU GET TWO FEATS AT 1ST LEVEL
Three if you're human

Agile Maneuvers	If you're a Dexterity-focused monk, this feat will allow you to perform effective combat maneuvers. (*Core Rulebook* 117)
Improved Initiative	This feat improves your chances of acting first, allowing you to use the Stunning Fist feat on your enemies before they can act. (*Core Rulebook* 127)
Toughness	This feat lets you absorb powerful hits without flinching—add 3 to your total hit points, plus an additional 1 for every Hit Die you possess or gain beyond 3. (*Core Rulebook* 135)
Weapon Focus	This feat increases your chances of hitting with your main weapon. It gives you a +1 bonus on attacks made with that weapon. You can, and probably should, enhance your unarmed strikes with this feat. (*Core Rulebook* 136)

In addition to the feats listed above, consider Blind Fight (*Core Rulebook* 118) and Nimble Moves (*Core Rulebook* 131).

	Consider Catch Off-Guard (*Core Rulebook* 119), Combat Reflexes (*Core Rulebook* 119), or Dodge (*Core Rulebook* 122).
	Take Deflect Arrows (*Core Rulebook* 121), Improved Grapple (*Core Rulebook* 127), or Scorpion Style (*Core Rulebook* 132).

CLASS FEATURES

Armor Class Bonus: When unarmored, a monk adds his Wisdom modifier to his Armor Class (AC). This bonus (and the additional Armor Class bonuses he gains at higher levels) apply even against touch attacks and when he is flat-footed.

Flurry of Blows: Instead of attacking once, you can take your whole turn to attack twice (take a −1 penalty on both attack rolls). As you gain levels, you will gain more attacks, bonuses instead of penalties on the attack rolls, and higher potential damage (*Core Rulebook* 57).

Stunning Fist: You gain Stunning Fist as a bonus feat. If you damage a foe with this special unarmed attack, the foe must attempt a Fortitude save (DC = 10 + half your character level [minimum 1] + your Wisdom modifier). If the foe fails this save, it's stunned for 1 round (until you begin your next turn). A stunned character drops everything it's holding, can't take any actions, loses its Dexterity bonus to AC, and takes an additional −2 penalty to AC. As you gain levels, you can also use this feat to inflict other crippling conditions on your target.

Unarmed Strike: You can strike effectively with your fists and feet, even if you're holding things. If you hit, you deal 1d6 points of damage. As you gain levels, the base damage you deal increases; eventually your strikes will be more deadly than a greatsword.

 TIP All of these class features gain power as you level up, so be patient if they don't seem as mighty as a paladin's smite or a barbarian's rage at 1st level.

SUGGESTED STARTING GEAR

Monks start with 35 gp.

Maneuver Specialist: Kama, nunchaku, javelins (4), backpack, silk rope (50 ft.), sunrod, trail rations (4 days), waterskin; *Cost* 25 gp (9 gp left); *Weight* 28 lbs. (Medium) or 15 lbs. (Small).

Martial Warrior: Quarterstaff, kama (2), sai (2), siangham (2), shuriken (20), backpack, sunrod, trail rations (4 days), waterskin; *Cost* 23 gp (12 gp left); *Weight* 25 lbs. (Medium) or 14 lbs. (Small).

FAVORED CLASS BONUS

For each monk level you attain, gain:

+1 *to hp total*

Adding to your hit points helps you survive combat.

OR

+1 *skill rank*

Diversify your skill set.

LEVELING UP

The next few pages explain the abilities you get at 2nd level and higher. Some of these abilities are just additions to your 1st-level abilities, and are noted in a Level Up bar: additional hit points and skill ranks, increased flurry of blows attacks and bonuses, and increases to your base attack bonus, Fortitude save bonus, Reflex save bonus, and Will save bonus.

The information about what you gain at each level is also presented as Table 3–10: Monk on page 58 of the *Core Rulebook*.

MANEUVER SPECIALIST
(PAGE 22)

MARTIAL WARRIOR
(PAGE 22)

Leveling up as a monk is relatively straightforward, but there are a few things to consider. Selecting feats that help you specialize in one area, such as a specific combat maneuver or attack style, are going to be more valuable than spreading your choices around to cover multiple styles. In addition, always be on the lookout for gear and magic items to enhance your Armor Class and attacks. Since you can't wear armor, magic amulets and rings are the easiest way to boost your defenses.

2nd Level

HP	SKILL RANKS	BAB	FORT	REF	WILL	FLURRY OF BLOWS
1d8 + Con	4 + Int	+1	+1	+1	+1	+0/+0

Your hit points increase by a number equal to 1d8 + your Constitution modifier. Unlike at 1st level, you must roll for these hit points.

You also gain a number of skill ranks equal to 4 + your Intelligence modifier. If you're human, don't forget the bonus skill rank per level.

Your base attack bonus, flurry of blows attack bonuses, Fortitude save bonus, Reflex save bonus, and Will save bonus increase by 1.

Bonus Feat: You gain another monk feat.

Evasion: Instead of taking half the normal damage from many spells and effects that deal damage when you fail a Reflex save, you take no damage.

3rd Level

HP	SKILL RANKS	BAB	FORT	REF	WILL	FLURRY OF BLOWS
1d10 + Con	4 + Int	+1	—	—	—	+1/+1

Feat: You gain another feat. You should consider some of the same choices you had at 1st level, but your higher base attack bonus opens up several more good options.

 Consider taking Power Attack now or at the next available opportunity. Your higher attack bonus will compensate for the feat's penalty, and you can use a two-handed weapon like a quarterstaff to deal considerably more damage.

 If your intelligence score is 13 or higher, consider selecting Combat Expertise. Not only does the feat allow you to boost your Armor Class when needed, but it's also a prerequisite for powerful combat maneuver feats.

Fast Movement: You can move much more quickly than other members of your race, gaining +10 feet of movement to your base move speed.

Maneuver Training: You can now use your monk level in place of your base attack bonus when calculating your combat maneuver bonus. This is especially important for maneuver specialist monks.

Still Mind: You gain a +2 bonus on saving throws against enchantment effects.

4th Level

HP	SKILL RANKS	BAB	FORT	REF	WILL	FLURRY OF BLOWS
1d8 + Con	4 + Int	+1	+1	+1	+1	+2/+2

Ability Score Increase: You gain a permanent +1 increase to one ability score of your choice. This should be added to an ability score that's important to you—like Strength—especially if you have an odd number in that score, as your modifier increases at even numbers.

Armor Class Bonus: When you're not wearing armor, your Armor Class and combat maneuver defense increase by 1.

Ki Pool: You gain a daily pool of ki points that you can use to increase your speed, make an extra attack, or drastically improve your Armor Class. This ability also allows your unarmed strikes to ignore progressively tougher types of damage reduction—at 4th level, your unarmed attacks bypass the same damage reduction as magic weapons. You will gain several more abilities that use ki as you gain monk levels. Remember that you also gain an additional point of ki for every 2 levels that you gain, starting at 6th level.

Slow Fall 20 Feet: When you fall along a wall or other surface, you can slow your fall, subtracting 20 feet from the fall height when calculating damage.

Unarmed Strike Damage Increase: Your unarmed strikes now deal 1d8 points of damage, making them equivalent to a heavy mace.

5th Level

	HP	SKILL RANKS	BAB	FORT	REF	WILL	FLURRY OF BLOWS
	1d8 + Con	4 + Int	—	—	—	—	+3/+3

Feat: You gain another feat. If you find yourself running out of ki regularly, consider selecting Extra Ki.

High Jump: Your ability to jump using the Acrobatics skill improves drastically, and you can spend ki to gain a huge bonus on such checks.

Purity of Body: You're now immune to all diseases, including magical or supernatural ones.

6th Level

	HP	SKILL RANKS	BAB	FORT	REF	WILL	FLURRY OF BLOWS
	1d8 + Con	4 + Int	+1	+1	+1	+1	+4/+4/−1

Bonus Feat: You gain another monk feat, and several new feats are added to your list of choices.

Fast Movement: Your speed increases by an additional 10 feet per round.

Flurry of Blows: When using flurry of blows, you gain yet another attack.

Slow Fall 30 Feet: The distance that you can safely fall increases by 10 feet.

7th Level

	HP	SKILL RANKS	BAB	FORT	REF	WILL	FLURRY OF BLOWS
	1d8 + Con	4 + Int	+1	—	—	—	+5/+5/+0

Feat: You gain another feat.

Ki Pool (cold iron and silver): Your unarmed strikes are now treated as cold iron and silver weapons for the purposes of overcoming damage reduction.

Wholeness of Body: By spending 2 ki points, you can heal yourself for a number of hit points equal to your monk level. This is most useful in an emergency or when you're taking bleed damage, which is negated by healing effects.

 A monk loses his special monk Armor Class bonuses if he's immobilized or helpless, when he's armored, or when he's carrying a shield or a medium or heavy load.

8th Level

	HP	SKILL RANKS	BAB	FORT	REF	WILL	FLURRY OF BLOWS
	1d8 + Con	4 + Int	+1	+1	+1	+1	+6/+6/+1/+1

Ability Score Increase: You gain a permanent +1 increase to an ability score of your choice.

Attack Bonus: Now that your base attack bonus is +6, you get a second attack (at an attack bonus +1) whenever you make a full attack (see page 122). From now on, any bonuses to your BAB apply to this attack as well.

Armor Class Bonus: When you're not wearing armor, your Armor Class and combat maneuver defense increase by an additional 1.

Flurry of Blows: When using flurry of blows, you now gain yet another attack.

Slow Fall 40 Feet: The distance that you can safely fall increases by 10 feet.

Unarmed Strike Damage Increase: Your unarmed strikes now deal 1d10 points of damage, making them the equivalent of a greatclub.

9th Level

	HP	SKILL RANKS	BAB	FORT	REF	WILL	FLURRY OF BLOWS
	1d8 + Con	4 + Int	—	—	—	—	+7/+7/+2/+2

Feat: You gain another feat. Because your base attack bonus is now +6, several very attractive feats are available. Lunge is excellent for many monks because flurry of blows is so important; this feat grants you extra reach, which means that even more foes are in range of your flurry of blows.

 Greater Bull Rush and Greater Grapple are both excellent feats. If you selected Combat Expertise at an earlier level, you probably qualify for Greater Disarm and Greater Trip.

Fast Movement: Your speed increases by an additional 10 feet per round.

Improved Evasion: Not only do you take no damage on most successful Reflex saves, but you now take only half the normal amount of damage even if you fail the saving throw.

10th Level

	HP	SKILL RANKS	BAB	FORT	REF	WILL	FLURRY OF BLOWS
	1d8 + Con	4 + Int	+1	+1	+1	+1	+8/+8/+3/+3

Bonus Feat: You gain another monk feat.

Ki Pool (lawful): Your unarmed strikes are now treated as lawful weapons for the purposes of overcoming damage reduction.

Slow Fall 50 Feet: The distance that you can safely fall increases by 10 feet.

11th Level

	HP	SKILL RANKS	BAB	FORT	REF	WILL	FLURRY OF BLOWS
	1d8 + Con	4 + Int	+1	—	—	—	+9/+9/+4/+4/–1

Feat: You gain another feat. Because your base attack bonus is now +8, you qualify for Improved Critical. This is an excellent feat, particularly considering the high number of attacks you can make each round.

Diamond Body: You're now immune to all poisons, sparing you from one of the most common sources of ability damage.

Flurry of Blows: When using flurry of blows, you now gain yet another attack.

12th Level

	HP	SKILL RANKS	BAB	FORT	REF	WILL	FLURRY OF BLOWS
	1d8 + Con	4 + Int	+1	+1	+1	+1	+10/+10/+5/+5/+0

Ability Score Increase: You gain a permanent +1 increase to an ability score of your choice.

Abundant Step: You can now spend ki to teleport short distances.

Armor Class Bonus: When you're not wearing armor, your Armor Class and combat maneuver defense increase by an additional 1.

Fast Movement: Your speed increases by an additional 10 feet per round.

Slow Fall 60 Feet: The distance that you can safely fall increases by 10 feet.

Unarmed Strike Damage Increase: Your unarmed strikes now deal 2d6 points of damage, making them equivalent to a greatsword.

 One of the defining features of the monk is his facility with combat maneuvers—battlefield tricks such as tripping, disarming, or grappling an opponent. You can learn more about combat maneuvers on page 132.

13th Level

	HP	SKILL RANKS	BAB	FORT	REF	WILL	FLURRY OF BLOWS
	1d8 + Con	4 + Int	—	—	—	—	+11/+11/+6/+6/+1

Feat: You gain another feat.

Diamond Soul: You gain an amount of spell resistance equal to 10 + your monk level. That's enough to make about 50% of spells fail against you automatically, depending on the level of the caster.

14th Level

	HP	SKILL RANKS	BAB	FORT	REF	WILL	FLURRY OF BLOWS
	1d8 + Con	4 + Int	+1	+1	+1	+1	+12/+12/+7/+7/+2

Bonus Feat: You gain another monk feat.

Slow Fall 70 Feet: The distance that you can safely fall increases by 10 feet.

15th Level

	HP	SKILL RANKS	BAB	FORT	REF	WILL	FLURRY OF BLOWS
	1d8 + Con	4 + Int	+1	—	—	—	+13/+13/+8/+8/+3/+3

Attack Bonus: Now that your base attack bonus is +11, you gain a third attack (at an attack bonus of +1) whenever you make a full attack (see page 122). From now on, any bonuses to your BAB apply to this attack as well.

Feat: You gain another feat. Even more critical feats are open to you now.

Fast Movement: Your speed increases by an additional 10 feet per round.

Flurry of Blows: When using flurry of blows, you now gain yet another attack.

Quivering Palm: You gain the ability to strike a creature dead with a single strike (*Core Rulebook* 60).

16th Level

	HP	SKILL RANKS	BAB	FORT	REF	WILL	FLURRY OF BLOWS
	1d8 + Con	4 + Int	+1	+1	+1	+1	+14/+14/+9/+9/+4/+4/−1

Ability Score Increase: You gain a permanent +1 increase to an ability score of your choice.

Armor Class Bonus: When you're not wearing armor, your Armor Class and combat maneuver defense increase by an additional 1.

Flurry of Blows: When using flurry of blows, you gain yet another attack.

Ki Pool (adamantine): Your unarmed strikes are now treated as adamantine weapons for the purposes of overcoming damage reduction and bypassing hardness.

Slow Fall 80 Feet: The distance that you can safely fall increases by 10 feet.

Unarmed Strike Damage Increase: Your unarmed strikes now deal 2d8 points of damage, which is the equivalent of an oversized greatclub.

Ex-Monks: If a monk's alignment becomes non-lawful, he can't gain new levels as a monk but retains all of his monk abilities. Check with your GM to see what sort of acts she considers significant enough to trigger an alignment change.

17th Level

	HP	SKILL RANKS	BAB	FORT	REF	WILL	FLURRY OF BLOWS
	1d8 + Con	4 + Int	—	—	—	—	+15/+15/+10/+10/+5/+5/+0

Feat: You gain another feat.

Timeless Body: You're now virtually immune to aging. This is a fun ability for campaigns that span many years, though the average adventurer might not get much use out of it.

Tongue of the Sun and Moon: You can now communicate with any living creature.

18th Level

	HP	SKILL RANKS	BAB	FORT	REF	WILL	FLURRY OF BLOWS
	1d8 + Con	4 + Int	+1	+1	+1	+1	+16/+16/+11/+11/+6/+6/+1

Bonus Feat: You gain another monk feat.

Fast Movement: Your speed increases by an additional 10 feet per round.

Slow Fall 90 Feet: The distance that you can safely fall increases by 10 feet.

19th Level

	HP	SKILL RANKS	BAB	FORT	REF	WILL	FLURRY OF BLOWS
	1d8 + Con	4 + Int	+1	—	—	—	+17/+17/+12/+12/+7/+7/+2

Feat: You gain another feat.

Empty Body: You can now become ethereal—this makes you invisible and able to move like a ghost through walls—by spending ki.

20th Level

	HP	SKILL RANKS	BAB	FORT	REF	WILL	FLURRY OF BLOWS
	1d8 + Con	4 + Int	+1	+1	+1	+1	+18/+18/+13/+13/+8/+8/+3

Ability Score Increase: You gain a permanent +1 increase to an ability score of your choice.

Armor Class Bonus: When you're not wearing armor, your Armor Class and combat maneuver defense increase by an additional 1.

Perfect Self: You have transcended your corporeal limitations, and are now treated as an **outsider** (a creature from another plane). Additionally, you ignore the first 10 points of damage from nonchaotic weapons.

Slow Fall Any Distance: You can fall any distance along a flat surface without taking damage.

Unarmed Strike Damage Increase: Your unarmed strikes now deal 2d10 points of damage, which is off the charts.

Unlike other outsiders, a 20th-level monk can still be brought back from the dead as if he were a member of his previous creature type.

PALADIN

Paladins are noble warriors who bear divine power into battle against chaos and evil. Your paladin might be a mighty crusader carrying a blessed weapon or a glorious knight riding a majestic steed.

 CRUSADER (PAGE 18)　　 **KNIGHT** (PAGE 21)

ABILITY SCORES

You'll want a high Strength score to deal lots of damage in melee combat, and a high Constitution score to stay alive. Your magical abilities are based on your Charisma score, so that should be a priority as well.

> **Knight**: If you're playing a knight, you'll want at least an average Dexterity score, as mounted combat sometimes requires nimble maneuvering.

SKILLS

Paladins' high Charisma and Strength scores make them perfectly suited to handle both martial and social challenges, and their sterling reputations mean they're good choices to deal with rulers and nobility.

 **SKILL RANKS PER LEVEL:** 2 + Intelligence modifier

Class Skills for Paladins

Craft
Diplomacy
Handle Animal
Heal
Knowledge (nobility, religion)
Profession
Ride
Sense Motive
Spellcraft

- Your high Charisma score gives you a natural aptitude for dealing with people, and you may want to further enhance that by putting a rank into Diplomacy.
- If you want to be knowledgeable about heraldry and the rulers of the land, put a rank into Knowledge (nobility).
- Put a rank into Sense Motive to be better at sensing others' lies.
- Even though it's not a class skill, you may want to put a rank into Perception to make it harder for enemies to sneak up on you.

 Remember, if you put at least 1 rank into any of your class skills, you get a +3 bonus to your total for that skill to represent your class training. At 1st level, you can't put more than 1 rank in a particular skill. If you're human, you get an additional skill rank to spend at each level, including 1st level.

ALIGNMENT
All paladins are lawful good.

HIT DIE
Your Hit Die is a d10. At 1st level, you have 10 hit points plus your Constitution modifier.

BASE ATTACK BONUS **+1**
Your base attack bonus is +1, and it will increase every time you gain a level.

SAVING THROWS
A paladin has to be physically and mentally strong in the face of great evil.

FORTITUDE **+2**
Your Fortitude save bonus is +2 plus your Constitution modifier.

REFLEX **+0**
Your Reflex save bonus is +0 plus your Dexterity modifier.

WILL **+2**
Your Will save bonus is +2 plus your Wisdom modifier.

WEAPON AND ARMOR PROFICIENCIES

Your combat training means you can freely use most kinds of weapons and armor. You should use either one big melee weapon (such as a greatsword), which can deal a lot of damage, or a one-handed weapon (such as a longsword or warhammer) with a wooden shield, which makes it harder for enemies to hit you.

Wear the heaviest armor you can afford—at 1st level, that's probably scale mail or chainmail. Your armor is going to slow down your movement (see Speed on page 150 of the *Core Rulebook*), but you'll need the extra protection. As soon as you can afford it, get banded mail, half-plate, or full plate.

FEATS

As a paladin, you should choose feats that enhance your combat abilities.

YOU GET ONE FEAT AT 1ST LEVEL
Two if you're human

Power Attack	Want to eliminate an enemy with a single blow? Trade accuracy for power—take a –1 penalty on melee attack rolls to gain a +2 bonus on damage rolls. (*Core Rulebook* 131)
Weapon Focus	Get a +1 bonus on attacks made with your main weapon. (*Core Rulebook* 136)
	Select one of the two feats suggested above.
	A lance is a powerful weapon for a knight, so you may want to choose Weapon Focus (lance) (*Core Rulebook* 136) even if you don't yet have a mount. If you want to get a head start on becoming a mounted warrior, choose Mounted Combat (*Core Rulebook* 131).

CLASS FEATURES

Aura of Good: Your aura makes it slightly easier for anyone using magic to detect good creatures to notice you.

Code of Conduct: A paladin's code requires that she be of lawful good alignment. She loses all of her paladin class features (except the weapon and armor proficiencies) if she ever willingly commits an evil act. In addition, her code requires her to respect legitimate authority, act with honor, help those in need, and punish those who harm innocents.

Detect Evil: As a move action, you can concentrate on a single item or creature within 60 feet and determine whether it's evil. You can use this ability as often as you want. Remember that just because a person is evil doesn't mean you can kill him for no reason!

Smite Evil: This is your main special attack. Once per day as a swift action, you can choose one target within your sight to smite. If the target is evil, you add your Charisma modifier to your attack rolls, your paladin level to damage rolls, and your Charisma modifier to your AC against this creature. If your target isn't evil, the smite is wasted.

 TIP At 1st level you can use smite only once per day, so save it for powerful enemies or emergencies.

79

LEVELING UP

The next few pages explain the abilities you get at 2nd level and higher. Some of these abilities are just additions to your 1st-level abilities, and are noted in a Level Up bar: additional hit points and skill ranks, and increases to your base attack bonus, Fortitude save bonus, Reflex save bonus, and Will save bonus.

The information about what you gain at each level is also presented as Table 3–11: Paladin on page 62 of the *Core Rulebook*.

 CRUSADER (PAGE 18)   **KNIGHT** (PAGE 21)

When selecting your feats, spells, and class features as you go up in level, you should focus on enhancing those abilities that allow you to best help the rest of your party. If you're primarily a melee combatant, you should take feats that increase your accuracy or help you deal extra damage. Alternatively, if you're the primary healer in the group, taking a feat like Extra Lay on Hands will give you more healing to spread around to the group.

2nd Level

HP	SKILL RANKS	BAB	FORT	REF	WILL
1d10 + Con	2 + Int	+1	+1	—	+1

Your hit points increase by 1d10 + your Constitution modifier. Unlike at 1st level, you must roll for these hit points.

You also gain a number of skill ranks equal to 2 + your Intelligence modifier. If you're human, don't forget the bonus skill rank per level.

Your base attack bonus, Fortitude save bonus, and Will save bonus each increase by 1.

Divine Grace: You now add your Charisma bonus to all three of your saving throws (only your bonus—if you have a penalty, don't subtract it from your saving throws). You should write this bonus under Misc. Bonus on your character sheet and adjust your saving throws.

Lay on Hands: This ability allows you to heal yourself or others with a touch. You can use this ability a number of times per day equal to 1/2 your paladin level + your Charisma modifier (if your modifier is negative, it reduces the number of times you can use this ability per day). At 2nd level, this ability will heal 1d6 points of damage each time you use it. You can also use this ability as a touch attack against an undead creature to deal 1d6 points of damage to it.

 Ex-Paladins: In addition to losing all her other class abilities, a paladin who violates her code of conduct loses the services of her mount. She can regain her abilities by seeking atonement (*Core Rulebook* 64).

3rd Level

HP	SKILL RANKS	BAB	FORT	REF	WILL
1d10 + Con	2 + Int	+1	—	+1	—

Feat: You gain another feat. You should consider some of the same choices you had at 1st level. In addition, if you're using a shield, you might want to consider Shield Focus, a feat that adds to your Armor Class when using a shield. Extra Lay on Hands is a good feat if you want more daily uses of that ability.

	If you took Power Attack at 1st level, you might want to consider Cleave, a feat that lets you hit two enemies with one attack.
	If you took Mounted Combat at 1st level, Ride-By Attack gives you a bit more mobility while making attacks from your mount.

Aura of Courage: This ability makes you immune to fear and grants nearby allies a bonus on saving throws against fear effects.

Divine Health: You're now immune to all diseases, including magical and supernatural ones.

Mercy: When you heal yourself or an ally with your lay on hands ability, you also remove a condition from the target of your healing. Now, you can choose fatigued, shaken, or sickened. Consider selecting shaken or sickened, as these conditions are fairly common at low levels. All future mercies you select will stack with this one, eventually making your lay on hands ability remarkably powerful.

4th Level

	HP	SKILL RANKS	BAB	FORT	REF	WILL
	1d10 + Con	2 + Int	+1	+1	—	+1

Ability Score Increase: You gain a permanent +1 increase to one ability score of your choice. This should be added to an ability score that's important to you—like Strength or Charisma—especially if you have an odd number in either of them, as your modifier increases at even numbers.

Channel Positive Energy: You can use your lay on hands ability to heal everyone within 30 feet of you. This requires two of your daily uses of lay on hands, and heals enemies in the area too, so be careful when you use it.

Lay on Hands: You can use this ability one additional time per day, and it now heals 2d6 points of damage each time you use it.

Smite Evil: You can use this ability one additional time per day.

Spells: Each day, you can pray or meditate for 1 hour to prepare a limited number of divine spells from the paladin spell list (*Core Rulebook* 232). You can cast each spell you prepare once per day (although you can prepare multiple "copies" of the same spell if you can cast multiple spells of that level per day). In order to cast a spell, your Charisma score must be at least 10 + the spell level (for example, in order to cast a 2nd-level spell, a paladin must have a Charisma of at least 12). Paladins with high Charisma scores can prepare additional spells per day (*Core Rulebook* 17). At 4th level, a paladin with a Charisma score of 12 or higher can prepare one 1st-level spell (a paladin with a Charisma score of 20 or higher can cast two 1st-level spells per day). If your Charisma score is below 12, you can't prepare spells until you reach 5th level. When you do gain the ability to prepare spells, you should consider *bless* (which gives you and all your allies a boost), *divine favor* (which gives a bigger boost, but only to you), or *protection from evil* (which increases the target's defenses against evil opponents). The Difficulty Class (DC) for a saving throw against your spells is 10 + the spell level + your Charisma modifier.

5th Level

	HP	SKILL RANKS	BAB	FORT	REF	WILL
	1d10 + Con	2 + Int	+1	—	—	—

Feat: You gain another feat. While considering your previous options, you should also consider Selective Channel, which allows you to channel positive energy to heal your allies during combat without also healing your enemies.

 If you haven't taken Mounted Combat yet, you should do so now.

Divine Bond: This powerful ability allows you to imbue your weapon with holy power or to summon a faithful steed to serve you in battle.

 You should select the ability to bond with a celestial spirit that enhances your weapon. Since you can use this ability only once per day at 5th level, you should save it for critical fights.

 You should select the ability to bond with a mount. Although you can summon the mount only once per day, it remains at your side for as long as you need, allowing you to ride it into combat.

Spells: If your Charisma is 11, you can prepare one 1st-level paladin spell each day. Otherwise, you can prepare one additional 1st-level spell each day.

6th Level

	HP	SKILL RANKS	BAB	FORT	REF	WILL
	1d10 + Con	2 + Int	+1	+1	+1	+1

Attack Bonus: Now that your base attack bonus is at +6, you get a second attack (at an attack bonus of +1) whenever you make a full attack (see page 122). From now on, any bonuses to your BAB apply to this attack as well.

Lay on Hands: You can use this ability one additional time per day, and it heals 3d6 points of damage each time you use it.

Mercy: Select another mercy. In addition to the choices at 3rd level, you can also select from dazed, diseased, and staggered. Of those, staggered is probably the most useful one to choose, unless you've encountered a lot of diseases during your adventures.

7th Level

	HP	SKILL RANKS	BAB	FORT	REF	WILL
	1d10 + Con	2 + Int	+1	—	—	—

Feat: You gain another feat. In addition to your previous choices, consider Vital Strike, a feat that lets you deal additional damage when you make a single attack on your turn.

Smite Evil: You can use this ability one additional time per day.

Spells: If your Charisma score is 14 or higher, you can prepare one 2nd-level spell per day (if not, you can't prepare 2nd-level paladin spells until 8th level). Consider preparing *bull's strength*, which allows you to deal more damage with melee attacks, or *resist energy*, which protects you from one type of energy damage (such as the fire from a *fireball* spell).

8th Level

	HP	SKILL RANKS	BAB	FORT	REF	WILL
	1d10 + Con	2 + Int	+1	+1	—	+1

Ability Score Increase: You gain a permanent +1 increase to an ability score of your choice.

Aura of Resolve: This ability makes you immune to charm spells and gives nearby allies a +4 bonus on saves against such spells and effects.

Lay on Hands: You can use this ability one additional time per day, and it heals 4d6 points of damage each time you use it.

Spells: If your Charisma is under 14, you can prepare one 2nd-level spell each day. Otherwise, you can prepare one additional 2nd-level spell each day.

9th Level

	HP	SKILL RANKS	BAB	FORT	REF	WILL
	1d10 + Con	2 + Int	+1	—	+1	—

Feat: You gain another feat.

Mercy: You gain an additional mercy. In addition to your previous choices, you can select from cursed, exhausted, frightened, nauseated, and poisoned. Consider taking frightened or poisoned, as these are the most common conditions encountered at this level.

Spells: You can prepare one additional 1st-level spell per day.

10th Level

	HP	SKILL RANKS	BAB	FORT	REF	WILL
	1d10 + Con	2 + Int	+1	+1	—	+1

Lay on Hands: You can use this ability one additional time per day, and it heals 5d6 points of damage each time you use it.

Smite Evil: You can use this ability one additional time per day.

Spells: If your Charisma is 16 or higher, you can prepare one 3rd-level spell per day (if not, you can't prepare 3rd-level spells until 11th level).

 Greater magic weapon is a good choice for your 3rd-level spell, as is *prayer*.

 If your mount takes damage frequently, consider *heal mount*.

11th Level

	HP	SKILL RANKS	BAB	FORT	REF	WILL
	1d10 + Con	2 + Int	+1	—	—	—

Attack Bonus: Now that your base attack bonus is at +11, you gain a third attack (at an attack bonus of +1) whenever you make a full attack (see page 122). From now on, any bonuses to your BAB apply to this attack as well.

Feat: You gain another feat.

Aura of Justice: You can expend two uses of smite evil to let your nearby allies smite evil too.

Spells: If your Charisma is under 16, you can prepare one 3rd-level spell each day. Otherwise, you can prepare one additional 3rd-level spell each day.

12th Level

	HP	SKILL RANKS	BAB	FORT	REF	WILL
	1d10 + Con	2 + Int	+1	+1	+1	+1

Ability Score Increase: You gain a permanent +1 increase to an ability score of your choice.

Lay on Hands: You can use this ability one additional time per day, and it heals 6d6 points of damage each time you use it.

Mercy: Select one additional mercy. In addition to your previous choices, you can select from blinded, deafened, paralyzed, or stunned. From your new options, paralyzed and stunned are both good choices.

Spells: You can prepare one additional 2nd-level spell per day.

13th Level

	HP	SKILL RANKS	BAB	FORT	REF	WILL
	1d10 + Con	2 + Int	+1	—	—	—

Feat: You gain another feat.

Smite Evil: You can use this ability one additional time per day.

Spells: You can prepare one additional 1st-level spell per day. If your Charisma is 18 or higher, you can prepare one 4th-level spell per day (if not, you can't prepare 4th-level spells until 14th level). *Holy sword* is a good choice for a 4th-level spell.

14th Level

HP	SKILL RANKS	BAB	FORT	REF	WILL
1d10 + Con	2 + Int	+1	+1	—	+1

Aura of Faith: Your weapons, and those of your nearby allies, are better at damaging evil creatures such as demons and devils.

Lay on Hands: You can use this ability one additional time per day, and it heals 7d6 points of damage each time you use it.

Spells: If your Charisma is under 18, you can prepare one 4th-level spell each day. Otherwise, you can prepare one additional 4th-level spell each day.

15th Level

HP	SKILL RANKS	BAB	FORT	REF	WILL
1d10 + Con	2 + Int	+1	—	+1	—

Feat: You gain another feat.

Mercy: Select another mercy.

Spells: You can prepare one additional 3rd-level spell per day.

16th Level

HP	SKILL RANKS	BAB	FORT	REF	WILL
1d10 + Con	2 + Int	+1	+1	—	+1

Ability Score Increase: You gain a permanent +1 increase to an ability score of your choice.

Attack Bonus: Now that your base attack bonus is at +16, you gain a fourth attack (at an attack bonus of +1) whenever you make a full attack (see page 122). From now on, any bonuses to your BAB apply to this attack as well.

Lay on Hands: You can use this ability one additional time per day, and it heals 8d6 points of damage each time you use it.

Smite Evil: You can now use this ability one additional time per day.

Spells: You can prepare one additional 2nd-level spell per day.

17th Level

HP	SKILL RANKS	BAB	FORT	REF	WILL
1d10 + Con	2 + Int	+1	—	—	—

Feat: You gain another feat.

Aura of Righteousness: You gain damage reduction 5/evil, which means all physical attacks (but not spells) deal 5 fewer points of damage to you unless they are from an evil source. You're also immune to compulsions.

Spells: You can prepare one additional 1st-level spell per day.

18th Level

HP	SKILL RANKS	BAB	FORT	REF	WILL
1d10 + Con	2 + Int	+1	+1	+1	+1

Lay on Hands: You can use this ability one additional time per day, and it heals 9d6 points of damage each time you use it.

Mercy: Select another mercy.

Spells: You can prepare one additional 4th-level spell per day.

19th Level

HP	SKILL RANKS	BAB	FORT	REF	WILL
1d10 + Con	2 + Int	+1	—	—	—

Feat: You gain another feat.

Smite Evil: You can now use this ability one additional time per day.

Spells: You can prepare one additional 3rd-level spell per day.

20th Level

HP	SKILL RANKS	BAB	FORT	REF	WILL
1d10 + Con	2 + Int	+1	+1	—	+1

Ability Score Increase: You gain a permanent +1 increase to an ability score of your choice.

Holy Champion: You become a divine conduit for your deity. Your damage reduction increases to 10/evil, and your smite evil ability can banish demons, devils, and other evil outsiders.

Lay on Hands: You can use this ability one additional time per day, and it heals 10d6 points of damage each time you use it.

Spells: You can prepare one additional 4th-level spell and one additional 2nd-level spell per day.

RANGER

Talented trackers and versatile wilderness warriors, rangers are adept at bringing down their favored enemies. Your ranger might be a deadeye archer or a dual-weapon whirlwind of destruction.

 ARCHER (PAGE 15)

 DUAL-WEAPON WARRIOR (PAGE 19)

ABILITY SCORES

A ranger values Strength to improve melee attacks and damage with melee weapons and composite bows. A high Dexterity score improves your Armor Class and chance of hitting with ranged weapons.

 TIP A high Constitution score boosts hit points to help you survive; a high Wisdom score strengthens your spellcasting and class abilities.

SKILLS

Rangers are masters of their environments, in touch with the flora and fauna of their home turf. You'll likely be the party's guide, tracker, animal wrangler, and scout. You also get a 1st-level ability that acts like the Diplomacy skill, but with animals.

 **SKILL RANKS PER LEVEL**
6 + Intelligence modifier

Class Skills for Rangers

Climb	Perception
Craft	Profession
Handle Animal	Ride
Heal	Spellcraft
Intimidate	Stealth
Knowledge	Survival
(dungeoneering,	Swim
geography, nature)	

- Put a rank in Climb or Swim to move more effectively in your chosen environment.
- Handle Animal helps you train and command animals more effectively, so invest a rank there.
- Your party will likely look to you as the wilderness expert, so put a rank in Knowledge (nature) to help you identify animals, plants, and hazards.
- Put a rank in Perception so you can spot your enemies before they can surprise you.
- Stealth lets you scout undetected, so invest a rank in it.
- You can't guide your party or track your enemies if you're lost, so put a rank in Survival to keep your bearings in the wilderness.

 Remember, if you put at least 1 rank into any of your class skills, you get a +3 bonus to your total for that skill to represent your class training. At 1st level, you can't put more than 1 rank in a particular skill. If you're human, you get an additional skill rank to spend at each level, including 1st level.

ALIGNMENT
You can be of any alignment.

HIT DIE
Your Hit Die is a d10. At 1st level, you have 10 hit points plus your Constitution modifier.

BASE ATTACK BONUS **+1**
Your base attack bonus is +1, and it will increase every time you gain a level.

SAVING THROWS
A ranger must be able to shrug off punishing conditions and dodge out of the way of natural hazards.

FORTITUDE **+2**
Your Fortitude save bonus is +2 plus your Constitution modifier.

REFLEX **+2**
Your Reflex save bonus is +2 plus your Dexterity modifier.

WILL **+0**
Your Will save bonus is +0 plus your Wisdom modifier.

WEAPON AND ARMOR PROFICIENCIES

You're proficient with light armor, medium armor, and shields; the important trade-off is defense versus speed. Choose light armor if you prefer speed, or choose medium armor if you prefer defense and don't have a very high Dexterity score.

You're proficient with all simple and martial weapons, giving you a wide range of weapons from which you can select.

	Purchase a longbow as well as one or two melee weapons.
	Purchase either a one-handed weapon and a light weapon, or a double weapon. It's a good idea to purchase a ranged weapon as well.

FEATS

Rangers gain extra feats quite often. Most rangers specialize in dealing damage either from afar or up close, but a ranger is also a skill-focused character. Keep your goals in mind as you consider the feats below.

YOU GET ONE FEAT AT 1ST LEVEL
Two if you're human

Nimble Moves	Take a 5-foot step in difficult terrain, which could be the difference between making many attacks or just one. (*Core Rulebook* 131)
Power Attack	Want to eliminate an enemy with a single blow? Trade accuracy for power—take a –1 penalty on melee attack rolls to gain a +2 bonus on damage rolls. It's even more effective when you use a weapon with two hands! (*Core Rulebook* 131)
Quick Draw	Draw a weapon as a free action, or a hidden weapon as a move action; switching weapons quickly may be important if an enemy you're shooting at gets close. (*Core Rulebook* 131)
Weapon Focus	Increase your chances of hitting with your main weapon—get a +1 bonus on attacks made with that weapon. (*Core Rulebook* 136)
	Consider Point-Blank Shot. This provides a reliable boost to ranged attacks and damage, and it's a vital prerequisite for most other archery feats.
	Consider Exotic Weapon Proficiency if you want to use a double weapon other than the quarterstaff, or Two-Weapon Fighting. These improve your melee combat effectiveness.

CLASS FEATURES

Favored Enemy: Choose a category of enemy. This ability grants you a +2 bonus on attack rolls, damage rolls, and many skill checks against creatures in that category (the *Core Rulebook* has a complete list of favored enemy categories on page 64). This ability will improve as you gain ranger levels, and you will also select additional favored enemy categories.

Track: You gain a bonus equal to half your ranger level (minimum 1) on Survival checks to track creatures. This is a specialty of the ranger, and you will gain more tracking abilities as you gain levels.

Wild Empathy: This ability allows you to calm wild animals and magical beasts, much like Diplomacy does with intelligent creatures.

 TIP Because favored enemy is such a central ability for the ranger, it's a good idea to ask your GM what types of favored enemy would make the most sense. If in doubt, humanoid (human), outsider (evil), and undead are common enemy categories in a typical campaign.

ʼNG UP

ain the abilities you get at 2nd level and higher. Some of these abilities are just additions to your 1st-level
:evel Up bar: additional hit points and skill ranks, and increases to your base attack bonus, Fortitude save bonus,
ʼave bonus.

you gain at each level is also presented as Table 3–12: Ranger on page 66 of the *Core Rulebook*.

ARCHER
(PAGE 15)

DUAL-WEAPON WARRIOR
(PAGE 19)

, you will choose a combat style that will dictate many of the other choices you can make later in your career.
ence the sort of gear and magic items that are most valuable to your character. If you're an archer, magic bows
ost. If you're a dual-weapon warrior, on the other hand, you should upgrade your weapons whenever possible.
such as feats and spells, should be made to complement your combat style whenever possible.

	HP	SKILL RANKS	BAB	FORT	REF	WILL
	1d10 + Con	6 + Int	+1	+1	+1	—

d10 + your Constitution modifier. Unlike at 1st level, you must roll for these hit points.

nks equal to 6 + your Intelligence modifier. If you're human, don't forget the bonus skill rank per level.

itude save bonus, and Reflex save bonus each increase by 1.

ose a combat style and select your first of many bonus feats from a thematic list. As an added benefit, you don't
erequisites for these feats, so you can take Two-Weapon Fighting even if your Dexterity is low.

tyle and select Point-Blank Shot if you haven't yet, and select either Precise Shot or Rapid Shot if you have. You
acquire Far Shot, as it's far more situational.

pon combat style and Two-Weapon Fighting (if you don't have it already). If you already have that feat, select
Draw. Choose Improved Shield Bash only if you intend to fight with a shield and a weapon.

Feats that may not seem that strong by themselves sometimes serve as prerequisites for more
powerful feats. Consider using some of your bonus feats to work your way through feat chains and get
access to the formidable feats at the end of the chain.

	HP	SKILL RANKS	BAB	FORT	REF	WILL
	1d10 + Con	6 + Int	+1	—	—	+1

You should consider some of the same choices you had at 1st level that you haven't taken yet, but you'll gain
advance in level, so leave yourself a few good bonus feat options for later on.

which enhances your damage at the cost of accuracy.

n Defense, which improves your Armor Class.

nce as a bonus feat.

arn how to hide, navigate, and take stock of your surroundings better in a terrain type of your choice (see page
complete list of favored terrain types). Just like when you chose a favored enemy, this is a good time to talk
ommendations about what would fit in the campaign. If you're in doubt, forest, underground, and urban are
 regularly in most campaigns.

4th Level

	HP	SKILL RANKS	BAB	FORT	REF	WILL
	1d10 + Con	6 + Int	+1	+1	+1	—

Ability Score Increase: You gain a permanent +1 increase to one ability score of your choice. This should be added to an ability score that's important to you—like Strength or Dexterity—especially if you have an odd number in either of them, as your modifiers increase at even numbers.

Hunter's Bond: You develop a strong bond with either an animal companion or your comrades.

 Choose the animal companion. The animal can engage your enemies in close combat, keeping them from closing with you. Good animal companion choices include the bird, small cat, and wolf. Alternatively, you could choose a horse, camel, or other mount to perform mounted archery, though this requires at least 1 rank in Ride and the Mounted Combat and Mounted Archery feats to perform properly.

 Choose the companion bond. This will help your allies strike your favored enemies, and because using the ability takes only a move action, it's a great way to strengthen your allies as you wait for the enemy to approach.

Spells: Each day, you can pray or meditate for 1 hour to prepare a limited number of divine spells from the ranger spell list (*Core Rulebook* 232). You can cast each spell you prepare once per day (although you can prepare multiple "copies" of the same spell if you can cast multiple spells of that level per day). In order to prepare or cast a spell, your Wisdom must be at least 10 + the spell level (for example, in order to prepare a 2nd-level spell, a ranger must have a Wisdom of at least 12). Rangers with high Wisdom scores get additional bonus spells per day (*Core Rulebook* 17), enabling those with Wisdom scores of 12 or higher to cast one 1st-level spell when they reach 4th level (rangers with a Wisdom score of 20 or more can cast two 1st-level spells per day). If your Wisdom score is below 12, you can't cast spells until you reach 5th level. Ranger spells tend to enhance mobility, provide basic healing, and modify animals and plants. If you gain spells at this level, consider *delay poison*, *jump*, *longstrider*, and *resist energy*. The Difficulty Class (DC) for a saving throw to resist your spells is 10 + the spell level + your Wisdom modifier.

5th Level

	HP	SKILL RANKS	BAB	FORT	REF	WILL
	1d10 + Con	6 + Int	+1	—	—	—

Feat: You gain another feat.

Second Favored Enemy: You gain a second favored enemy with a +2 bonus, and one of your two favored enemy bonuses increases to +4.

Spells: If your Wisdom is 11, you can prepare one 1st-level spell each day. Otherwise, you can prepare one additional 1st-level spell each day.

6th Level

	HP	SKILL RANKS	BAB	FORT	REF	WILL
	1d10 + Con	6 + Int	+1	+1	+1	+1

Attack Bonus: Now that your base attack bonus is +6, you gain a second attack (at an attack bonus of +1) whenever you make a full attack (see page 122). From now on, any bonuses to your BAB apply to this attack as well.

Combat Style Feat: You gain another bonus feat, and your list of options expands.

 Choose Improved Precise Shot to ignore most obstacles or Multishot to increase your damage.

 Choose Improved Two-Weapon Fighting to gain an additional off-hand attack (see page 123).

7th Level

	HP	SKILL RANKS	BAB	FORT	REF	WILL
	1d10 + Con	6 + Int	+1	—	—	—

Feat: You gain another feat.

 Because you have a base attack bonus of +7, you qualify for the Lunge feat, which grants you extra reach and allows you to take a full-attack action even if your target isn't adjacent to you.

Hunter's Bond (animal companion): You're now treated as a 4th-level druid for the purpose of calculating your animal companion's abilities. At this level, many of your possible animal companions become much stronger.

Woodland Stride: You can now walk easily through difficult terrain caused by undergrowth, which both improves your movement speed and gives you a tactical edge while fighting others in those areas.

Spells: If your Wisdom is 14 or higher, you can prepare one 2nd-level spell per day (if not, you can't prepare 2nd-level ranger spells until 8th level). Consider *barkskin*, *cat's grace*, and *wind wall*.

8th Level

	HP	SKILL RANKS	BAB	FORT	REF	WILL
	1d10 + Con	6 + Int	+1	+1	+1	—

Ability Score Increase: You gain a permanent +1 increase to an ability score of your choice.

Second Favored Terrain: You gain a second favored terrain with a +2 bonus, and one of your two favored terrain bonuses increases to +4 (see the 3rd-level section for advice).

Swift Tracker: You can now follow tracks without slowing down.

Spells: If your Wisdom is under 14, you can prepare one 2nd-level spell each day. Otherwise, you can prepare one additional 2nd-level spell each day.

9th Level

	HP	SKILL RANKS	BAB	FORT	REF	WILL
	1d10 + Con	6 + Int	+1	—	—	+1

Feat: You gain another feat. Because you have a base attack bonus of +9, you qualify for the Improved Critical feat, which doubles the critical threat range of your attacks with one type of weapon.

Evasion: Instead of taking half the normal damage from spells and effects that deal damage on a successful Reflex save, you take no damage.

Spells: You can prepare one additional 1st-level spell per day.

10th Level

	HP	SKILL RANKS	BAB	FORT	REF	WILL
	1d10 + Con	6 + Int	+1	+1	+1	—

Combat Style Feat: You gain another bonus feat, and your list of options expands.

 Choose Shot on the Run to become a better skirmisher, or a feat from earlier lists. Consider Pinpoint Targeting if you're having trouble hitting your targets.

 Choose Greater Two-Weapon Fighting to gain another off-hand attack.

Third Favored Enemy: You gain a third favored enemy with a +2 bonus, and one of your three favored enemy bonuses increases by 2. See the favored enemy class feature description on page 85 for advice.

Spells: If your Wisdom is 16 or higher, you can prepare one 3rd-level spell per day (if not, you can't prepare 3rd-level spells until 11th level). Consider *darkvision*, *diminish plants*, and *plant growth*.

11th Level

	HP	SKILL RANKS	BAB	FORT	REF	WILL
	1d10 + Con	6 + Int	+1	—	—	—

Attack Bonus: Now that your base attack bonus is +11, you gain a third attack (at an attack bonus of +1) whenever you make a full attack (see page 122). From now on, any bonuses to your BAB apply to this attack as well.

Feat: You gain another feat.

Quarry: You can boost your tracking and combat bonuses against one creature that you designate.

Spells: If your Wisdom is under 16, you can prepare one 3rd-level spell each day. Otherwise, you can prepare one additional 3rd-level spell each day.

12th Level

	HP	SKILL RANKS	BAB	FORT	REF	WILL
	1d10 + Con	6 + Int	+1	+1	+1	+1

Ability Score Increase: You gain a permanent +1 increase to an ability score of your choice.

Camouflage: While in one of your favored terrains, you don't need cover or concealment to hide using Stealth checks.

Spells: You can prepare one additional 2nd-level spell per day.

13th Level

	HP	SKILL RANKS	BAB	FORT	REF	WILL
	1d10 + Con	6 + Int	+1	—	—	—

Feat: You gain another feat.

Third Favored Terrain: You gain a third favored terrain with a +2 bonus, and one of your three favored terrain bonuses increases by +2. See the 3rd-level section for advice.

Spells: You can prepare one additional 1st-level spell per day. If your Wisdom is 18 or higher, you can prepare one 4th-level ranger spell per day (if not, you can't prepare 4th-level spells until 14th level). Consider *animal growth*, *commune with nature*, and *freedom of movement*.

14th Level

HP	SKILL RANKS	BAB	FORT	REF	WILL
1d10 + Con	6 + Int	+1	+1	+1	—

Combat Style Feat: You gain another bonus feat from the earlier lists.

Spells: If your Wisdom is under 18, you can prepare one 4th-level spell each day. Otherwise, you can prepare one additional 4th-level spell each day.

15th Level

HP	SKILL RANKS	BAB	FORT	REF	WILL
1d10 + Con	6 + Int	+1	—	—	+1

Feat: You gain another feat.

Fourth Favored Enemy: You gain a fourth favored enemy with a +2 bonus, and one of your four favored enemy bonuses increases by 2. See the favored enemy class feature description on page 85 for advice.

Spells: You can prepare one additional 3rd-level spell per day.

16th Level

HP	SKILL RANKS	BAB	FORT	REF	WILL
1d10 + Con	6 + Int	+1	+1	+1	—

Ability Score Increase: You gain a permanent +1 increase to an ability score of your choice.

Attack Bonus: Now that your base attack bonus is +16, you gain a fourth attack (at an attack bonus of +1) whenever you make a full attack (see page 122). From now on, any bonuses to your BAB apply to this attack as well.

Improved Evasion: Not only do you take no damage on most successful Reflex saves, you now only take half the normal damage even if you fail the saving throw.

Spells: You can prepare one additional 2nd-level spell per day.

17th Level

HP	SKILL RANKS	BAB	FORT	REF	WILL
1d10 + Con	6 + Int	+1	—	—	—

Feat: You gain another feat.

Hide in Plain Sight: While in one of your favored terrains, you gain the ability to hide even while someone is watching you.

Spells: You can prepare one additional 1st-level spell per day.

18th Level

HP	SKILL RANKS	BAB	FORT	REF	WILL
1d10 + Con	6 + Int	+1	+1	+1	+1

Combat Style Feat: You gain another bonus feat from the earlier lists.

Fourth Favored Terrain: You gain a fourth favored terrain with a +2 bonus, and one of your four favored terrain bonuses increases by +2. See the 3rd-level section for advice.

Spells: You can prepare one additional 4th-level spell per day.

19th Level

HP	SKILL RANKS	BAB	FORT	REF	WILL
1d10 + Con	6 + Int	+1	—	—	—

Feat: You gain another feat.

Improved Quarry: You can now select a quarry as a free action, your bonus on attack rolls against your quarry increases to +4, and more.

Spells: You can prepare one additional 3rd-level spell per day.

20th Level

HP	SKILL RANKS	BAB	FORT	REF	WILL
1d10 + Con	6 + Int	+1	+1	+1	—

Ability Score Increase: You gain a permanent +1 increase to an ability score of your choice.

Fifth Favored Enemy: You gain a fifth favored enemy with a +2 bonus, and you can increase your existing bonus against one favored enemy by 2. The earlier advice about selecting a favored enemy still applies.

Master Hunter: You become even faster when tracking, but more importantly, you gain the ability to kill a favored enemy with one hit.

Spells: You can prepare one additional 4th-level spell and one additional 2nd-level spell per day.

ROGUE

Stealthy assassins, cunning troubleshooters, and agile acrobats, rogues are equally talented at outwitting their opponents and stabbing them in the back! Your rogue might be a sneaky opportunist or a master of many skills.

 SHADOW (PAGE 23)   **THIEF (PAGE 25)**

SHADOW (PAGE 23)
THIEF (PAGE 25)

ABILITY SCORES

Rogues value Dexterity because it improves many of their skills, and helps them move faster and strike more accurately.

 TIP Every ability score can be helpful depending on your theme and style.

Shadow: High Strength and Constitution scores will help you hit harder and take a few hits without falling.

Thief: You may want good Intelligence, Wisdom, and Charisma scores to gain more skill points, spot danger more reliably, and trick others into believing you, respectively.

SKILLS

Rogues are good at pretty much everything, skill-wise. Given their vast number of class skills and generous allotment of skill ranks, it makes sense to have a rogue be the party's jack of all trades, though she'll still have to specialize somewhat to use her skill ranks most effectively.

 **SKILL RANKS PER LEVEL**
8 + Intelligence modifier

Class Skills for Rogues

Acrobatics	Disable Device	Linguistics	Stealth
Appraise	Disguise	Perception	Swim
Bluff	Escape Artist	Perform	Use Magic Device
Climb	Intimidate	Profession	
Craft	Knowledge	Sense Motive	
Diplomacy	(dungeoneering, local)	Sleight of Hand	

- Put a rank in Acrobatics so you can jump, tumble, and balance with ease, especially to get in position to sneak attack foes.
- You're likely to be the party spokesperson, or "face" (see page 146), so put a rank in Bluff, Diplomacy, or Intimidate so you can convince people more effectively.
- Put a rank in Climb or Swim to help you move even more effectively.
- People will look to you to pick locks and disarm traps, so put a rank in Disable Device.
- A rank in Knowledge (local) will give you information about local legends, hazards, and customs.
- Put a rank in Perception so you can spot traps and other hazards.
- A rank in Sleight of Hand will help you swipe small objects without being noticed.
- Put a rank in Stealth so you can move about undetected and sneak attack your enemies.

 Remember, if you put at least 1 rank into any of your class skills, you get a +3 bonus to your total for that skill to represent your class training. At 1st level, you can't put more than 1 rank in a particular skill. If you're human, you get an additional skill rank to spend at each level, including 1st level.

ALIGNMENT

You can be of any alignment.

HIT DIE

Your Hit Die is a d8. At 1st level, you have 8 hit points plus your Constitution modifier.

BASE ATTACK BONUS **+0**

Your base attack bonus is +0, but it will increase at most levels.

SAVING THROWS

A rogue must be exceptionally quick to avoid traps and other nasty surprises.

FORTITUDE +0

Your Fortitude save bonus is +0 plus your Constitution modifier.

REFLEX +2

Your Reflex save bonus is +2 plus your Dexterity modifier.

WILL +0

Your Will save bonus is +0 plus your Wisdom modifier.

WEAPON AND ARMOR PROFICIENCIES

You're proficient with all simple weapons and several particularly roguish martial weapons, giving you a healthy selection to choose from. Almost every rogue can make good use of a rapier, though Strength-focused rogues might prefer a morningstar. Also purchase a few daggers for emergencies, plus a good ranged weapon like a light crossbow or shortbow. If you want to be able to knock out enemies instead of killing them, buy a sap.

You're proficient with light armor, which protects you well enough from the occasional attack, but isn't enough to save you if you charge ahead alone. As a shadow rogue, consider studded leather armor or a chain shirt for extra protection. As a thief, stick to leather armor for now; it won't interfere with your skill checks.

FEATS

A shadow specializes in dealing damage and moving quickly about the battlefield, whereas a thief is best with skills.

YOU GET ONE FEAT AT 1ST LEVEL
Two if you're human

Combat Expertise	Take a –1 penalty on attack rolls and combat maneuver checks to gain a +1 bonus to your Armor Class. This is a prerequisite for several other interesting feats. (*Core Rulebook* 119)
Improved Initiative	Gain a +4 bonus on initiative checks, and deal sneak attack damage before your enemy even knows combat has begun. (*Core Rulebook* 127)
Nimble Moves	Take a 5-foot step in difficult terrain, which helps you to flank foes and deal sneak attack damage. (*Core Rulebook* 131)
Weapon Finesse	Use your Dexterity for melee attack rolls instead of your Strength. If your Dexterity is high and your Strength is low, this feat is very useful. (*Core Rulebook* 136)

Consider Point Blank Shot or Weapon Focus to improve your combat skills, Great Fortitude or Iron Will to improve your saving throw bonuses, and Toughness or Dodge to increase your chances of survival. Alternatively, consider Skill Focus, Alertness, Deceitful, Persuasive, or Stealthy to improve your skills.

	Take Dodge, Improved Initiative, or Two-Weapon Fighting. These increase your defenses, speed, and offense, respectively.
	Consider Skill Focus (Disable Device), which makes you more likely to bypass locks and traps, or Weapon Finesse, which increases your accuracy in melee.

CLASS FEATURES

Sneak Attack: This ability adds 1d6 extra points of damage whenever you attack a distracted or unaware creature; usually this happens when you surprise a target at the very beginning of combat or when you flank it with the help of an ally. As you gain levels, this extra damage increases.

Trapfinding: This ability gives you a +1 bonus on Perception checks when you're looking for traps and does the same for your Disable Device checks when you're disarming traps. It also allows you to disarm magical traps, which is something nobody else can do. Remember that if you want to spot traps, you still need to actively look for them, so you'll need to tell your GM when and where you're looking. Focus on doors, hallways, treasure chests, and intersections.

 TIP Some kinds of creatures are immune to sneak attack damage—for example, swarms of bees, giant blobs, and creatures made of pure fire don't take sneak attack damage.

SUGGESTED STARTING GEAR

Rogues start with 140 gp.

Shadow: Rapier, daggers (2), sap, shortbow with 20 arrows, leather armor, backpack, bedroll, belt pouch, flint and steel, grappling hook, silk rope (50 ft.), smokestick, sunrod, thieves' tools, tindertwigs (2), trail rations (4 days), waterskin; *Cost* 138 gp (2 gp left); *Weight* 53 lbs. (Medium) or 27 lbs. (Small).

Thief: Rapier, daggers (6), leather armor, sunrod, backpack, belt pouch, bedroll, bullseye lantern, flint and steel, grappling hook, oil (5 flasks), ink (1 vial), inkpen, paper (10 sheets), scroll case, silk rope (50 ft.), thieves' tools, trail rations (4 days), waterskin; *Cost* 128 gp (12 gp left); *Weight* 63 lbs. (Medium) or 42 lbs. (Small).

FAVORED CLASS BONUS

For each rogue level you attain, gain:

+1 *to hp total*

Adding to hit points helps a shadow survive combat.

OR

+1 *skill rank*

All rogues benefit from investing in skills.

LEVELING UP

The next few pages explain the abilities you get at 2nd level and higher. Some of these abilities are just additions to your 1st-level abilities, and are noted in a Level Up bar: additional hit points and skill ranks, additional sneak attack damage dice, and increases to your base attack bonus, Fortitude save bonus, Reflex save bonus, and Will save bonus.

The information about what you gain at each level is also presented as Table 3–13: Rogue on page 69 of the *Core Rulebook*.

 SHADOW (PAGE 23)   **THIEF** (PAGE 25)

One of the keys to leveling up your rogue is careful allotment of your skill ranks. While putting the maximum number of ranks in certain key skills, such as Disable Device or Stealth, should always be a top priority, dabbling in a few other areas, such as Bluff, Diplomacy, or even Knowledge (local) will give you the ability to talk your way out of a tricky situation or serve as the negotiator for the party.

2nd Level

	HP	SKILL RANKS	BAB	FORT	REF	WILL	SNEAK ATTACK
	1d8 + Con	8 + Int	+1	—	+1	—	—

Your hit points increase by 1d8 + your Constitution modifier. Unlike 1st at level, you must roll for these hit points.

You also gain a number of skill ranks equal to 8 + your Intelligence modifier. If you're human, don't forget the bonus skill rank per level.

Your base attack bonus and Reflex save bonus each increase by 1.

Evasion: This ability reduces damage you take from area-effect attacks like a *burning hands* spell or dragon breath. Instead of taking half the normal damage if you succeed at your save, you take no damage at all.

Rogue Talent: You learn a special trick that sharpens your skills, confounds your enemies, or hones your combat abilities. You gain an additional rogue talent at each even level. Trap spotter is a very useful talent for any rogue, for it allows you to automatically attempt a Perception check when you get close to a trap (even when you're not actively searching). However, traps can be rare in some campaigns, so this may not be a good choice (ask the GM whether traps are common enough that this talent is worth taking).

 Consider bleeding attack, combat trick, finesse rogue, or weapon training. All of these make you a more effective combatant.

 Consider fast stealth, ledge walker, or rogue crawl, help you to move faster in difficult conditions. Alternatively, quick disable helps you perform your skills more quickly, and minor magic lets you acquire magical tricks.

3rd Level

	HP	SKILL RANKS	BAB	FORT	REF	WILL	SNEAK ATTACK
	1d8 + Con	8 + Int	+1	+1	—	+1	+1d6

Feat: You gain another feat. You should consider some of the same choices you had at 1st level. If you have Combat Expertise, consider Improved Feint, which allows you to distract your enemies and use sneak attack. If you have Dodge, consider Mobility to move around the battlefield more safely. If you have Nimble Moves, consider Acrobatic Steps, which increases the distance that you can move in difficult terrain. If you have Point Blank Shot, consider Precise Shot (to shoot accurately around your allies) or Rapid Shot (to let you shoot more quickly—even before the enemy has acted).

Trap Sense +1: This ability lets you dodge traps more easily, and it improves every 3 levels. It's still probably not a good idea to trigger traps unless you have to.

4th Level

	HP	SKILL RANKS	BAB	FORT	REF	WILL	SNEAK ATTACK
	1d8 + Con	8 + Int	+1	—	+1	—	—

Ability Score Increase: You gain a permanent +1 increase to one ability score of your choice. This should be added to an ability score that's important to you—like Strength or Dexterity—especially if you have an odd number in either of them, as your modifiers increase at even numbers.

Rogue Talent: You gain another rogue talent. If you took minor magic earlier, consider taking major magic to expand your toolbox of arcane tricks.

Trapfinding: Your bonus on Perception checks to locate traps and Disable Device checks to disable them increases to +2.

Uncanny Dodge: Your senses are so sharp that you react to danger instinctively, making it virtually impossible to catch you unaware. You cannot be caught flat-footed, and you only rarely lose your Dexterity bonus to Armor Class.

 Feats that may not seem that strong by themselves sometimes serve as prerequisites for more powerful feats. Consider using the combat trick rogue talent to gain extra feats and work your way through feat chains to get access to the formidable feats at the end of the chain.

5th Level

	HP	SKILL RANKS	BAB	FORT	REF	WILL	SNEAK ATTACK
	1d8 + Con	8 + Int	—	—	—	—	+1d6

Feat: You gain another feat.

6th Level

	HP	SKILL RANKS	BAB	FORT	REF	WILL	SNEAK ATTACK
	1d8 + Con	8 + Int	+1	+1	+1	+1	—

Rogue Talent: You gain another rogue talent.

Trapfinding: Your bonus on Perception checks to locate traps and Disable Device checks to disable them increases to +3.

Trap Sense +2: The bonuses from your trap sense ability increase by 1.

7th Level

	HP	SKILL RANKS	BAB	FORT	REF	WILL	SNEAK ATTACK
	1d8 + Con	8 + Int	+1	—	—	—	+1d6

Feat: You gain another feat.

8th Level

	HP	SKILL RANKS	BAB	FORT	REF	WILL	SNEAK ATTACK
	1d8 + Con	8 + Int	+1	—	+1	—	—

Ability Score Increase: You gain a permanent +1 increase to an ability score of your choice.

Attack Bonus: Now that your base attack bonus is +6, you gain a second attack (at an attack bonus of +1) whenever you make a full attack (see page 122). From now on, any bonuses to your BAB apply to this attack as well.

Improved Uncanny Dodge: You become impossible to flank, unless it's by a rogue who's much more powerful than you.

Rogue Talent: You gain another rogue talent.

Trapfinding: Your bonus on Perception checks to locate traps and Disable Device checks to disable them increases to +4.

9th Level

	HP	SKILL RANKS	BAB	FORT	REF	WILL	SNEAK ATTACK
	1d8 + Con	8 + Int	—	+1	—	+1	+1d6

Feat: You gain another feat. If you have Two-Weapon Fighting, consider choosing Improved Two-Weapon Fighting, which grants you another off-hand attack.

Trap Sense +3: The bonuses from your trap sense ability increase by 1.

10th Level

	HP	SKILL RANKS	BAB	FORT	REF	WILL	SNEAK ATTACK
	1d8 + Con	8 + Int	+1	—	+1	—	—

Advanced Talents: You gain access to a new set of options that you can choose from every time you gain a new rogue talent. Slippery mind is a valuable talent for any rogue, as it grants you a second chance to break free of an enchantment spell or effect. Improved evasion is attractive because it means you never take full damage from spells and effects that deal only half the normal damage if you succeed at a Reflex saving throw. However, your Reflex save bonus is probably good (which means your chance of failing a Reflex save is low), so this might not be the best choice for you. Using a rogue talent to gain a feat is often a good idea—particularly once you've grabbed the other talents that you really want.

Consider crippling strike to quickly weaken any enemy you sneak attack. Opportunist is excellent for allowing you to make even more attacks each round. Defensive roll gives you a way to escape in emergencies that may save your life.

Skill mastery is an excellent talent. By now your bonuses for your favorite skills are probably exceptional, so taking 10 would still mean success. It also means is that you are unlikely to fail if you roll a low number. For a dedicated thief, this talent may be worth taking at least one more time.

Rogue Talent: You gain another rogue talent. This can be used to choose from the advanced talents to which you now have access (see above), or you can choose another (non-advanced) rogue talent.

Trapfinding: Your bonus on Perception checks to locate traps and Disable Device checks to disable them increases to +5.

11th Level

	HP	SKILL RANKS	BAB	FORT	REF	WILL	SNEAK ATTACK
	1d8 + Con	8 + Int	+1	—	—	—	+1d6

Feat: You gain another feat.

12th Level

	HP	SKILL RANKS	BAB	FORT	REF	WILL	SNEAK ATTACK
	1d8 + Con	8 + Int	+1	+1	+1	+1	—

Ability Score Increase: You gain a permanent +1 increase to an ability score of your choice.

Rogue Talent: You gain another rogue talent.

Trapfinding: Your bonus on Perception checks to locate traps and Disable Device checks to disable them increases to +6.

Trap Sense +4: The bonuses from your trap sense ability increase by 1.

13th Level

	HP	SKILL RANKS	BAB	FORT	REF	WILL	SNEAK ATTACK
	1d8 + Con	8 + Int	—	—	—	—	+1d6

Feat: You gain another feat.

14th Level

	HP	SKILL RANKS	BAB	FORT	REF	WILL	SNEAK ATTACK
	1d8 + Con	8 + Int	+1	—	+1	—	—

Rogue Talent: You gain another rogue talent.

Trapfinding: Your bonus on Perception checks to locate traps and Disable Device checks to disable them increases to +7.

15th Level

	HP	SKILL RANKS	BAB	FORT	REF	WILL	SNEAK ATTACK
	1d8 + Con	8 + Int	+1	+1	—	+1	+1d6

Attack Bonus: Now that your base attack bonus is +11, you gain a third attack (at an attack bonus of +1) whenever you make a full attack (see page 122). From now on, any bonuses to your BAB apply to this attack as well.

Feat: You gain another feat. If you have Improved Two-Weapon Fighting, consider Greater Two-Weapon Fighting, which grants a third attack with your off-hand weapon (see page 123).

Trap Sense +5: The bonuses from your trap sense ability increase by 1.

16th Level

	HP	SKILL RANKS	BAB	FORT	REF	WILL	SNEAK ATTACK
	1d8 + Con	8 + Int	+1	—	+1	—	—

Ability Score Increase: You gain a permanent +1 increase to an ability score of your choice.

Rogue Talent: You gain another rogue talent.

Trapfinding: Your bonus on Perception checks to locate traps and Disable Device checks to disable them increases to +8.

17th Level

	HP	SKILL RANKS	BAB	FORT	REF	WILL	SNEAK ATTACK
	1d8 + Con	8 + Int	—	—	—	—	+1d6

Feat: You gain another feat.

18th Level

	HP	SKILL RANKS	BAB	FORT	REF	WILL	SNEAK ATTACK
	1d8 + Con	8 + Int	+1	+1	+1	+1	—

Rogue Talent: You gain another rogue talent.

Trapfinding: Your bonus on Perception checks to locate traps and Disable Device checks to disable them increases to +9.

Trap Sense +6: The bonuses from your trap sense ability increase by 1.

19th Level

	HP	SKILL RANKS	BAB	FORT	REF	WILL	SNEAK ATTACK
	1d8 + Con	8 + Int	+1	—	—	—	+1d6

Feat: You gain another feat.

20th Level

	HP	SKILL RANKS	BAB	FORT	REF	WILL	SNEAK ATTACK
	1d8 + Con	8 + Int	+1	—	+1	—	—

Ability Score Increase: You gain a permanent +1 increase to an ability score of your choice.

Master Strike: You have perfected the art of the sneak attack to the point that every such attack can instantly knock out, paralyze, or kill the target.

Rogue Talent: You gain another rogue talent.

Trapfinding: Your bonus on Perception checks to locate traps and Disable Device checks to disable them increases to +10.

SORCERER

Sorcerers' instinctive command of eldritch power is a birthright, and their bloodlines give them unique powers that distinguish them from other spellcasters with a wealth of additional abilities and benefits.

 ANGEL-BORN (PAGE 14)   **DRAGON-CHILD** (PAGE 18)   **FIRE-BLOODED** (PAGE 19)

ABILITY SCORES

Gaining conscious control over inborn powers takes unshakeable confidence and a forceful personality, so you'll want a high Charisma score. Low hit points and lack of armor make both Constitution and Dexterity good scores to boost.

 You'll want a high Strength score as well, because your abilities make you a good melee fighter.

TIP Intelligence and Wisdom are not critical ability scores, but Intelligence boosts your skill points.

SKILLS

Sorcerers' high Charisma often causes their companions to turn to them to lead social interactions, and their inborn magical affinity lends them understanding of the workings of the arcane. As a sorcerer, you gain one additional class skill based on your bloodline (see Class Features).

 SKILL RANKS PER LEVEL
2 + Intelligence modifier

Class Skills for Sorcerers
Appraise
Bluff
Craft
Fly
Intimidate
Knowledge (arcana)
Profession
Spellcraft
Use Magic Device

- Put a rank in Bluff or Intimidate to trick others or coerce them into following your instructions.
- A rank in Spellcraft will allow you to identify magic items and spell effects.
- Put a rank into your bloodline's skill to better embrace your theme.

 Remember, if you put at least 1 rank into any of your class skills, you get a +3 bonus to your total for that skill to represent your class training. At 1st level, you can't put more than 1 rank in a particular skill. If you're human, you get an additional skill rank to spend at each level, including 1st level.

ALIGNMENT
You can be of any alignment.

HIT DIE
Your Hit Die is a d6. At 1st level, you have 6 hit points plus your Constitution modifier.

BASE ATTACK BONUS **+0**
Your base attack bonus is +0. It will increase at every even level.

SAVING THROWS
A sorcerer must have a strong will to control magic.

FORTITUDE **+0**
Your Fortitude save bonus is +0 plus your Constitution modifier.

REFLEX **+0**
Your Reflex save bonus is +0 plus your Dexterity modifier.

WILL **+2**
Your Will save bonus is +2 plus your Wisdom modifier.

WEAPON AND ARMOR PROFICIENCIES

You're proficient with simple weapons, providing you a respectable assortment of options, but nothing too powerful. A dagger is a versatile weapon, and the longspear can give you extra reach to help fight without getting too close to the enemy. At low levels, it can be wise to conserve your spells and attack with a light crossbow or other ranged weapon. You gain no armor proficiencies, and wearing armor of any kind interferes with your spellcasting.

FEATS

Most sorcerers focus strongly on spellcasting, so they favor feats that boost their magical abilities. The dragon-child theme also favors melee combat, and should consider feats that would appeal to barbarians and fighters.

YOU GET ONE FEAT AT 1ST LEVEL
Two if you're human

Combat Casting	Gain a +4 bonus on concentration checks to prevent enemies from interrupting spells as you cast them. (*Core Rulebook* 119)
Improved Initiative	Gain a +4 bonus on initiative checks, allowing you to hit a group of opponents with an area spell before they scatter. (*Core Rulebook* 127)
Spell Focus	Strengthen your spells and make your enemies less likely to resist them. Spell focus (conjuration) is also a prerequisite for Augment Summoning, which is a great feat for sorcerers with *summon monster* spells. Enchantment, evocation, and illusion may also be effective. (*Core Rulebook* 127)
Toughness	Add 3 to your total hit points, plus an additional 1 for every Hit Die you possess or gain beyond 3. (*Core Rulebook* 135)
Metamagic Feats	Metamagic feats, which allow you to get extra use out of low-level spells, are very powerful for a sorcerer, particularly because you may have plenty of high-level spell slots but a lower number of high-level spells known. You probably won't want to start taking metamagic feats until you reach 7th level. (*Core Rulebook* 112)
	Consider Dodge because you'll be in melee combat a lot, and improving your Armor Class helps you survive. (*Core Rulebook* 122)
	Spell Focus (evocation), which raises saving throw DCs on your evocation spells, is a natural choice to ensure you do maximum damage. (*Core Rulebook* 134)

CLASS FEATURES

Bloodline: Every sorcerer chooses a bloodline at 1st level. Your bloodline represents the background or ancestor from which your magical abilities arise, and determines which additional abilities you get. Be sure to write your bloodline, bloodline arcana, and 1st-level bloodline power on your character sheet.	
	Choose the celestial bloodline. An excellent bloodline for a generalist spellcaster, it also makes your summoned creatures stronger.
	Choose the draconic (blue) or draconic (bronze) bloodline. These bloodlines grant you elemental and melee abilities, including a powerful bonus to spells with the electricity descriptor.
	Choose the elemental (fire) bloodline, which grants you extra fire-based abilities as well as the ability to change acid, cold, and electricity spells into fire spells, increasing your list of theme-appropriate spells.
Bloodline Power: Gain an additional combat option that does not expend your spell slots, giving you some interesting magical options even when you're running low on spells.	
	You gain heavenly fire, which allows you to damage evil creatures or heal good creatures.
	You gain claws, which allows you to grow claws and attack with them twice in a round.
	You gain elemental ray, which allows you to shoot a ray of fire at an enemy.
Eschew Materials: You gain Eschew Materials as a bonus feat. This represents the inherent magical ability that allows you to ignore most components for spells. You may still need expensive or valuable material components for some spells (like having a crystal ball to magically spy on someone far away).	

SPELLS AND CANTRIPS

Sorcerers cast **arcane spells**—spells that come through their bloodline and are under their power. Unlike most other spellcasting classes, you don't need to choose and prepare your spells ahead of time. You know a certain number of spells by heart, and when you want to cast a spell, you choose it from among these known spells right before you cast it. When you've cast all your spells for the day, you need 8 hours of sleep to refresh your magical energies.

Each day, you need to spend 15 minutes concentrating and focusing your powers to be able to cast spells that day. You know fewer spells than a wizard or cleric, but you can cast each of your spells multiple times and in any combination, choosing them on the fly. As you level up, you'll gain more spells known, and be able to cast grander spells. In order to cast a spell, your Charisma score must be at least 10 + the spell's spell level; for instance, you must have a Charisma score of 12 or higher to cast 2nd-level sorcerer spells. The Difficulty Class for saves against your spell's effects is 10 + the spell's spell level + your Charisma modifier.

At 1st level, you choose two different 1st-level spells that you know, and can cast a total of three 1st-level spells each day, choosing which of the two spells you're casting each time you cast. You'll also learn four different **cantrips** (0-level spells that you can cast as often as you want). If your Charisma score is 12 or higher, you can cast additional spells per day (see Table 1–3 on page 17 of the *Core Rulebook*).

0-Level Spells (cantrips): Good choices for all themes include *detect magic*, *light*, *prestidigitation*, and *read magic*.

1st-Level Spells: *Magic missile* is a powerful spell that improves as you gain levels, always hits, has a good range, and deals damage that few creatures can resist. Even if you don't learn it at 1st level, strongly consider learning it at some point. *Mage armor* lasts a long time and grants a good bonus to AC (dragon-child sorcerers learn *mage armor* for free at 3rd level). It's important to know spells that use different types of saving throws, such as *burning hands* (Reflex save) and *chill touch* (Fortitude save), since different enemies will be good at different types of saves.

	Consider *charm person*, *color spray*, *protection from evil*, and *summon monster I*. These give you good options for social encounters, disabling multiple enemies, and defending against common threats.
	Consider *chill touch*, *enlarge person*, *shield*, and *shocking grasp*. These grant you potent combat bonuses and several types of touch-range spells. *Shocking grasp* is particularly powerful with your bloodline arcana.
	Consider *grease*, *shocking grasp*, and *ray of enfeeblement*. These grant you several good damaging and debilitating spells.

 TIP Since you know fewer spells than a wizard or cleric, you need to be smart about which spells you choose to learn. If you don't think you'll use a spell on a daily basis, consider getting a few scrolls of that spell rather than learning it.

⬆ LEVELING UP

The next few pages explain the abilities you get at 2nd level and higher. Some of these abilities are just additions to your 1st-level abilities, and are noted in a Level Up bar: additional hit points and skill ranks, as well as increases to your base attack bonus, Fortitude save bonus, Reflex save bonus, and Will save bonus.

The information about what you gain at each level is also presented as Table 3–14: Sorcerer on page 72 of the *Core Rulebook*.

 **ANGEL-BORN** (PAGE 14)   **DRAGON-CHILD** (PAGE 18)   **FIRE-BLOODED** (PAGE 19)

As a sorcerer, your bloodline will inform many of the decisions you make as you go up in level. Due to your limited list of spells known, you should carefully consider which spell is the right one to take at each level of play. The bonus spells will help in shaping your selections, but you should try to round out your spell list to give you as much versatility as possible. For a sorcerer, having both *fireball* and *lightning bolt* is a bit of a waste, as you have so few spells known. Consider picking up *fly*, *haste*, or *slow* to give you more tools to tackle any encounter. Finally, consider feats that allow you to get the most out of your spellcasting or otherwise enhance your defenses. Sorcerers are very fragile in combat, so any edge you can get is welcome.

2nd Level

	HP	SKILL RANKS	BAB	FORT	REF	WILL
	1d6 + Con	2 + Int	+1	—	—	+1

Your hit points increase by 1d6 + your Constitution modifier. Unlike at 1st level, you must roll for these hit points.

You gain a number of skill ranks equal to 2 + your Intelligence modifier. If you're human, don't forget the bonus skill rank per level.

Your base attack bonus (BAB) and Will save bonus each increase by 1.

Spells: You gain another 0-level spell known and can cast an additional 1st-level spell per day.

3rd Level

	HP	SKILL RANKS	BAB	FORT	REF	WILL
	1d6 + Con	2 + Int	—	+1	+1	—

Feat: You gain another feat. You should consider some of the same choices you had at 1st level.

 If you selected Spell Focus (conjuration) earlier, you can now learn Augment Summoning, which drastically empowers your summoned creatures.

 You now qualify for Power Attack, which allows you to trade accuracy for extra damage. Arcane Strike is another good choice, as it grants you a slightly lower but more reliable boost to damage.

Bloodline Power: You gain another ability tied to your bloodline.

 You gain resist acid 5 and resist cold 5, which lets you subtract 5 from cold or acid damage you take.

 You gain resist electricity 5, which lets you subtract 5 from electricity damage you take, and a +1 natural armor bonus.

 You gain resist fire 10, which lets you subtract 10 from fire damage you take.

Bloodline Spell: You gain a bonus spell known based on your bloodline. Sometimes this is a spell that no other sorcerer can learn.

 You learn *bless*, which lasts a minute per sorcerer level and gives your allies a +1 bonus on attack rolls and saves against fear.

 You learn *mage armor*, which lasts an hour per sorcerer level and gives you a +4 armor bonus to Armor Class.

 You gain *burning hands*, which blasts your enemies with fire for 1d4 points of damage per sorcerer level.

Spells: You gain another 1st-level spell known and can cast an additional 1st-level spell per day.

4th Level

	HP	SKILL RANKS	BAB	FORT	REF	WILL
	1d6 + Con	2 + Int	+1	—	—	+1

Ability Score Increase: You gain a permanent +1 increase to one ability score of your choice. This should be added to an ability score that's important to you—like Charisma—especially if you have an odd number in it, as your modifiers increase at even numbers.

Spells: You gain one 2nd-level spell known and one 0-level spell known; you can cast three 2nd-level spells per day (four if your Charisma score is 14 or higher; five if it's 22 or higher) and one additional 1st-level spell per day. You can also exchange one spell you know for a different spell of the same level. For example, if you know *unseen servant* but haven't really been using it, you can unlearn it and learn *charm person* instead. *See invisibility* and *glitterdust* and are both good 2nd-level spell choices; the former lets you point out invisible enemies to your allies, and the latter reveals invisible creatures and causes blindness.

 Consider *invisibility* and *summon monster II*. Spells that don't directly harm or target another creature in a harmful way allow you to stay invisible, so summoning monsters works very well when you're invisible.

 Consider *bull's strength*, *false life*, and *mirror image*. The first gives you a big boost on attack and damage rolls. The second gives you more hit points. The third is almost better than having a good armor class; it makes multiple successful hits actually miss you entirely.

 Consider *acid arrow*, *blindness/deafness*, and *flaming sphere*. *Flaming sphere* allows you to deal damage each round as a move action, so it can greatly improve the punishment you inflict each round.

5th Level

	HP	SKILL RANKS	BAB	FORT	REF	WILL
	1d6 + Con	2 + Int	—	—	—	—

Feat: You gain another feat. Consider taking Craft Wondrous Item to allow you to create various simple magic items.

Bloodline Spell: You gain a bonus spell known based on your bloodline.

 You learn *resist energy*, which protects a creature against up to 10 points of acid, cold, electricity, or fire damage.

 You learn *resist energy*, which protects a creature against up to 10 points of acid, cold, electricity, or fire damage.

 You learn *scorching ray*, which blasts a target with a ray of fire for 4d6 points of damage. (As you level up, you gain additional rays.)

Spells: You gain another 1st-level spell and another 2nd-level spell known, and can cast an additional 2nd-level spell per day.

 Don't forget your bloodline spells, especially if you're the only spellcaster in your party. Your bloodline may give you access to magic not normally available to arcane casters (such as divine healing spells for the Celestial-blooded sorcerer) or sorcerers (such as arcane bonds for the Arcane bloodline).

6th Level

	HP	SKILL RANKS	BAB	FORT	REF	WILL
	1d6 + Con	2 + Int	+1	+1	+1	+1

 At 6th level you likely qualify for the dragon disciple prestige class (*Core Rulebook* 380), which trades some of your spellcasting ability for extra combat abilities. The following progression assumes you have not taken levels in that prestige class, but remember that it's an option.

Spells: You gain one 3rd-level spell known and one 0-level spell known; you can cast three 3rd-level spells per day (four if your Charisma score is 16 or higher; five if it's 24 or higher) and one additional 2nd-level spell per day. You can also exchange one spell you know for a different spell of the same level (see the 4th-level section for advice). *Dispel magic*, *fly*, and *haste* are excellent 3rd-level spell choices for any sorcerer. In particular, *haste* allows everyone in your party to attack more often, which can be even more effective than an explosive spell.

 Consider *major image*, *slow*, and *suggestion*. *Major image* is extraordinarily versatile for the creative spellcaster, and *slow* can cut down your enemies' actions severely. *Summon monster* spells are still good choices for you, but consider replacing several of your lower-level summoning spells with more useful choices; one celestial eagle from a *summon monster I* probably won't scare any enemies you face once you're 8th level or higher.

 Consider *heroism* to boost your dice rolls and *lightning bolt* to damage multiple targets.

 Consider *fireball* and *lightning bolt* to blast many enemies at once.

7th Level

	HP	SKILL RANKS	BAB	FORT	REF	WILL
	1d6 + Con	2 + Int	—	—	—	—

Feat: You gain another feat. Consider enhancing your spells with a metamagic feat such as Empower Spell or Extend Spell.

Bloodline Feat: You gain a bonus feat selected from a list provided by your bloodline.

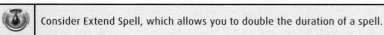 Consider Extend Spell, which allows you to double the duration of a spell.

Consider Blind-Fight, Improved Initiative, or Toughness to improve your defenses, speed, or durability.

Consider Empower Spell, which allows you to drastically increase the damage dealt by a spell.

Bloodline Spell: You gain a bonus spell known based on your bloodline.

You learn *magic circle against evil*, which can protect many targets against evil creatures, spells, and effects.

You learn *fly*, which grants you or an ally the ability to fly.

You learn *protection from energy*, which grants you or an ally a powerful ward against acid, cold, electricity, or fire.

Spells: You gain another 3rd-, 2nd-, and 1st-level spell known, and can cast an additional 3rd- and 2nd-level spell per day.

8th Level

	HP	SKILL RANKS	BAB	FORT	REF	WILL
	1d6 + Con	2 + Int	+1	—	—	+1

Ability Score Increase: You gain a permanent +1 increase to an ability score of your choice.

Spells: You gain one 4th-level spell known and one 0-level spell known; you can cast three 4th-level spells per day (four if your Charisma is 18 or higher; five if it's 26 or higher) and one additional 3rd-level spell per day. You can exchange one spell you know for a different spell of the same level (see the 4th-level section for advice).

Consider *charm monster*, *confusion*, *dimensional anchor*, and *resilient sphere* to command and trap your enemies.

Consider *fire shield* and *stoneskin* to improve your defenses.

Consider *enervation*, *wall of fire*, and *wall of ice* to debilitate and separate your enemies.

9th Level

	HP	SKILL RANKS	BAB	FORT	REF	WILL
	1d6 + Con	2 + Int	—	+1	+1	—

Feat: You gain another feat.

Bloodline Power: You gain another ability tied to your bloodline.

You gain the ability to fly for a short time.

You gain the ability to breathe electricity in a line.

You gain an elemental blast that deals fire damage to a large number of enemies and makes them vulnerable to fire damage (meaning they take 50% more damage) for one round.

Bloodline Spell: You gain a bonus spell known based on your bloodline.

You learn *remove curse*, useful for removing debilitating conditions.

You learn *fear*, which can cause multiple enemies to panic and run.

You learn *elemental body I*, which allows you to turn into a Small elemental.

Spells: You gain another 4th-, 3rd-, and 2nd-level spell known, and can cast an additional 4th- and 3rd-level spell per day.

10th Level

	HP	SKILL RANKS	BAB	FORT	REF	WILL
	1d6 + Con	2 + Int	+1	—	—	+1

Spells: You gain one 5th-level spell known and one 0-level spell known; you can cast three 5th-level spells per day (four if your Charisma is 20 or higher; five if it's 28 or higher) and one additional 4th-level spell per day. You can exchange one spell you know for a different spell of the same level (see the 4th-level section for advice). For all themes, *wall of force* is a very powerful wall spell that's nearly impossible to destroy.

 Consider *cone of cold*, *dismissal*, and *hold monster*.

 Consider *beast shape III* and *interposing hand* to increase your combat options.

 Consider *cloudkill*, *cone of cold*, and *overland flight*.

11th Level

	HP	SKILL RANKS	BAB	FORT	REF	WILL
	1d6 + Con	2 + Int	—	—	—	—

Feat: You gain another feat.

Bloodline Spell: You gain a bonus spell known based on your bloodline.

 You learn *flame strike*, which blasts creatures with fire and divine damage.

 You learn *spell resistance*, which protects against many spells.

 You learn *elemental body II*, which allows you to turn into a Medium elemental.

You gain another 5th-, 4th-, 3rd-, and 2nd-level spell known, and can cast an additional 5th- and 4th-level spell per day.

12th Level

	HP	SKILL RANKS	BAB	FORT	REF	WILL
	1d6 + Con	2 + Int	+1	+1	+1	+1

Ability Score Increase: You gain a permanent +1 increase to an ability score of your choice.

Attack Bonus: Now that your base attack bonus is +6, you gain a second attack (at an attack bonus of +1) whenever you make a full attack (see page 122). From now on, any bonuses to your BAB apply to this attack as well.

Spells: You gain one 6th-level spell known; you can cast three 6th-level spells per day (four if your Charisma is 22 or higher; five if it's 30 or higher) and one additional 5th-level spell per day. You can also exchange one spell you know for a different spell of the same level (see the 4th-level section for advice). For all themes, *greater dispel magic* can destroy many enemy spells at once, and *true seeing* is able to completely negate illusion magic.

 Consider *planar binding* to command an outsider for a long period of time.

 Consider *chain lightning*, *greater heroism*, and *transformation* to massively boost your combat abilities.

 Consider *chain lightning*, *freezing sphere* and *disintegrate*—all powerful damaging spells.

13th Level

	HP	SKILL RANKS	BAB	FORT	REF	WILL
	1d6 + Con	2 + Int	—	—	—	—

Feat: You gain another feat.

Bloodline Feat: You gain a bonus feat selected from a list provided by your bloodline.

	Consider Iron Will, which gives you a +2 bonus on Will saving throws.
	Consider Quicken Spell, which allows you to cast two spells in a round.
	Consider Great Fortitude, Improved Initiative, or Lightning Reflexes to improve your weaker saving throws or act more quickly in combat.

Bloodline Spell: You gain a bonus spell known based on your bloodline.

	You learn *greater dispel magic*, which can destroy multiple enemy spells at once.
	You learn *form of the dragon I*, which transforms you into a Medium dragon.
	You learn *elemental body III*, which allows you to turn into a Large elemental.

Spells: You gain another 6th-, 5th-, and 4th-level spell known, and can cast an additional 6th- and 5th-level spell per day.

14th Level

	HP	SKILL RANKS	BAB	FORT	REF	WILL
	1d6 + Con	2 + Int	+1	—	—	+1

Spells: You gain one 7th-level spell known; you can cast three 7th-level spells per day (four if your Charisma score is 24 or higher) and one additional 6th-level spell per day. You can also exchange one spell you know for a different spell of the same level (see the 4th-level section for advice). For all themes, *power word blind* can quickly disable a single creature, and *limited wish* has many effects and can duplicate other spells—handy for a class that has a limited number of spells known.

	Consider *prismatic spray* and *reverse gravity* to decisively incapacitate many creatures at once.
	Consider *grasping hand* and *elemental body III* to better push around your enemies.
	Consider *delayed blast fireball* and *finger of death* to damage foes.

15th Level

	HP	SKILL RANKS	BAB	FORT	REF	WILL
	1d6 + Con	2 + Int	—	+1	+1	—

Feat: You gain another feat.

Bloodline Power: You gain another ability tied to your bloodline.

	You gain the ability to reroll one attack, save, or check once per day.
	You gain wings that allow you to fly at will.
	You increase your base speed by 30 feet per round.

Bloodline Spell: You gain a bonus spell known based on your bloodline.

	You learn *banishment*, which can instantly defeat an extraplanar outsider.
	You learn *form of the dragon II*, which transforms you into a Large dragon.
	You learn *elemental body IV*, which allows you to turn into a Huge elemental.

Spells: You gain another 7th-, 6th-, and 5th-level spell known, and can cast an additional 7th- and 6th-level spell per day.

16th Level

	HP	SKILL RANKS	BAB	FORT	REF	WILL
	1d6 + Con	2 + Int	+1	—	—	+1

Ability Score Increase: You gain a permanent +1 increase to an ability score of your choice.

Spells: You gain one 8th-level spell known; you can cast three 8th-level spells per day (four if your Charisma score is 26 or higher) and one additional 7th-level spell per day. You can also exchange one spell you know for a different spell of the same level. For all themes, *maze* can remove a creature from the battlefield without a saving throw, *mind blank* provides valuable defenses, and *moment of prescience* grants a large bonus to any one roll.

	Consider *greater planar binding*, *horrid wilting*, and *prismatic wall*.
	Consider *irresistible dance*, *iron body*, and *power word stun*.
	Consider *greater shout*, *incendiary cloud*, and *polar ray*.

17th Level

	HP	SKILL RANKS	BAB	FORT	REF	WILL
	1d6 + Con	2 + Int	—	—	—	—

Feat: You gain another feat.

Bloodline Spell: You gain a bonus spell known based on your bloodline.

	You learn *sunburst*, which can blind and damage enemies.
	You learn *form of the dragon III*, which transforms you into a Huge dragon.
	You learn *summon monster VIII*, which allows you to summon incredibly powerful elementals.

Spells: You gain another 8th- and 7th-level spell known, and can cast an additional 8th- and 7th-level spell per day.

18th Level

	HP	SKILL RANKS	BAB	FORT	REF	WILL
	1d6 + Con	2 + Int	+1	+1	+1	+1

Spells: You gain one 9th-level spell known; you can cast three 9th-level spells per day (four if your Charisma score is 28 or higher) and one additional 8th-level spell per day. You can also exchange one spell you know for a different spell of the same level. For all themes, *mage's disjunction* destroys practically any form of magic, *time stop* allows you to cast many spells while everyone else is frozen, and *wish* allows you to duplicate nearly any spell.

	Consider *dominate monster*.
	Consider *foresight* and *shapechange*.
	Consider *energy drain*, *meteor swarm*, and *wail of the banshee*.

 It may seem at first glance like *wish* and *limited wish* are the only spells a sorcerer needs, as they can duplicate nearly any other spell, but beware: both require expensive material components to cast, and can only duplicate the effects of lower-level spells. Versatility comes at a price!

19th Level

	HP	SKILL RANKS	BAB	FORT	REF	WILL
	1d6 + Con	2 + Int	—	—	—	—

Feat: You gain another feat.

Bloodline Feat: You gain a bonus feat selected from a list provided by your bloodline.

	Consider Dodge or Skill Focus (Knowledge [religion]).
	Consider Great Fortitude, Power Attack, or a feat from an earlier list.
	Consider Skill Focus (Knowledge [planes]) to learn more about outsiders (a common type of foe at this level), or any feat from an earlier list.

Bloodline Spell: You gain a bonus spell known based on your bloodline.

	You learn *gate*, which allows you to summon extraordinarily powerful creatures or travel to other planes.
	You learn *wish*, which allows you to create nearly any effect.
	You learn *elemental swarm*, which allows you to summon a small army of elementals.

Spells: You gain another 9th- and 8th-level spell known, and can cast an additional 9th- and 8th-level spell per day.

20th Level

	HP	SKILL RANKS	BAB	FORT	REF	WILL
	1d6 + Con	2 + Int	+1	—	—	+1

Ability Score Increase: You gain a permanent +1 increase to an ability score of your choice.

Bloodline Power: You gain another ability tied to your bloodline.

	You gain multiple resistances and immunities, unlimited flight, and the ability to speak with any creature.
	You gain immunity to electricity, paralysis, and sleep. You also gain blindsense 60 feet (*Core Rulebook* 561).
	You gain immunity to fire, sneak attacks, and critical hits.

Spells: You gain another 9th-level spell known, and can cast two additional 9th-level spells per day. You can exchange one spell you know for a different spell of the same level.

WIZARD

Wizards are masters of the arcane, able to bend reality to suit their needs. They're among the most devastating and versatile classes in the game.

 CONJURER
(PAGE 17)

 ILLUSIONIST
(PAGE 21)

 TRADITIONAL MAGE
(PAGE 26)

ABILITY SCORES

Wizards specialize in learning and unleashing powerful spells. You'll need a high Intelligence score to make the most of your spellcasting ability. A high Dexterity score will give you a bit of necessary defense and speed.

 TIP Having an above-average Constitution score will help you stay alive in combat.

SKILLS

Wizards' high intelligence and arcane knowledge make them experts on magic, and often give them expertise in other esoteric lore, like ancient dead languages, lost history, and the nature of unusual objects.

 SKILL RANKS PER LEVEL
2 + Intelligence modifier

Class Skills for Wizards

Appraise
Craft
Fly
Knowledge (all categories)
Linguistics
Profession
Spellcraft

- Put a rank into Knowledge (arcana).
- Having a rank in Spellcraft will help you identify magic items and spell effects.
- If you're a conjurer, put a rank in Linguistics so you can learn a language such as Abyssal, Celestial, or Infernal (see page 115), so you can give orders to the monsters you summon.

If you have more skill ranks, choose some other Knowledge skills that appeal to you or that your GM recommends as useful for the game. Consider Perception, as Perception checks are one of the most common checks you'll make. Alternatively, choose Fly, which you'll use in later levels as you gain spells that allow flight.

 Remember, if you put at least 1 rank into any of your class skills, you get a +3 bonus to your total for that skill to represent your class training. At 1st level, you can't put more than 1 rank in a particular skill. If you're human, you get an additional skill rank to spend at each level, including 1st level.

ALIGNMENT

You can be of any alignment.

HIT DIE

Your Hit Die is a d6. At 1st level, you have 6 hit points (like rolling a 6 on the d6) plus your Constitution modifier.

BASE ATTACK BONUS **+0**

Your base attack bonus is +0. It will increase at every even level—but your spells make up for it.

SAVING THROWS

A wizard's sharp mind helps him resist mental influences.

FORTITUDE **+0**

Your Fortitude save bonus is +0 plus your Constitution modifier.

REFLEX **+0**

Your Reflex save bonus is +0 plus your Dexterity modifier.

WILL **+2**

Your Will save bonus is +2 plus your Wisdom modifier.

WEAPON AND ARMOR PROFICIENCIES

You're proficient with the club, dagger, heavy crossbow, light crossbow, and quarterstaff, but not with any type of armor or shield. Buy a ranged weapon you can afford at low level, and a quarterstaff as a melee weapon just in case. You shouldn't wear armor, as it interferes with your spellcasting. That means you can use that money on other useful items instead—like a backpack, torches, and rope.

FEATS

As a wizard, you should choose a feat that enhances your knowledge and arcane abilities.

YOU GET ONE FEAT AT 1ST LEVEL
Two if you're human

Combat Casting	Gain a +4 bonus to concentration checks to prevent enemies from interrupting spells as you cast them. (*Core Rulebook* 119)
Fleet	Increase your move speed by 5 feet to outdistance foes. (*Core Rulebook* 124)
Improved Initiative	Gain a +4 bonus on initiative checks and hit a group of opponents with an area spell before they scatter. (*Core Rulebook* 127)
Toughness	Add 3 to your total hit points, plus an additional 1 for every Hit Die you possess or gain beyond 3. (*Core Rulebook* 135)

CLASS FEATURES

Arcane Bond: All wizards form a powerful bond with either an object (like an amulet, ring, staff, wand, or weapon) or a creature (known as a familiar). A bonded object allows you to cast an additional spell each day, but it's very hard to cast your spells if the item is lost or stolen. A familiar can scout for you and deliver touch-range spells, but could get killed—although you can replace it through a magical ritual. If this is your first wizard character, consider choosing a bonded object because it's an easier option to use than a familiar.

Arcane School: Magical effects belong to one of eight schools of magic: abjuration (protective magic), conjuration (summoning creatures from another plane), divination (discovering information), enchantment (influencing minds), evocation (creating energy or force out of nothing), illusion (false images and sounds), necromancy (manipulating life and death), and transmutation (changing the shape or properties of creatures and objects). Wizards can choose one of these as a **specialty school**, but will have trouble casting spells from two other schools, called your **opposition schools**.

	Choose conjuration as your specialty school. Choose abjuration and evocation as your opposition schools. You gain the summoner's charm ability, which increases how long your summoned creatures last. You also gain the ability to create an acid dart to shoot at opponents, which is useful when you're running low on spells.
	Choose illusion as your specialty school. Choose evocation and necromancy as your opposition schools. You gain the extended illusions ability, which makes illusion spells last longer after you stop concentrating. You also gain the ability to create a shimmering ray that blinds an opponent, which is useful for disabling foes so your stronger allies can defeat them.
	You don't have a specialty school—you're a dabbler, not a specialist. Wizards like you are called universalist wizards because they're easily able to learn any kind of spell. You gain the hand of the apprentice ability, which allows you to telekinetically throw your weapon at an opponent and have it automatically return to you.

Scribe Scroll: At 1st level, all wizards gain Scribe Scroll as a bonus feat. When you're not adventuring, you can spend gold to write down extra copies of spells to save for later, like an extra *fireball* or *invisibility* spell.

SPELLS AND CANTRIPS

Wizards cast **arcane spells**—spells they study and cast through their own power. You're defined by the arcane spells you know—these choices are far more important that what feats or skills you have. You cast spells drawn from the Wizard spell list (*Core Rulebook* 232). At first level, each day you may choose and prepare three different **cantrips** (0-level spells that you can cast as often as you want), and one 1st-level spell, which you may cast once per day. If your Wisdom score is 12 or higher, you can cast additional spells per day (see Table 1–3 on page 17 of the *Core Rulebook*).

To prepare your spells, you need to have slept for 8 hours to refresh your magical energies, and then spend an hour studying your spellbook (see below). Once you've cast a prepared spell, you can't cast it again until you prepare it again—though you can prepare multiple copies of a spell if you can cast multiple spells of that level per day. The Difficulty Class to resist the effects of your spells is equal to 10 + the spell's spell level + your Wisdom modifier.

As you level up, you'll gain access to grander spells, and increase the number of spells you can prepare each day. In order to cast a spell, your Intelligence score must be at least 10 + the spell's spell level; for instance, you need an Intelligence score of 12 or higher to cast 2nd-level wizard spells.

Spellbook: Your spellbook contains the spells from which you choose when preparing your spells for the day. It contains all the cantrips one pages 232–233 of the *Core Rulebook*, as well as the higher-level spells you have chosen to learn. At 1st level, you may choose three 1st-level spells plus an additional number of spells equal to your Intelligence modifier; for example, if your Intelligence modifier is +2, you choose a total of 5 1st-level spells for your spellbook. Each time you level up, add two more spells to your spellbook of any spell level you can cast. Any time you find another wizard's spellbook, you may copy the spells found in it into yours (*Core Rulebook* 78). There's no limit to how many spells you can learn!

	You get an additional 1st-level spell slot, but you can only use it to prepare a spell from your specialized school. If you want to prepare a spell from an opposition school, it takes up two spell slots instead of one.
	You get an additional 1st-level spell slot, but you can only use it to prepare a spell from your specialized school. If you want to prepare a spell from an opposition school, it takes up two spell slots instead of one.

0-Level Spells: Good choices for all wizards include *dancing lights* or *light* (useful if you or your compatriots don't see well in the dark), *detect magic*, *disrupt undead* (if you suspect you'll be fighting undead), and *read magic*.

1st-Level Spells: You should prepare one attack spell and one defense spell; change up the other spells per day based on what you expect to encounter. For example, you could prepare a second copy of your attack spell, or instead prepare a utility spell like *disguise self*.

	Summon monster I is a strong attack spell for you, especially as your summoner's charm school ability makes that spell last longer. *Mage armor* is a strong defensive spell. *Charm person*, *color spray*, and *protection from evil* are useful choices.
	Color spray and *silent image* are the core 1st-level illusion spells. *Charm person* and *sleep* are also good attack spell choices. Choose *mage armor* or *shield* as a defensive spell.
	Burning hands, color spray, magic missile, and *sleep* make for great attack spells. Choose *mage armor* or *shield* as a defensive spell.

⬆ LEVELING UP

The next few pages explain the abilities you get at 2nd level and higher. Some of these abilities are just additions to your 1st-level abilities, and are noted in a Level Up bar: additional hit points and skill ranks, additional spells in your spellbook (any two wizard/sorcerer spells of a level you can cast), and increases to your base attack bonus, Fortitude save bonus, Reflex save bonus, and Will save bonus.

The information about what you gain at each level is also presented as Table 3–16: Wizard on page 80 of the *Core Rulebook*.

As you adventure, always be on the lookout for new spells to add to your spellbook. More spells means more versatility when preparing your spells each morning. Also consider investing in some wands and scrolls to allow you to have the right spell for the task at hand, even if you did not think to prepare it that day.

 **CONJURER**
(PAGE 17)

 ILLUSIONIST
(PAGE 21)

 TRADITIONAL MAGE
(PAGE 26)

2nd Level

	HP	SKILL RANKS	BAB	FORT	REF	WILL	SPELLBOOK
	1d6 + Con	2 + Int	+1	—	—	+1	+2 spells

Your hit points increase by 1d6 + your Constitution modifier. Unlike at 1st level, you must roll for these hit points.

You gain a number of skill ranks equal to 2 + your Intelligence modifier. If you're human, don't forget the bonus skill rank per level.

Your base attack bonus and Will save bonus each go up by 1.

Spells: You can prepare one additional 0-level spell and one additional 1st-level spell per day.

 Add *sleep*, a powerful offensive solution for groups of lesser threats.

 Add *mage armor* if you often find yourself in danger of close combat, or *magic missile* if you're usually at a distance.

 Add *silent image* for deception and trickery, or *charm person* if your party needs help convincing prisoners to talk.

3rd Level

	HP	SKILL RANKS	BAB	FORT	REF	WILL	SPELLBOOK
	1d6 + Con	2 + Int	—	+1	+1	—	+2 spells

Feat: You gain an additional feat. Choose Spell Focus for your preferred school of spells to make your offensive spells more deadly by increasing the saving throw required to resist their effects.

Spells: You can prepare one 2nd-level spell per day. If your Intelligence score is 14 or higher, you can cast an additional 2nd-level spell per day; wizards with very high Intelligence scores may be able to cast more than one bonus 2nd-level spell (*Core Rulebook* 17).

 Glitterdust and *web* are excellent choices. The first reveals invisible and hidden foes, and the second traps creatures so your fighters can deal with smaller groups of monsters.

 Invisibility is the must-have spell here, but *hideous laughter* is also a great choice. *Mirror image* is a strong defensive choice, and *minor image* adds sound to your illusions.

 Levitate is a terrific for lifting you above the battlefield for a better view out of harm's way. Consider choosing *invisibility* or *web* if you want more control over the battlefield.

4th Level

	HP	SKILL RANKS	BAB	FORT	REF	WILL	SPELLBOOK
	1d6 + Con	2 + Int	+1	—	—	+1	+2 spells

Ability Score Increase: You gain a permanent +1 increase to one ability score of your choice. This should be added to an ability score that's important to you—like Intelligence—especially if you have an odd number in it, as your modifiers increase at even numbers.

Spells: You can prepare an additional 2nd-level spell and an additional 1st-level spell per day. For your new spells, *levitate, enlarge person, web, rope trick,* and *invisibility* are all good choices. You'll also want to make scrolls of your more situational spells so you don't have to prepare them each day; *knock* and *minor image* are good candidates for scrolls.

5th Level

	HP	SKILL RANKS	BAB	FORT	REF	WILL	SPELLBOOK
	1d6 + Con	2 + Int	—	—	—	—	+2 spells

Feat: You gain another feat. Consider taking Spell Focus in your specialized school if you haven't already, or diversify your talents by taking Spell Focus in a secondary school. Otherwise, take Extend Spell or Spell Penetration.

Bonus Feat: You gain an extra feat, but you must select either an item creation feat (which lets you create magic items; *Core Rulebook* 112), a metamagic feat (which modifies your prepared spells; *Core Rulebook* 112), or Spell Mastery (which lets you prepare a few spells if you lose your spellbook). Brew Potion is probably the most useful item creation feat at low levels, allowing the rest of your party to store useful spells from you or another caster. Also consider Craft Wondrous Item, which allows you to create a great variety of useful magic items to aid you and your allies, or Craft Wand, which allows you to make wands, the most cost-effective magic items that can be crafted.

 When you reach 8th level, you'll get the ability to add a metamagic feat to a spell for free, so consider choosing Enlarge Spell, Extend Spell, Silent Spell, or Still Spell as your bonus feat now so you can make use of that ability later.

Spells: You can prepare one 3rd-level spell per day (or two if your Intelligence score is 16 or higher). *Dispel magic*, *fly*, and *haste* are excellent choices for any wizard. In particular, *haste* allows everyone in your party to attack more often, which can be even more effective than an explosive spell.

 You have some great choices for 3rd-level spells, including *sleet storm*, *stinking cloud*, *summon monster III*, and even *phantom steed*. Choose whichever one you're most excited about.

 Suggestion is useful, but it requires some creativity and the ability to speak the target creature's language. *Invisibility sphere* is great for sneaking your party around. *Wind wall* is a good defense against *stinking cloud* and projectile weapons.

 Fly is a game-changing spell that provides a powerful defense against melee opponents. *Haste* will make your allies quite happy. *Slow* is useful for hampering opponents. Also consider area-effect spells such as *fireball* or *stinking cloud*.

6th Level

	HP	SKILL RANKS	BAB	FORT	REF	WILL	SPELLBOOK
	1d6 + Con	2 + Int	+1	+1	+1	+1	+2 spells

Spells: You can prepare an additional 3rd-level spell and an additional 2nd-level spell per day. *Displacement* can protect you or a melee-focused ally. The *magic circle against chaos/evil/good/law* spells are great if you often encounter creatures with enchantment attacks. (Note that those are four different spells!)

 While exploring, pay attention to how your party arranges itself. As a wizard, you're usually better off staying in the middle of the pack and letting other characters enter a room first or last. It pays to keep someone armored between you and potential danger!

7th Level

	HP	SKILL RANKS	BAB	FORT	REF	WILL	SPELLBOOK
	1d6 + Con	2 + Int	—	—	—	—	+2 spells

Feat: You gain another feat.

Consider Augment Summoning if you have Spell Focus (conjuration).

Consider Spell Focus (enchantment) or Spell Focus (illusion), or Greater Spell Focus if you already have Spell Focus for one of these schools.

Improved Familiar can be useful if you have a familiar. Otherwise, consider Spell Focus or Greater Spell Focus for your most common spell school.

Spells: You can prepare one 4th-level spell per day (or two if your Intelligence score is 18 or higher) and an additional 1st-level spell per day.

Black tentacles can end combats very quickly (and is especially effective against opposing spellcasters), and *summon monster IV* allows you to call upon fierce dire apes, big rhino bruisers, giant flying wasps, and Medium elementals.

Phantasmal killer can instantly kill one opponent. *Confusion* can turn your enemies against each other. *Fear* helps split the enemy ranks.

Stoneskin requires expensive dust every time you cast it, but it's an extremely good defensive spell. *Arcane eye* is a great scouting spell. *Enervation* takes big foes down a peg without a saving throw. *Resilient sphere* is great for capturing prisoners (or protecting yourself in a battle gone wrong). *Ice storm* and *wall of ice* are also worth consideration.

8th Level

	HP	SKILL RANKS	BAB	FORT	REF	WILL	SPELLBOOK
	1d6 + Con	2 + Int	+1	—	—	+1	+2 spells

Ability Score Increase: You gain a permanent +1 increase to an ability score of your choice.

Spells: You can prepare an additional 4th-level spell and an additional 3rd-level spell per day.

 You gain the dimensional steps ability, which allows you to teleport short distances. Because you don't provoke attacks of opportunity for teleporting, this ability is useful for getting away from a dangerous opponent or moving an ally to a better position on the battlefield.

 You gain the invisibility field ability, which allows you to turn invisible for a short time. Unlike the lower-level *invisibility* spell, you can attack or cast spells without breaking your invisibility.

 You gain the metamagic mastery ability, which lets you apply any one metamagic feat that you know to a spell you're about to cast. (If you don't know any metamagic feats, select one when you reach 9th level.) This ability doesn't alter the level of the spell or the casting time. You can use this ability once per day at 8th level and one additional time per day for every 2 wizard levels you have beyond 8th. This ability interfaces with some complex rules; see page 112 in the *Core Rulebook* for information on metamagic feats and page 82 of the *Core Rulebook* for the full description of the metamagic mastery ability.

9th Level

	HP	SKILL RANKS	BAB	FORT	REF	WILL	SPELLBOOK
	1d6 + Con	2 + Int	—	+1	+1	—	+2 spells

Feat: You gain another feat.

Spells: You can prepare one 5th-level spell per day (or two if your Intelligence score is 20 or higher) and an additional 2nd-level spell per day. *Overland flight* and *teleport* make long-distance travel and exploration relatively trivial for you and your allies.

 Cloudkill, summon monster V, and *lesser planar binding* are very useful, but *teleport* is the key spell at this level—even if you just use it to teleport back to town, resupply, and teleport back.

 Feeblemind and *dominate person* are powerful control spells, and *persistent image* is a versatile illusion that requires no concentration to maintain.

 Take *permanency* if you have the budget to make permanent spells for the party, and don't skimp out on *magic jar, telekinesis,* or *wall of force. Telepathic bond* provides a link between everyone if the group, making it practical to split up when needed.

10th Level

	HP	SKILL RANKS	BAB	FORT	REF	WILL	SPELLBOOK
	1d6 + Con	2 + Int	+1	—	—	+1	+2 spells

Bonus Feat: As at 5th level, you gain another bonus item creation feat, metamagic feat, or Spell Mastery. You now have enough spell levels that some of the more powerful metamagic feats become useful. For example, a quickened *magic missile* takes up a 5th-level slot, but sometimes that extra 5d4+5 points of damage on top of your other attacks is just what you need. If your allies are willing to pay the costs of crafting, consider taking Craft Magic Arms and Armor so you can make or upgrade their gear.

Spells: You can prepare an additional 5th-level spell and an additional 4th-level spell per day.

11th Level

	HP	SKILL RANKS	BAB	FORT	REF	WILL	SPELLBOOK
	1d6 + Con	2 + Int	—	—	—	—	+2 spells

Feat: You gain another feat.

Spells: You can prepare one 6th-level spell per day (or two if your Intelligence score is 22 or higher) and an additional 3rd-level spell per day. *Greater dispel magic* is a terrific counter to magic-heavy opponents you'll see at these levels.

 Planar binding is great, and many creatures you can conjure with this spell have magic that you can use to your advantage. *Summon monster VI* is also excellent.

 Mass suggestion can turn mob encounters into trivial obstacles. *Programmed image* requires no concentration and can keep foes engaged for a long time while you do something else. *Shadow walk* is good for visiting places that you haven't yet seen when

12th Level

	HP	SKILL RANKS	BAB	FORT	REF	WILL	SPELLBOOK
	1d6 + Con	2 + Int	+1	+1	+1	+1	+2 spells

Ability Score Increase: You gain a permanent +1 increase to an ability score of your choice.

Attack Bonus: Now that your base attack bonus is at +6, you get a second attack (at an attack bonus of +1), whenever you make a full attack (see page 122). From now on, any bonuses to your BAB apply to this attack as well.

Spells: You can prepare an additional 6th-level spell and an additional 5th-level spell per day.

13th Level

	HP	SKILL RANKS	BAB	FORT	REF	WILL	SPELLBOOK
	1d6 + Con	2 + Int	—	—	—	—	+2 spells

Feat: You gain another feat. Maximize Spell is a good choice to optimize some of your lower-level attack spells.

Spells: You can prepare one 7th-level spell per day (or two if your Intelligence score is 24 or higher) and an additional 4th-level spell per day. *Greater teleport* never misses. *Limited wish* lets you duplicate almost any spell, so it's great when you don't have the right spell prepared.

 Summon monster VII is a must-have spell.

 Project image is a great spell that lets you attack around corners or from concealment.

 Reverse gravity and *greater arcane sight* are very effective.

14th Level

	HP	SKILL RANKS	BAB	FORT	REF	WILL	SPELLBOOK
	1d6 + Con	2 + Int	+1	—	—	+1	+2 spells

Spells: You can prepare an additional 7th-level spell and an additional 6th-level spell per day. Consider adding divinations (such as *scrying*) and abjurations (such as *anti-magic sphere* and *greater dispel magic*) to round out your spell repertoire—these are also great choices to scribe onto scrolls for emergencies.

 As you reach higher wizard levels and gain additional higher-level spells per day, remember that metamagic feats can make lower-level spells as effective as higher-level ones.

15th Level

	HP	SKILL RANKS	BAB	FORT	REF	WILL	SPELLBOOK
	1d6 + Con	2 + Int	—	+1	+1	—	+2 spells

Feats: You gain another feat.

Bonus Feat: As at 5th level, you gain another bonus feat: item creation, metamagic, or Spell Mastery.

Spells: You can prepare one 8th-level spell per day (or two if your Intelligence score is 26 or higher) and an additional 5th-level spell per day. The must-have spells include *maze* (no save), *prismatic wall* (great defense), and *clone* (a literal lifesaver). Consider *sunburst* to blind huge numbers of enemies and eliminate undead easily, or consider *irresistible dance* or *form of the dragon III* for more focused power.

 Maze traps an enemy without allowing for a saving throw to resist it!

 Irresistible dance humiliates and incapacitates an opponent for at least 1 round.

 Clenched fist provides cover, which can also push or attack opponents.

16th Level

	HP	SKILL RANKS	BAB	FORT	REF	WILL	SPELLBOOK
	1d6 + Con	2 + Int	+1	—	—	+1	+2 spells

17th Level

	HP	SKILL RANKS	BAB	FORT	REF	WILL	SPELLBOOK
	1d6 + Con	2 + Int	—	—	—	—	+2 spells

Feat: You gain another feat.

Spells: You can prepare one 9th-level spell per day (or two if your Intelligence score is 28 or higher) and an additional 6th-level spell per day. You can now access the most powerful spells in the game, and you have many options for attack, defense, and utility. *Mage's disjunction* can tear apart enemy magic, *summon monster IX* can conjure extremely powerful expendable minions, and *time stop* gives you several rounds to set up some amazing spell combos. Don't forget *wish*—it costs 25,000 gp worth of materials to cast, but it can do nearly anything.

18th Level

	HP	SKILL RANKS	BAB	FORT	REF	WILL	SPELLBOOK
	1d6 + Con	2 + Int	+1	+1	+1	+1	+2 spells

Spells: You can prepare an additional 9th-level spell and an additional 8th-level spell per day. *Meteor swarm* is a fun spell that affects a very large area; its main drawback is that it deals fire damage, which many monsters are immune to by the time you reach this level. *Prismatic sphere* is a fantastic defense that you can move into and out of without harm.

19th Level

	HP	SKILL RANKS	BAB	FORT	REF	WILL	SPELLBOOK
	1d6 + Con	2 + Int	—	—	—	—	+2 spells

Feat: You gain another feat.

Spells: You can prepare an additional 9th-level spell and an additional 7th-level spell per day. Now that you can cast three 9th-level spells per day, any additional 9th-level spell in your spellbook is bound to be useful in some way.

20th Level

	HP	SKILL RANKS	BAB	FORT	REF	WILL	SPELLBOOK
	1d6 + Con	2 + Int	+1	—	—	+1	+2 spells

Ability Score Increase: You gain a permanent +1 increase to an ability score of your choice.

Bonus Feat: As at 5th level, you gain another bonus feat: item creation, metamagic, or Spell Mastery.

 Your 1st-level summoner's charm ability gets an upgrade—you can make any summon monster spell you cast permanent, giving you a permanent minion, though only one spell at a time.

Your 1st-level extended illusions ability gets an upgrade—you can make any illusion spell you cast permanent, so it remains even after you stop concentrating, though only one spell at a time.

Spells: You can prepare one additional 9th-level spell and one additional 8th-level spell per day.

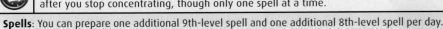

ADDITIONAL DETAILS

Once you've recorded your character's race and class, it's time to finish your character. There are a few of details to work out at this point, some of which can be finalized only once your other choices have been made.

Grab your character sheet and follow along as this section guides you through the process of completing your character. The circled letters in the following pages refer to character sheet on pages 38–39.

Important Statistics

By this point, you should have recorded some of the key information that relate to your character, like your ability scores, hit points, base attack bonus, skill ranks, and feats. Now it's time to fill in all of the other numbers that rely upon those choices.

(A) **Class, Race, and Level**: Before you begin, make sure you've recorded all of the relevant information (such as any bonuses to ability scores or skills) from your race, class, and level.

(C) **Initiative**: Initiative determines who acts first in combat (see page 120). Each time you begin a combat encounter, the GM will ask you to roll initiative. To figure out your initiative, roll a d20 and add your initiative modifier. Your base initiative modifier is equal to your Dexterity modifier, but effects from various feats, spells, and other abilities can change this.

Write this total down in the Initiative Modifier section—you'll use it at the beginning of every combat.

(G) **Speed**: Your speed represents how far you can move each turn in combat. Moving from one square to the next on a combat map represents 5 feet of movement. Your base speed is determined by your race, though your armor, feats, spells, and other factors may affect it. Most player characters have a speed of 30 feet (6 squares), but dwarves, gnomes, and halflings have a speed of only 20 feet (4 squares).

(D) **Armor Class**: Once you've selected your gear and filled out the AC Items section, you can calculate your **Armor Class** (**AC**), which reflects both how good you are at getting out of the way of attacks and how well your armor protects you from harm. A character's AC starts at 10 and is modified by factors like armor and Dexterity modifiers, a size modifier if the character is Small, and so on. Your character sheet provides spaces for these modifiers (see page 126 for more).

> **Armor Class** (AC) = 10 + armor bonus + shield bonus + Dexterity modifier + size modifier + natural armor + deflection modifier + other bonuses and penalties
>
> **Touch Armor Class** (touch AC) = 10 + Dexterity modifier + size modifier + deflection modifier + other bonuses and penalties
>
> **Flat-footed Armor Class** (flat-footed AC) = 10 + armor bonus + shield bonus + size modifier + natural armor bonus + deflection modifier + other bonuses and penalties

Some spells and other attacks don't need to pierce your armor to take full effect; the attacker merely needs to touch you or your clothing to succeed. Your **touch Armor Class** represents how difficult you are to touch with such an attack. Your armor, shield, and natural armor bonuses won't help you against touch attacks since touching armor is no more difficult than touching skin, but your Dexterity and deflection bonuses do since they help you to dodge out of the way.

Your **flat-footed Armor Class** represents how difficult you are to hit when you're caught by surprise and before you act in combat. All your normal Armor Class bonuses apply, but since you weren't ready for the attack, your Dexterity modifier doesn't count when you're flat-footed, unless it's lower than 0.

If you get a bonus to your AC under certain conditions (such as dwarves' bonus against giants), write that in the Modifier box so you remember to use it.

UNITING THE NUMBERS AND THE STORY

While you can select feats and class options based solely on their combat value, you might want to consider tying your choices to your character's personality and backstory. A graceful elven bard, for example, might choose the Nimble Moves feat to ensure that he can dodge past any obstacle. You may also consider making choices that defy expectations: the iconic Pathfinder ranger, Harsk, is a dwarf who feels more at home in forests, fields, and mountains (his favored terrain choices) than in underground tunnels and caverns.

For more information on the various types of armor, from treated leather to metal plate armor, see pages 149–151 of the *Core Rulebook*.

There are a lot of different sorts of weapons, from swords to bows. See pages 142–143 of the *Core Rulebook* to see how they stack up.

For a list of the most common languages, see pages 101–102 of the *Core Rulebook*.

E Saving Throws: After you've entered your base saving throw bonuses from your class, fill in the Ability Modifier boxes for each: Constitution modifier for Fortitude, Dexterity modifier for Reflex, and Wisdom modifier for Will. If you have any racial bonuses or bonuses from feats, like Lightning Reflexes or Iron Will, put those in the Misc Modifier box. The bonuses from any magic items you eventually acquire also go in the Magic Modifier box. For each saving throw, add up the numbers in each row and put that total in the Total box.

If you have a class or racial ability that affects only certain kinds of saving throws (such as the elven bonus against enchantment spells and effects), write that in the large Modifiers box and apply it only when relevant.

F CMB and CMD: Your **Combat Maneuver Bonus** (CMB) represents how good you are at performing certain types of actions likes grabbing or tripping an opponent. **Combat Maneuver Defense** (CMD) represents and how good you are at resisting those specialized assaults. CMB works like a weapon attack bonus—you roll a d20 and add your CMB to determine how well you do. CMD is more like Armor Class—it mostly stays the same and opponents compare their combat maneuver checks to it. See pages 132–135 for more on combat maneuvers.

Combat Maneuver Bonus (CMB) = your base attack bonus + your Strength modifier + your size modifier
Combat Maneuver Defense (CMD) = 10 + your CMB + your Dexterity modifier

If you have bonuses on specific types of maneuvers (such as from the Improved Bull Rush feat) or to your CMD under certain conditions (such as dwarves' stability), enter those into the big Modifiers box.

F Weapons: If you didn't choose your weapons while going through your class guide, do so now. Information about different weapons can be found on pages 142–143 of the *Core Rulebook*. Fill in one Weapon section box for each weapon you choose. See page 37 for information on how to calculate your weapon attack bonuses. If your weapon requires ammunition (such as arrows for a bow or bolts for a crossbow), record how many pieces of ammunition you have for that weapon in the Ammunition box.

H Skills: Make sure you've spent all of your skill ranks, as granted by your class. If you put a rank in any skill listed as a class skill, add a +3 bonus to the Misc. Mod. column for that skill. Then enter your ability modifiers into the Ability Mod. column and add any bonuses from feats or other class features to the Misc. Mod. column. Any skills based on Dexterity or Strength may take a penalty based on the armor you're wearing (see the Armor Check Penalty section on page 150 of the *Core Rulebook*). Add all the numbers together in the Total Bonus column. If you get conditional bonuses to certain skills (such as dwarves' stonecunning racial ability), note that in the Conditional Modifiers section.

H Languages: In this section, write "Common," any languages you automatically know because of your race, and any other special languages from your class (for example, all druids know Druidic). If your Intelligence modifier is +1 or higher, you can pick a number of additional languages equal to your Intelligence modifier. These languages have to come from the list of bonus languages for your race. If you have ranks in the Linguistics skill, select one additional language for each Linguistics rank you have—these don't need to be on your bonus language list.

BACKSTORY

In addition to basic details, consider creating a backstory for your character. A backstory is the tale of your character before she became an adventurer. For most, this is a look back at the character's family, formative years, and education.

A rich backstory not only gives you some hooks to help shape your character's personality, but also gives your GM some ideas to help make your character a more seamless part of the world. When writing your character's backstory, consider the following questions.

Upbringing: How was the character educated? Did the character pursue a different career before leaving to become a hero?

Catalyst: What caused the character to set out on a life of danger and adventure? Was this change a choice or due to circumstance?

Events: What important events from your character's youth are worth noting? How did they shape her into the hero she is today?

Family: Who are the character's parents? What do they do for a living? Are they still alive? Does the character have any siblings? Where are they and what are they doing?

Friends: What childhood friends or relationships are worth noting? Who of those people is still a part of the character's life?

Personal Details

Ⓐ Details like your character's name, hair color, eye color, deity, and homeland are up to you. Think about your character's race and the game's setting, and ask your GM if you need suggestions. If your character is a cleric, her deity determines which domains are available to her (*Core Rulebook* 43), but for other characters it has no effect.

Though gender may affect your character's height and weight, it has no bearing on your ability scores or class choices—anyone can be any class. Your character's gender doesn't have to be the same as your real-life gender.

Your character's height, weight, and age mainly factor in to roleplaying, and rarely have an impact on the rules. For example, your half-orc character could be tall or short for her race, but her height doesn't affect how far she can swing a sword. Growing older does eventually affect a character's ability scores (*Core Rulebook* 169), but otherwise age has little game effect.

You can determine your height and weight randomly (*Core Rulebook* 170), or choose values from within the ranges listed for your race and gender. Remember that your height affects the possible weight range for your PC. If you want a height or weight outside these ranges, take with your GM.

Similarly, you can either choose your age or determine it randomly based on your race and class (*Core Rulebook* 169). You can't choose an age younger than the minimum random result for your race and class. Think carefully before picking a starting age that's middle age or older, as that affects your ability scores. Talk with the GM if you'd like to choose an age outside your race's typical range for adulthood.

Gear

Ⓙ Your class guide has suggested starting gear for your theme, but you may want to purchase additional items with your leftover gold pieces (gp), especially if your campaign is going to be taking place in specialized environments. For example, if you will be venturing into snowy mountains, you may want to purchase climbing gear or a cold-weather outfit. If you'll be camping outside in dangerous areas, it might be wise to purchase bear traps so you can strew them around your camp to hinder enemies or creatures who might try to catch you sleeping.

Though 1st-level characters don't start play with much money, you'll likely earn a lot more as you adventure, so don't despair if you can't immediately afford an item you want. That said, find out from your GM how often you'll have the opportunity to buy things, and buy all the important gear you can afford if you'll be away from civilization for an extended period of time.

Record your purchases on your character sheet. Information on and prices for normal equipment are in Chapter 6 of the *Core Rulebook*. Total the weight of all your gear, and make sure it's not too heavy—if you have a low Strength score, a pile of heavy gear could encumber your movement (*Core Rulebook* 169).

Money

Ⓘ Write down in any money you have left over in this section, as well as any earned in later adventures.

Experience Points

ⓙ New adventurers start with 0 **experience points** (**XP**). As you gain XP, add that to the Experience Points box on your character sheet. For the Next Level box, ask your GM how she plans to award experience points and leveling up. Many GMs use the values in Table 3–1: Character Advancement and Level-Dependent Bonuses on page 30 of the *Core Rulebook*, but some GMs don't track XP, and instead award levels based purely on story events and milestones.

> After you've finished recording all of this information, take a moment to review all of your choices and make sure you're satisfied with the results. When you're happy with your character, it's time to grab some dice and play—you're ready for adventure!

GOING BEYOND!

The options in this book are just a fraction of those available. There's a wealth of other sources you can consult for other character ideas and options, from feats and spells to entirely new classes and ways to play your character. Below are just some of the options that will expand your Pathfinder Roleplaying Game experience.

Prestige Classes

Prestige classes—special classes that are available at later levels—unlock unique and powerful abilities not available to the classes detailed here. See page 374 of the *Core Rulebook* for prestige classes like the arcane archer (who infuses his arrows with magical energy) and the shadowdancer (who can teleport through shadows, hide in plain sight, and animate her shadow to fight alongside her).

Archetypes

An archetype is a variation of an existing class, trading several of the base class' abilities for others that better match a particular concept—like the crafty urban druid or the deadly sniper rogue. Archetypes are introduced in the *Advanced Player's Guide*, and many other books for the Pathfinder Roleplaying Game include unique archetypes.

Other Classes

The *Advanced Player's Guide* introduces six new classes, including the ingenious alchemist and the shrewd witch, and the *Advanced Class Guide* introduces 10 more classes, such as the fearsome bloodrager and the canny investigator. *Ultimate Magic* introduces the magus, and *Ultimate Combat* introduces the gunslinger, ninja, and samurai. These classes are full-fledged character roles, just like the 11 classes in the *Core Rulebook*, but present new options and play styles. Future books in the Pathfinder RPG line may contain additional classes with other abilities.

And Much, Much More!

The books listed above (as well as the books in the Pathfinder Player Companion and Pathfinder Campaign Setting lines) include many new feats, spells, and kinds of equipment. Other books enable you to play new races such as fiend-blooded begins called tieflings, pyromaniacal goblins, shadow-infused fetchlings, and other fantastical beings.

PATHFINDER SOURCEBOOKS

Pathfinder offers a wide number of sourcebooks aimed at giving players and GMs alike a variety of options to enhance your games. Here are just some of the sourcebooks in the Pathfinder RPG line.

Advanced Player's Guide: This handy resource contains six new character classes: the alchemist, cavalier, inquisitor, oracle, summoner, and witch. It also contains new feats and spells suitable for any character.

Advanced Race Guide: Full of new rules and options for characters of any race, this book also contains a number of new races for you to try, from the shifty kitsune to the bloodthirsty orc!

Ultimate Combat: A complete guide to martial techniques and equipment, this sourcebook has a mountain of options for characters focused on combat. It also introduces three new classes: the gunslinger, the ninja, and the samurai!

Ultimate Magic: This mysterious guide is brimming with tools for spellcasting characters, including a wide number of spells for every kind of spellcaster. It also contains the magus class—a sword-wielding arcane spellcaster.

Ultimate Equipment: This mighty book is packed from cover to cover with new armor, weapons, gear, and magic items for your game.

PLAYING THE GAME

In a typical game session, the Game Master (GM) and the players work together to create a story in which the players act as the story's main characters (known as player characters, or PCs) and the GM creates goals for them to reach and challenges for them to overcome, playing the parts of villains, allies, bystanders, and other characters (all known as non-player characters, or NPCs), as well as the environment itself. Dice rolls determine whether characters succeed and add an element of chance to the story. Over time, the characters gain new powers and abilities and find treasures, tools, and other loot to help them on their quests.

For a sense of how a Pathfinder RPG game session might play out, see the example of play on pages 13–14 of the *Core Rulebook*.

BEYOND HACKING AND SLASHING

Combat mode can be used for any situation that requires structure, or in which the GM wants players to feel the urgency of a time limit, such as a chase or a contest.

Starting a Game Session

In your first game session, the GM may give your group's characters a reason to meet and plan a strategy, or immediately start combat to give your characters a reason to work together to defeat a common threat. If the session is a continuation of an earlier session, the GM should start with a quick recap of what happened last time.

In either case, the GM then describes where the characters are and gives the players time to familiarize themselves with that location. Play proceeds with exploration, talking, and combat as needed, with the GM providing clues or instructions about where the adventure is supposed to go and the players deciding what to do next.

Modes of Play

GMs use a lot of different tools to make their adventures exciting, atmospheric, and intriguing, and play in a Pathfinder session can take a lot of different forms, but most of those forms fall into one of two modes: combat mode and narrative mode. A single game session might jump between these modes many times.

Combat Mode: In combat mode, the players take turns performing combat actions in an order determined by their initiative (see page 120). Sometimes players choose to start combat, perhaps by sneaking up on a dragon and taking the first shot. At other times, the GM may start it, such as when the dragon ambushes the PCs and attacks. Either way, you'll know you've entered combat mode because the GM will ask everyone to roll initiative. Then it's your chance to swing a sword, cast powerful spells, dodge explosions, and show off what's on your character sheet!

Remember that your opponents can think and reason, and not every combat needs to end with one side completely annihilating the other. Enemies might try to surrender or flee if battle isn't going their way. Keeping a villain's minions from escaping to warn him might give you the element of surprise, and accepting a creature's surrender opens up opportunities for roleplaying and investigation.

 Make the Numbers Come Alive: Instead of saying "I hit AC 16 for 7 points of damage," try "I whomp the goblin over the head for 7 points of payback! Not so tough now, are you?"

Narrative Mode: In narrative mode, the GM creates a framework for the story and lets the players choose how to respond to the setup and explore.

Description, exploration, and investigation, which are often referred to as "roleplaying," give you a chance to express yourself in the game, and provide context for combat encounters. When the GM describes the appearance of a dungeon or you banter with a bartender or explore a pristine wilderness, that's narration. It can involve puzzles, traps, riddles, or negotiation, and may not even require rolling dice. Narration mode usually doesn't use initiative order.

Narration often provides opportunities to use your skills to be a hero outside of battle. A rogue well-versed in Disable Device might disarm a deadly trap and save the group from a grisly demise, or a character with a high Perception bonus might notice a different route that avoids it entirely. Roleplaying encounters invite creative solutions regardless of the character classes involved—even a group of less trap-savvy PCs might figure out a clever way to safely neutralize a trap. One character might take the lead for a particular challenge, but everyone can contribute.

 Cooperation Isn't Just for Characters: There's nothing wrong with players offering each other advice. A druid's player might have a sneaking suspicion about likely places for traps, and warn the rogue's player to attempt some Perception checks before her character opens that treasure chest.

COMBAT VERSUS NARRATIVE

COMBAT MODE	NARRATIVE MODE
Is highly structured.	Can be structured or unstructured.
Usually involves conflict between two or more creatures.	May involve description, character interaction, exploration, or other activities.
Divides play time into rounds, in which each player takes a turn in initiative order.	Does not generally involve turns or rounds.
Strictly limits character movement and may use a grid.	May place only very general movement limits on characters (e.g., miles per day).
Limits the types of actions a character can take.	Does not usually limit the types of actions a character can take.
Generally ends when all creatures on one side of the conflict die, fall unconscious, flee, or surrender, or when both sides declare a truce.	Ends when combat begins, or when a game session ends or pauses.

Ending a Game Session

When you end the game session, the GM might award experience points to each character or tell you to level up, which makes your character more powerful and gives you new abilities. If your characters are in a safe place, such as a town or fortress, the end of a session is often a good time to buy more equipment and supplies, rest to regain hit points, and to level up your character. If your characters aren't safe, ending the session may be a cliffhanger, and you'll start the next session exactly where you left off!

THE MOST IMPORTANT RULE

The purpose of all the rules in the Pathfinder RPG is to help you breathe life into your characters and the world they explore. There's no "right" or "wrong" balance of combat and narrative modes in a Pathfinder game session. The right balance is the one most enjoyable to your particular players and Game Master. The rules are your toolset, and you can adapt them to suit the type of play you most enjoy. Above all, have fun!

DOWNTIME

A roleplaying game is a social experience, and many people use the downtime before and after games or during breaks to socialize. For many players, hanging out to chat before and after the game or taking a break mid-game to grab dinner together is as integral to their experience as rolling dice.

Downtime is also used to handle aspects of the game that aren't really part of the action, like leveling up characters. Players often use downtime to decide how to divide up loot and spend their hard-earned wealth, breaking out rulebooks and gleefully perusing the pages for cool equipment to purchase.

COMBAT

In the Pathfinder Roleplaying Game, conflict largely consists of combat between the PCs and their adversaries. Once battle breaks out, the possible actions, options, and ramifications can be complex. Learning to act decisively and effectively in combat is a key element of mastering the Pathfinder RPG.

In combat, you'll attempt to reduce the **hit points** (**hp**) of the creatures you're fighting to below 0, rendering them unconscious or dead, before they can do the same to you and your allies. Alternatively, you may win the battle by capturing your enemies , frightening them into fleeing, or otherwise convincing them to stop fighting.

BASE RULES ONLY

Unless the text states otherwise, this section does not account for class abilities, feats, etc. In other words, this is how the combat rules normally work, but characters, monsters, and magic may bend or break some of these rules.

COMBAT IN GAME TIME

A round of combat represents 6 seconds in the game world, but may take longer to resolve in real life.

CHANGING TURN ORDER

Certain types of actions, such as delaying or readying an action (see below), can change the initiative order. Surprise rounds don't, even though some characters can't act in the surprise round.

ATTACKS OF OPPORTUNITY

Sometimes, another creature will do something that gives you a chance to attack it immediately. See page 129.

STANDARD ACTION? SWIFT ACTION?

See page 124 for action types and an explanation of how actions work.

Beginning Combat

Combat happens when all of the following occur.

- Two or more potential adversaries meet.
- At least one side is aware of the other.
- At least one side resorts to aggressive measures.

Entering combat doesn't need to be a mutual decision—all it takes is one creature deciding to attack.

Combat Rounds

Combat is divided into rounds. Each creature gets one turn per round in initiative order (see below), then everyone goes back to the beginning and follows that order again.

On your turn, you can move a certain distance and take a certain number of specific action types (see page 124). When you've used up your actions or decided not to take them, the turn moves on to the next participant.

Ending Combat

Combat ends when all creatures on one side of the fight are unconscious or dead, or have surrendered or fled. It may also end if all participants agree to a truce and are willing to drop out of combat mode (which means they can't attack unless they initiate combat again).

COMBAT CONCEPTS

There are a number of important concepts to familiarize yourself with before you end up in a fight.

Initiative Order: A creature's **initiative** represents how fast it can react and determines the order in which combat participants take their turns in a combat round. Initiative order is determined by each creature's initiative check, which is rolled as the fight begins; the creature with the highest initiative goes first. Once a creature has taken a turn, the creature with the next highest initiative takes its turn. When all participants in the combat have taken a turn, a new round begins at the start of the initiative order.

 Your initiative = d20 + your initiative modifier

TIP **That thing is fast!** You may not discover an opponent's initiative until after the creature has taken its first turn. Don't count on acting before it does.

Ambushes and Surprises: If not all participants were expecting to fight, the first round is a special mini-round called a **surprise round**. Only creatures who aren't surprised get a turn in the surprise round, which is played like a normal round, except participants can take only one action each. Additionally, if you haven't had the chance to act yet in a combat—in either a surprise round or a normal first round—you're **flat-footed**, meaning you're particularly vulnerable to certain attacks. If you're attacked while flat-footed, subtract your Dexterity bonus from your AC.

Extra-Long Actions: Some actions take longer than a full round—these finish just before your turn in the next round. Some particularly complicated tasks, such as disarming traps, take additional full-round actions on later rounds.

Waiting to See What Happens: Sometimes you want to wait to see what others do before you act—this is called **delaying**. Delaying doesn't count as an action. You can delay for as long as you want, and jump back into the fight at any time. When you jump back in, you'll go after whoever is currently taking a turn, and your new initiative position will be right after that person's. If two people stop delaying at the same time, the GM decides who acts first. If you're flat-footed due to not having taken a turn yet in combat, and have the chance to act on your turn but choose to delay, you're no longer flat-footed because you had the *opportunity* to act—you're essentially no longer caught off-guard.

Waiting for a Specific Event: Sometimes you want to react to a specific action rather than going on your turn—this is a special standard action called **readying**. To ready an action, you choose a condition that triggers your response, and state what action you'll take if triggered. If that condition happens, you take the action, even if it's in the middle of another person's turn. You can ready only a single standard, move, or swift action, though you can take a 5-foot step (see Moving on page 122) as part of the readied action, even if you didn't specify it ahead of time. Readied actions can be declared only once combat has begun and initiative has been rolled. If your action is triggered, you resolve its consequences, then finish the turn of the creature that triggered it. Your new initiative position is right before that creature's. If your action isn't triggered, you lose your turn and the next round you act in your normal initiative order.

Melee versus Ranged Attacks: **Melee** attacks are attacks made in hand-to-hand combat. **Ranged** attacks involve shooting or throwing a weapon at a foe who's at a distance.

Saving Throws: Some spells and circumstances give you a chance to try to escape their effects by attempting a **saving throw** (or **save**). If your total equals or exceeds the difficulty class (DC) of the challenge (see page 7), you're successful. For more information, see page 180 of the *Core Rulebook*.

> **Saving throw** = d20 + base save bonus + ability modifier + class ability bonus + racial trait modifiers + any other bonuses or penalties

There are three different types of saving throws, and you may have a different bonus on each of them.

Will saving throws are made against certain types of spells, such as those that affect your mind or perception. A Will saving throw represents the strength of mind you use to disbelieve illusions, fight back against mental control, and so on. Generally, a successful Will saving throw allows you to avoid negative effects entirely.

Fortitude saving throws are made to resist the effects of toxins, diseases, and similar effects. A Fortitude saving throw represents your physical resilience. Generally, a successful Fortitude save allows you to avoid negative effects entirely.

Reflex saving throws are made to jump out of the way of traps and disasters, stop yourself from falling, and avoid being hit by area effects like fireballs. A Reflex saving throw represents your agility. Generally, a successful Reflex save allows you to take only half the damage you'd take on a failure, though some feats and abilities that affect your Reflex saving throw allow you to evade damage entirely on a success.

Automatic Failure and Success: If the number rolled on the die is a 1 (before adding in your save bonus or any other modifiers), this is called a **natural 1**—that's always a failure, even if your bonus and modifiers would otherwise allow you to succeed. On the other hand, a 20 on the die roll (a **natural 20**) is always a success!

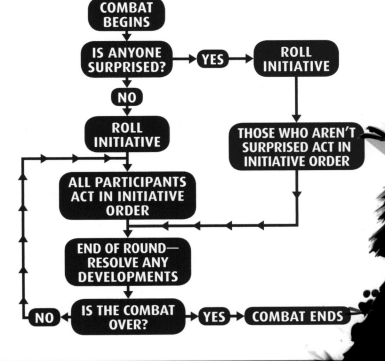

COMBAT BEGINS
↓
IS ANYONE SURPRISED? → YES → ROLL INITIATIVE
↓
NO
↓
ROLL INITIATIVE

THOSE WHO AREN'T SURPRISED ACT IN INITIATIVE ORDER

ALL PARTICIPANTS ACT IN INITIATIVE ORDER
↓
END OF ROUND— RESOLVE ANY DEVELOPMENTS
↓
IS THE COMBAT OVER? — NO / YES → COMBAT ENDS

READIED ACTION TRIGGERS

Conditions that trigger readied actions can be somewhat broad, such as "if an enemy casts a spell" or "if one of my allies gets wounded." How general you can be is up to your GM. Your response action, however, must be specific, such as "I counterspell" or "I attack with my greatsword."

ACTIONS

See page 124 for descriptions of action types and how to use them, and page 126 for information on how to make attacks and what happens when you're attacked.

YOUR TURN

- YOUR TURN BEGINS
- RESOLVE ANY ACTION THAT SHOULD FINISH BEFORE YOUR TURN
- CHECK DURATION ON EFFECTS
- RESOLVE ANY ONGOING EFFECTS
- TAKE YOUR ACTIONS (STANDARD, MOVE, SWIFT)
- RESOLVE ANY END-OF-TURN EFFECTS
- YOUR TURN ENDS

YOUR TURN

While the actions you can take in combat are limited, there are several different ways your character can make an attack, and multiple ways to combine attacking and movement. The most common method is an attack action—a standard action to deliver one melee or ranged attack—but there are a lot of other ways to bring an opponent to its knees. This section provides an overview of how your turn works and what you can do during a turn.

Turn Basics

Most combat turns consist of some combination of moving around the battlefield and making attacks. On each turn, your primary options are as follows.

- Make a full attack (give up your move action to potentially attack more than once).
- Move and take a standard action (often, this standard action is an attack).
- Move twice (substitute a second move action for your standard action).

Moving

Your **speed** represents how far you can move with one move action. Your speed is determined by your race, and is modified by your character class, your armor, any abilities or feats you have that let you move farther, the effects of any spells that affect your movement, and even the terrain. It's a good idea to write down your base speed on your character sheet for quick reference, but make sure that on your turn, you add or subtract any movement bonuses or penalties that apply in that specific situation (such as those from spells, magic items, or other sources).

If you're using a map with a 1-inch-by-1-inch grid for combat, each square on the grid represents a 5-foot-by-5-foot square, also referred to as a **5-foot square**. In general, the number of squares you can move on your turn with one move action is equal to your speed divided by 5. For example, if you have a speed of 30, you can move 6 squares per move action.

Moving Diagonally: A diagonal movement between squares is longer than moving between adjacent squares. When moving between diagonal squares, simply count your first diagonal movement as 5 feet (or 1 square), the second one as 10 feet (or 2 squares), the third one as 5 feet (or 1 square), and so on.

Moving and 5-Foot Steps: If you use your move action to move, you can't take a free 5-foot step. However, if you use your move action for something that doesn't involve leaving your square, like opening a door or standing up, you can still take a 5-foot step.

Difficult Terrain: Difficult terrain is an area that's challenging to move through, such as heavy undergrowth. When you're figuring out how far you can move, 1 square of difficult terrain counts as 2 squares of normal terrain, and moving diagonally between squares of difficult terrain counts as moving through 3 squares of normal terrain. You can't take a 5-foot step into difficult terrain.

Moving and Attacking

If you want to use your standard action to attack and you also want to move out of your square on your turn, you have two options for moving: taking a move action or taking a 5-foot step. You can move either before or after your attack.

Making Multiple Attacks

Certain PCs and many monsters can use a full-round action to deliver multiple attacks. This is called a **full attack** (or a **full-attack action**). Normally, you can take a standard action to make a single attack; if you want to attack multiple times on your turn, you have to take a full-attack action. Because a full attack is a full-round action, you can't also take a move action in the same round that you make a full attack. However, since a 5-foot step doesn't count as an action, you can still take a 5-foot step when you make a full attack. You can take a 5-foot step before, between, or after your attacks.

COMBAT TECHNIQUES

Want to try something more sophisticated than just hitting an opponent with a sword or an arrow? Having trouble deciding between your dagger and your longsword? Do you feel like jumping into a bare-fisted brawl? There are many options beyond single-weapon combat.

 Getting Tricky: Sometimes you may want to trip or grab an opponent. This is called a **combat maneuver** (see page 132 for more information).

Two-Weapon Fighting

Show off your martial prowess with a weapon in each hand! When using two-weapon fighting, you can make a full attack to attack with both weapons. You pick one weapon to be your "primary-hand" weapon, and the other is your "off-hand" weapon; you can change which is which from round to round. Your primary-hand weapon gets your full Strength bonus on damage rolls, but your off-hand weapon gets only 1/2 your Strength bonus on damage rolls (if you have a Strength penalty, your off-hand weapon takes the full penalty, not half).

Two-weapon fighting opens up several options: you could wield a weapon in one hand and bash with a shield in the other; wield a weapon in one hand and use a weapon that doesn't use a hand (such as armor spikes) as your off-hand attack; or even wield a double weapon with both hands. Be warned, however—using two-weapon fighting also adds big penalties to both attack rolls!

For more information on two-weapon fighting, see page 202 of the *Core Rulebook*.

 Two-Weapon Feats: Feats like Double Slice and Improved Two-Weapon Fighting can help you reduce or negate two-weapon penalties, or even give you extra attacks with your off-hand weapon.

Attacking with Natural Weapons

Monsters and characters with the ability to change shape (such as druids and dragon-child sorcerers) may be able to attack with their claws, tails, or teeth. If you have natural weapons, as a full-attack action you can attack with a manufactured weapon such as a longsword and follow up with attacks from your natural weapons. You attack with the manufactured weapon normally, then make your natural attacks, but you take a –5 penalty on attack rolls for the natural attacks and you apply only 1/2 your Strength bonus.

Sometimes the form of the natural weapon prevents you from attacking with it on the same round that you make an attack with a manufactured weapon. For example, if you have claws on your hands, but you're using one of your hands to hold a longsword, you can't use the hand holding the weapon to make a claw attack (you'd have to drop or put away the sword to free up that hand in order to use it for claw attacks).

For more information on attacking with natural weapons, see page 182 of the *Core Rulebook*.

Attacking without a Weapon

Any PC can punch or kick an opponent; this sort of attack is called an **unarmed strike**. Attacking with an unarmed strike provokes an attack of opportunity (see page 129) from the target of your attack. Unarmed strikes are otherwise like weapon attacks—you can even use two-weapon fighting to attack with a weapon in one hand and punch with your other hand (or you can kick instead, which functions just like a punch for this purpose).

If you're using a two-handed weapon such as a greatsword, you can't use two-weapon fighting to attack with an unarmed strike (even if it's a kick instead of a punch).

Monks and Unarmed Strikes: When making unarmed strikes, monks don't provoke attacks of opportunity, and they have a special attack type that lets them make extra unarmed strikes during a full-attack action (see page 73).

For more information on unarmed strikes, see page 182 of the *Core Rulebook*.

SWITCHING IT UP

Sometimes the circumstances change in the midst of a full-attack action, such as when you kill your opponent with your first hit and no one is in range of your next attack. As long as you've made only your first attack and haven't made any additional attacks, you can cancel the full-attack action and treat the attack as a standard action. This allows you to take a move action on the same turn. Similarly, you can decide to change a single attack into a full-attack action, as long as you haven't taken your move action yet. Keep this flexibility in mind during battle!

NATURAL ADVANTAGES

Although most natural weapons don't have the damage potential of normal weapons, they still offer some distinct advantages. First off, they can't be taken away from you, disarmed, or otherwise lost. They also don't have to be readied at the beginning of a fight—you've always got them on-hand. Perhaps the biggest advantage, though, is that they allow you to make more attacks than you could otherwise. Combining attacks with your normal weapons with natural attacks can be an especially deadly strategy.

For more information on the different types of actions, see pages 181–182 of the *Core Rulebook*.

TURN TACTICS

You can use the actions in your turn in any order you want, and you will often find situations in which using them in a certain order gives you an advantage.

For example, if you're fighting a badly wounded foe, you might want to take your standard action first to make an attack, hoping to knock them out of the fight. If you succeed, you might find that you have a much wider variety of options to take with your move action, such as retrieving a potion or moving to a safe location. Had you tried to use your move action first, you might have allowed your foe to take a free swing at you.

If you're a spellcaster, this is particularly important. Casting a spell is delicate work, and it's best to move away from foes before casting so they can't disrupt your spell before it goes off. Even taking a 5-foot step is usually enough to give you the room you need to work your magic.

ACTION TYPES

During your turn, you can take a standard action, a move action, and a swift action, which we'll explain below. There are also other types of actions that interact with these three actions.

Standard Action

Standard actions are the most important actions in most combat encounters, as they're the ones with the most potential to shape the battle's outcome. Most of the time, you'll use your standard action to cast a spell or make an attack. You can take only one standard action during your turn. Below are some examples of common standard actions.

Activate a magic item	Concentrate to maintain an active spell	Read a scroll
Aid another	Dismiss a spell	Ready an action
Apply an oil	Draw a hidden weapon	Stabilize someone
Attack (melee)	Drink a potion	Use a skill that takes a standard action
Attack (ranged)	Escape a grapple	Use a spell-like ability
Attack (unarmed)	Feint	Use a supernatural ability
Cast a normal spell	Light a torch with a tindertwig	Use an extraordinary ability
Channel energy	Lower spell resistance	Use total defense

Move Action

A move action either lets you move a distance that's less than or equal to your speed (the most common move action) or allows you to manipulate your environment, equipment, or position in some way. You can use your standard action to perform a move action instead, in which case it's possible for you to take two move actions on your turn. Below are some examples of common move actions.

Close a door	Move a heavy object
Control a frightened mount	Open or close a door
Direct or redirect an active spell	Pick up an item
Draw a weapon	Ready or drop a shield
Load a hand crossbow or light crossbow	Retrieve a stored item
Mount or dismount from a steed	Sheathe a weapon
Move	Stand up from a prone position

Full-Round Action

A full-round action is complicated enough that it ties up almost all of your activity for the round. When you take a full-round action, it uses up your standard action and move action (but not your swift action). Below are some examples of common full-round actions.

Cast a full-round spell	Lock or unlock a weapon in a locked gauntlet
Charge	Make a full-round attack
Deliver a coup de grace	Prepare to throw a splash weapon
Escape from a net	Run
Extinguish flames	Use a skill that takes 1 round
Light a torch	Use a touch spell on up to six allies
Load a heavy or repeating crossbow	Withdraw

Swift Action

Swift actions are special, extra-fast actions, usually granted by class abilities or magic items. For example, activating a paladin's smite evil ability is a swift action. You can take only one swift action per round, and you can't use any other action to perform a swift action. Below are some examples of swift actions.

Cast a quickened spell	Use a class or item ability that takes a swift action

Free Action

Free actions require very little time or effort. The rules don't limit the number of free actions you can take in a round, but your GM can limit you (and you should restrain yourself) to what can reasonably accomplished in a single 6-second round. Below are some examples of common free actions.

Cease concentration on a spell	Drop to the floor
Draw an arrow from a quiver	Prepare spell components to cast a spell
Drop an item	Speak

Immediate Action

A few spells and abilities are immediate actions, which means they can be used during another creature's turn, possibly interrupting that creature mid-action. When an immediate action is taken, resolve it, then continue with any action that was interrupted. If that activity is no longer valid, the interrupted creature's action is wasted. If you use an immediate action when it's not your turn, you give up your next turn's swift action. If you use an immediate action during your own turn, it uses your swift action for that turn. Below are some examples of common immediate actions.

Cast a spell whose casting time is an immediate action	Cast *feather fall*

No Action

A few activities don't use an action.

Delay	Take a 5-foot step

Variable Action Types

Some activities, such as using a feat or performing a combat maneuver, may vary with respect to the type of action you take to use them. A feat's description tells you what sort of action it takes. Combat maneuvers can substitute for melee attacks, be used as attacks of opportunity, or be used as separate actions—see the particular combat maneuver's description to find out what type of action it takes.

Perform a combat maneuver
Use a feat

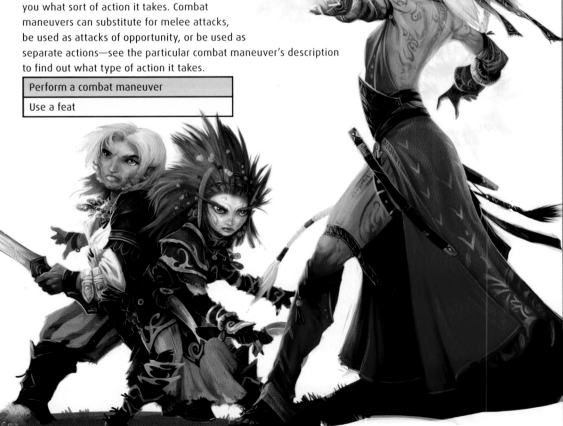

5-FOOT STEP

A 5-foot step is a special action you can take if you haven't otherwise moved during your turn. As the name suggests, it lets you move 5 feet, and you do so without provoking attacks of opportunity (see page 129). You can take your 5-foot step before, between, or after your other actions. You can even take it during certain full-round actions, such as while making a full attack or delivering a touch spell to multiple targets. Once you've taken a 5-foot step, you can't use your remaining actions to move, although you can still take move actions that don't require you to leave your square (for example, you could open a door). You can't take a 5-foot step to enter difficult terrain or if your movement is restricted by conditions.

USING ALL YOUR ACTIONS

Getting the most out of your actions is key to giving you an edge over your foes. While you can usually find a use for your move and standard action, keep in mind that you might have a class feature that you can use as a swift action, giving you a valuable boost.

ATTACKS AND DAMAGE

The most common way to make an attack is with an attack action: a standard action used to deliver one melee or ranged attack. If an attack hits, the target likely takes damage.

Some attacks, known as touch attacks, completely disregard armor. See page 179 of the *Core Rulebook* for more on touch attacks.

Certain creatures and magical effects can reduce ability scores when they damage a creature. For more information, see page 555 of the *Core Rulebook*.

The Weapons table on page 142 of the *Core Rulebook* lists the damage dice of most weapons.

See page 179 of the *Core Rulebook* for more on AC modifiers.

BOOSTING YOUR ARMOR CLASS

Taking hit after hit in combat can knock you out of a fight, but there are ways to boost your Armor Class. You might want to find a way to gain cover (which grants you an AC bonus) or concealment (which grants you a percentage chance the attack will miss). Both of these depend on the environment, so pay attention to your surroundings.

Making an Attack

To make an attack, you roll a d20, add any bonuses, and subtract any penalties—the result is called an **attack roll**. Your attack roll represents both how skilled you are with your weapon and the element of chance involved in battle. If your attack roll is equal to or higher than your opponent's Armor Class (see below), you hit!

MAKING AN ATTACK
Roll a d20. • If the die shows a 1, you automatically miss. • If it shows a 20, you automatically hit, and might deal extra damage (see Critical Hits on page 136). Otherwise, follow the steps below to determine what happens.
Add your attack bonus. Your attack bonus is usually the sum of the following: • Your base attack bonus (BAB), which is determined by your class and level • Your Strength modifier (if using a melee weapon) or your Dexterity modifier (if using a ranged weapon) • Your size modifier • Any bonuses from your specific weapon (if it's a masterwork weapon, a magical weapon, etc.) • Range penalty (if you're using ranged weapons)   Most of these variables don't change very often, so it's a good idea to calculate this bonus for each of your weapons ahead of time and write each bonus next to its respective weapon on your character sheet.
Add your attack bonus.
Add any other bonuses or penalties from conditions, spells, etc.
The GM compares the result to the Armor Class of your opponent.
If the result is equal to or higher than your opponent's Armor Class, you hit the creature and might damage it.

If you hit your opponent, it's time to figure out how much damage you deal. When you damage a creature, the amount of damage you deal is subtracted from its current hit points.

DETERMINING HOW MUCH DAMAGE YOU DEAL
Roll your damage dice. The type of dice you roll depends on the kind of weapon you're using.
If you're using a melee or thrown weapon, add your Strength modifier.
Factor in any multipliers (such as from a critical hit) and add any extra damage (such as from a sneak attack).
The result is the amount of damage you deal to your opponent. Some opponents may have abilities that reduce the amount of damage they take, especially if the damage is of a particular type (see the next page).

Being Attacked

When an opponent attacks you, you compare its attack roll to your Armor Class (AC). Your **Armor Class** represents the protection that your armor and shield (if you have one) give you against injury, your ability to dodge blows, and other factors that influence how likely you are to be hit and take damage.

Some of the other factors that can affect your Armor Class include the following:

• **Enhancement bonuses** to your armor (if you're wearing special or magical armor).
• **Deflection bonuses** such as the effects of spells that make you harder to hit.
• **Natural armor**, which is the term used to describe the scales or tough skin possessed by some creatures.
• **Dodge bonuses**, which represent your ability to actively avoid blows.
• **Size modifiers,** which represent how big of a target (and thus how easy to hit) you are.

 Your Armor Class = 10 + armor bonus + shield bonus + Dexterity modifier + other modifiers

If your opponent's attack roll equals or exceeds your Armor Class, the attack hits you. The GM rolls for damage and tells you the result. To determine your new hit point total after taking damage, perform the steps in the following table.

DETERMINING HOW MUCH DAMAGE YOU TAKE

Find out from the GM the amount of damage your opponent's attack deals to you.
If you have damage reduction or resistances, subtract the appropriate amount from the total.
Subtract the remaining amount from your hit point total. This is your new hit point total until you receive healing or rest (or until you take more damage).

Certain factors may prevent you from taking the full amount of damage.

- **Damage Reduction**: **Damage reduction (DR)** prevents you from taking the full amount of damage, allowing you to subtract a certain number of points from the total amount of damage dealt. Some class features or spells may give you damage reduction. For more information, see page 561 of the *Core Rulebook*.
- **Resistance to Weapon Damage Types**: Every weapon deals damage of a particular type, such as piercing, slashing, or bludgeoning, though some weapons allow you to choose which type they deal. Some forms of damage resistance are type-specific.
- **Resistance to Energy Types**: Spells, magical abilities, and some magic weapons deal damage with energy of a particular type, such as fire or electricity. Spells, class abilities, some forms of damage reduction, and some abilities can give you resistance to different types of energy.

If your new hit point total is 0, you're disabled. If it's below 0, you're dying. See page 137 for more information.

SAVING TIME AT THE TABLE

Attack and damage rolls can take up a lot of time at the table, but you can use a few simple tricks to speed up your turn and keep combat moving. Whenever you roll dice for an attack, roll the damage dice along with your d20. If you hit, you've already rolled the damage, and if you miss, you can just ignore the damage dice.

At higher levels of play when you have multiple attacks, you can still use this trick by having color-coded attack and damage dice. Then, if you roll a hit with your blue d20, you can just check the blue damage dice to determine the damage for that attack. Just remember to call out which color represents which attack before you roll.

Also, use the time between your turns to think about what you'll do next. Even if changing circumstances force you to change your plan by the time your turn comes around again, you'll be more prepared to act if you think ahead.

UNDERSTANDING YOUR SQUARE

Victory isn't always determined solely by your character's stats, or even by the weapons and equipment she brings to the battlefield. Understanding and controlling the space in which you're fighting can often mean the difference between triumph and defeat.

Occupying and Moving through Squares

Your **space** is the square or squares you occupy on the battlefield. If your space is 1 5-foot square (which is true for most creatures), it's often just called your **square**.

Allies' Squares: You can move through an ally's square freely, because it's assumed your ally will let you pass so you can get into a better tactical position in combat.

Opponents' Squares: You can't move through an opponent's square unless you either use the Acrobatics skill to tumble through it or attempt an overrun combat maneuver (see page 134) to force your way past.

Ending Movement: Generally, a creature must end its movement in an unoccupied square, though there are exceptions for very large and very small creatures. If you would be forced to end your movement in another creature's square, place yourself in the nearest open square instead.

Threatened Area

You **threaten** the squares around you—if a creature is in one of them, you can make a melee attack (see page 121) against it with a manufactured or natural weapon.

Most melee weapons give you enough reach that you can attack creatures in squares that are adjacent to your space (you can also attack creatures in your own square if necessary). For PCs, this usually means you threaten all squares that are adjacent to you, plus your own square.

Some melee weapons, such as the longspear, have the **reach weapon quality**, allowing you to attack foes 1 square farther away but preventing you from attacking creatures in adjacent squares or your own square. Most characters who use a reach weapon also keep a non-reach weapon to use against foes that are adjacent to them. For more information on reach, see page 145 of the *Core Rulebook*.

Gray Squares: The character doesn't threaten these squares with her reach weapon.

Green Squares: The character threatens these squares with her reach weapon, and can attack foes in them.

Dark Gray Squares: The character doesn't threaten these squares, but she receives an attack of opportunity against foes leaving them to move closer to her.

Some monsters have exceptional reach and threaten a larger area—they can attack you from farther away or close up. Monsters of at least Large size almost always threaten a larger area.

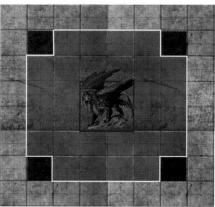

Green Squares: The monster threatens these squares and can attack foes in them.

Dark Gray Squares: The monster doesn't threaten these squares, but receives an attack of opportunity against foes leaving them to move closer to it.

SIZE MATTERS

If a creature is three or more sizes larger than another creature, it can end its movement while occupying the smaller creature's square.

FISTS OF FURY

If you're not holding a weapon, you don't threaten squares unless you're a monk or have the Improved Unarmed Strike feat.

See page 87 of the *Core Rulebook* for more information on using Acrobatics to avoid attacks of opportunity when passing through opponents' threatened squares.

REACH FOR IT

Your **reach** is the maximum distance from which you can hit opponents in melee combat.

TINY TERRORS

Very small monsters (Tiny and smaller) don't threaten adjacent squares; they have to move into their target's square to attack, and can end their movement in another creature's square.

Attacks of Opportunity

An **attack of opportunity** is a single extra attack you can make when an opponent lets its guard down in the area you threaten.

You make an attack of opportunity on your opponent's turn, and it doesn't count toward the number of attacks you can make on your turn. When you make an attack of opportunity, you briefly interrupt the action that provoked it, and may cause the action to fail entirely. For example, you might deal enough damage to kill your foe, thus preventing her attack, or disrupt a spell she's in the middle of casting. Each creature that threatens a provoking opponent's square gets to make an attack of opportunity against that opponent—so don't let yourself get surrounded!

See the Actions in Combat table on page 183 of the *Core Rulebook* for more actions that provoke an attack of opportunity.

Provoking an Attack of Opportunity: Many different actions can provoke an attack of opportunity. Here are some examples:

Casting a spell	Moving out of a threatened square
Drinking a potion	Picking up an item
Making an attack with a ranged weapon	Standing up from a prone position

Not all actions provoke attacks of opportunity, though—the following actions don't provoke an attack of opportunity:

Casting defensively (*Core Rulebook* 207)	Taking a 5-foot step (into or out of a threatened area)
Moving into a threatened square	Withdrawing (*Core Rulebook* 188)

Making an Attack of Opportunity: Most creatures can make only one attack of opportunity per round, but feats like Combat Reflexes allow you to make more.

- You don't have to make an attack of opportunity against an opponent if you don't want to.
- Your attack of opportunity is made at your normal attack bonus.
- You can't make an attack of opportunity if you're unable to act or if you're flat-footed.

    Avoiding Attacks of Opportunity: The easiest way to avoid attacks of opportunity is to not be in a threatened area. Often, you can take a 5-foot step away from an opponent into a square where you can act freely.

    Intentionally Provoking Attacks of Opportunity: Although it's not ideal to give your opponents extra chances to attack you, attacks of opportunity are still just attacks, and may even miss. If you're facing weak monsters and have enough hit points to take a hit, or your high Armor Class will protect you, it could be worth taking the chance if doing so gives you or your allies a tactical advantage or prevents a weaker ally from being hit.

Know Your Weapons: Since moving out of a threatened square provokes an attack of opportunity and reach weapons increase the number of threatened squares around you, reach weapons can give you many more chances for attacks of opportunity.

ATTACKS OF OPPORTUNITY REFERENCE

You *can* make an attack of opportunity if *all* of the following conditions are true.
- An opponent does something within your threatened area that provokes an attack of opportunity.
- You're armed with a melee or natural weapon, or have the Improved Unarmed Strike feat.
- You haven't made an attack of opportunity since your last turn, or you have the Combat Reflexes feat.
- You're not flat-footed and can take actions.

You *can't* make an attack of opportunity if *any* of the following conditions are true.
- Your opponent isn't in your threatened area.
- You're unarmed and don't have Improved Unarmed Strike.
- You've already made an attack of opportunity since your last turn (and don't have the Combat Reflexes feat).
- You're flat-footed or can't take actions.

ANALYZING THE BATTLEFIELD

When it's nearing your turn in combat, take a look at the battlefield and perform a quick analysis of the situation. Are you or any of your allies in trouble? Are any of your opponents vulnerable? How will this fight impact your objectives?

FIGHT OR FLIGHT?

Knowing when to back out of combat can mean the difference between victory and having to create a new character. Keeping track of the average amount of damage you've been taking each round can give you a feel for when it's time to retreat or call for help from a fellow player character.

WHEN TO RISK IT

Some players go to extraordinary lengths to avoid provoking attacks of opportunity. Remember that a foe only gets one attack of opportunity when you provoke, which limits the total amount of damage they can deal to you. If being targeted by one attack allows you to get to a more advantageous spot, it might be worth it.

PLAY IT SAFE

Sometimes it's a much better idea to stay in your current location rather than moving. If moving causes you to provoke multiple attacks of opportunity from numerous foes, it might be better to stay put and take your chances—especially if standing still lets you make a full attack. Also, always be wary when moving closer to foes. You don't want to make yourself vulnerable to charges or being flanked by multiple opponents.

Priorities and Opportunities

Keep the following variables in mind when deciding what to do on your turn.

YOURSELF	YOUR ALLIES
Are you badly hurt?	Are any badly hurt?
Are you in a threatened area?	Are any in danger from nearby opponents?
Are there dire consequences to staying put?	Can you make an ally more effective?
YOUR OPPONENTS	**YOUR MISSION**
Are any badly injured?	Are your mission goals in jeopardy?
Are any clustered together?	Can you take any actions to accomplish your goals?
Are any dangerous opponents not engaged by allies?	Could your allies take such actions?

Yourself

If you're badly hurt, here are some good choices.

- **Heal**: Use a potion or a spell to regain hit points.
- **Withdraw**: Withdrawing is a full-round action that allows you to move a distance equal to double your speed, and lets you leave a threatened square without provoking an attack of opportunity. For more information on withdrawing, see page 188 the *Core Rulebook*.
- **Go for Help**: Put yourself in a position where an ally can heal you.

If you can't get healing or move to safety, consider these options.

- **Fighting Defensively**: When you **fight defensively**, you take a –4 penalty on all attacks in a round but gain a +2 dodge bonus to your AC for the same round. For more information on fighting defensively, see pages 184 and 187 of the *Core Rulebook*.
- **Focus on Defending Yourself**: When you take the **total defense** action, you take a standard action to defend yourself and gain a +4 dodge bonus to your AC. You can't fight defensively or make attacks of opportunity while using total defense. For more information on taking the total defense action, see page 186 of the *Core Rulebook*.

Being in a threatened area limits your options, so if your square is threatened, consider moving to a better tactical position. Repositioning with a 5-foot step might take you out of the threatened area, giving you a wider range of options. Foes can still follow you with 5-foot steps of their own and then make full attacks on their turns, though, so try to gauge how dangerous taking a round of full attacks from your foes might be. If being hit by all those attacks would likely take you down, you might want to use a move action to reposition yourself farther away instead. Using a move action this way provokes attacks of opportunity, but it's often better to take that chance than to risk being targeted by lots of full attacks.

If you can't afford to take damage, the withdraw action makes leaving a threatened square safe—you won't provoke any attacks of opportunity—but it uses up a standard action that could otherwise shape the battle. Yet sometimes staying where you are is too dangerous to contemplate, and you have no choice but to leave—you might be in the middle of a damaging effect, in an area that's about to collapse, or badly outnumbered. At times like those, do what you must to reach safety, even if it means using up all your actions. After all, if you're dead, unconscious, or captured, you're not taking useful actions anyway.

 TIP Your first priority should usually be keeping yourself safe.

Your Allies

If an ally is about to go down, think about ways you can help—if no one else can come to the rescue before your ally's attackers finish him off, it's up to you to save him.

- Disarm, trip, or reposition the foes attacking your ally with combat maneuvers (see page 134).
- Heal your ally or cast a protective spell.
- Engage the attackers in melee combat.
- Block attackers' access to your ally by putting up a magical barrier like a *web* or *wall of fire*.
- Slow opponents down or incapacitate them with tanglefoot bags or spells like *sound burst*.

Once you've dealt with any immediate threats to your party, consider ways you can make yourself and your allies more effective. If you're in melee, look for a chance to take a 5-foot step so you and an ally can flank a foe. If it's early in the fight, consider giving your party an edge with helpful spells like *bless*—and use area enhancement spells if you're still close together. Conversely, if the fight's almost over, it may be time to stop using up rounds of limited-duration abilities like bardic performances and rage.

 Keep your allies alive and fighting—a dead or incapacitated ally can't contribute to the battle.

Your Opponents

Focusing fire wins battles. Wounded opponents fight just as effectively as unharmed opponents, so if you're in a good position to bring down a gravely wounded opponent, take the shot.

If your opponents are tightly clustered, use that to your advantage.

- Catch as many foes as you can in the area of a spell.
- If you fight in melee, position yourself so you're threatening multiple foes.
- You can also split the field of battle with spells like *wall of force*, leaving some foes cut off while your group finishes off the rest.

In many battles, one or two foes present the bulk of the threat. Keep your most dangerous opponents occupied so they can't target your most vulnerable allies.

- Engage the opponent in melee.
- Grapple the main foe or use other combat maneuvers (see pages 132–134) to stop her or isolate her from her allies.
- Rain down damage from afar.
- Neutralize spellcasters with spells like *silence*.

Your Mission

Failure of your mission might cost you financially, cause the deaths of innocents, or even endanger an entire world. Regardless of the consequences of failure, during your turn you should briefly consider why you are fighting so you don't forget your goals in the heat of battle. If your mission is in jeopardy, get it back on track or alert your allies to the situation. Conversely, if you find yourself free to accomplish an important objective, seize the moment.

 Victory requires keeping the big picture in mind.

KNOW YOUR FOE

In the course of an adventure, you may face the same type of foe multiple times. Make sure to pay close attention to that enemy's abilities and weaknesses so you're prepared for future conflicts. Remembering that your foes are vulnerable to fire, for example, can give you a huge advantage should you happen to face their kind again.

TARGET THE LEADER

While many fights are against a group of similar monsters, all too often you will encounter a group of minions following a powerful leader. This foe is usually far more dangerous than the minions under its command, so finding a way to hamper or take out this deadly foe can turn the tide of battle very quickly. Sometimes the minions will just outright flee the battle without the presence of their commander.

See page 198 of the *Core Rulebook* for more information on combat maneuvers.

WHAT KIND OF ACTION IS IT?

Disarm, sunder, and trip combat maneuvers can be performed in place of a melee attack (even an attack of opportunity). Bull rush, grapple, and overrun combat maneuvers are standard actions.

JUST LIKE AN ATTACK

A combat maneuver check is an attack roll, so you automatically miss if you roll a 1 and automatically succeed if you roll a natural 20. However, it can't be a critical threat (see page 136).

RISKY MANEUVER

Attempting a combat maneuver provokes an attack of opportunity from the target. If that attack hits, the damage is applied as a penalty on the combat maneuver check, which might make you fail the check.

COMBAT MANEUVERS

The best movie fight scenes don't just involve combatants repeatedly hitting each other with their weapons—they use tricky moves and unexpected gambits to try to gain an advantage. In the Pathfinder RPG, these tactics are known as combat maneuvers.

BEYOND SIMPLE ATTACKS

Combat maneuvers are special combat actions such as disarming, pushing, or tripping that let you bypass or hamper an opponent. Combat maneuvers are technically a kind of melee attack, so you can use them only against someone in your threatened area. Attempting a combat maneuver provokes an attack of opportunity from the target of your maneuver (although feats like Improved Disarm and other special abilities allow you to attempt a combat maneuver without provoking an attack of opportunity).

You perform a combat maneuver by making a **combat maneuver check**: Roll a d20 (as if you were making an attack) and add your **Combat Maneuver Bonus** (**CMB**), which represents your skill at performing these maneuvers. If the result is higher than your opponent's **Combat Maneuver Defense** (**CMD**), you succeed. Any bonuses or penalties on your attack rolls affect any combat maneuvers you attempt. If you provoke an attack of opportunity with a combat maneuver, any damage you take from that attack applies as a penalty on your combat maneuver check.

Using Weapons: When performing a disarm, sunder, or trip combat maneuver with a weapon, add the weapon's enhancement bonus to your combat maneuver check, as well as any other bonuses or penalties that apply when you wield that weapon (such as the benefits of Weapon Focus). You can use any weapon with these maneuvers—not just weapons with the trip or disarm special feature (*Core Rulebook* 144).

Tripping a Prone Target: You can't trip someone who's already prone. If a creature provokes an attack of opportunity by standing up, it can't be tripped with that attack because it's still considered prone until it finishes standing up.

Attacks of Opportunity and Combat Maneuvers: If someone hits you with an attack of opportunity while you're performing a combat maneuver, you must subtract the amount of damage dealt to you by that attack from the roll for your combat maneuver check.

Determining Combat Maneuver Bonus and Combat Maneuver Defense

Your Combat Maneuver Bonus is calculated using the formula below. The special size modifiers you're most likely to use are −1 for Small creatures, +0 for Medium creatures, and +1 for Large creatures. Some feats and abilities may grant bonuses on combat maneuver checks for specific maneuvers.

Your CMB = Your base attack bonus + your Strength modifier + your special size modifier

The formula below is used to find your Combat Maneuver Defense. The special size modifiers for a creature's CMD are the same as the ones for CMB above. If you have any circumstance, deflection, dodge, insight, luck, morale, profane, or sacred bonuses to your Armor Class, add them to your CMD as well. Any penalties to your Armor Class also apply to your CMD (if you're flat-footed, for example, your Dexterity modifier isn't added into your CMD).

Your CMD = 10 + your base attack bonus + your Strength modifier + your Dexterity modifier + your special size modifier

When Should You Use a Combat Maneuver?

Here are some good reasons to use a combat maneuver instead of making a normal attack.

Bull Rush: To push an opponent out of your way, closer to (or away from) an ally, or off the edge of a cliff.
Disarm: To leave your opponent unarmed or prevent use of a magic item.
Grapple: To keep an enemy from fleeing, interfere with spellcasting, or restrain a foe without killing it.
Overrun: To get past a foe that's blocking an exit or standing between you and your objectives.
Sunder: To break a dangerous weapon, shatter a shield to lower a foe's AC, or break a focus item to interfere with spellcasting.
Trip: To keep a foe from fleeing, or to leave it prone and more vulnerable to your attacks.

GRAPPLING

Sometimes it makes sense to try to immobilize foes so you can tie them up and question them, or to grab an attacker to keep him away from an ally. Attempting to restrain an opponent during combat is called **grappling**. Grappling is a powerful combat option, but it's also the most complicated combat maneuver to perform.

Grappler and Grappled: The creature who started a grapple (the grappler) has more options than the creature she has grappled. However, both have the **grappled condition**. Creatures with the grappled condition can't move or take actions that require two hands, and take big penalties to Dexterity, on attack rolls, and when spellcasting.

After Grappling an Opponent

A grapple requires a standard action each round to maintain and lasts until the grappler releases her opponent (a free action) or the grappled foe escapes. When you've grappled someone, as part of the standard action you take to maintain the grapple each round, you can also choose to perform one of the following three actions.

Damage: Deal the same amount of damage you'd deal with your unarmed strike, a natural attack, or an attack made with a light or one-handed weapon.

Move: Drag the grappled creature a distance equal to half your speed and place the foe in any square adjacent to you at the end of your move. Attempting to place your foe in a dangerous location (like in a fire) gives it a free check to escape with a +4 bonus.

Pin: Pin the grappled creature. Being pinned is like being grappled, but with even more restrictions. If the creature is already pinned, you can tie it up instead (assuming you have rope handy), but doing so imposes a penalty on your check to maintain the grapple.

 Wrestling Them into Submission: A grappled creature can still attack you, but a pinned one can't. Tying up a pinned foe while you're grappling him is tough, so get an ally to help you.

When You're the Target

If you're the one being grappled, you can attempt a combat maneuver check against the grappler's CMD to escape the grapple, or turn the tables on your opponent and become the grappler yourself!

If you just want to break free, you can attempt an Escape Artist skill check instead of a combat maneuver check, which is usually a better option if you have ranks in the Escape Artist skill and a high Dexterity score.

You can't fight with both hands while you're grappled, but you can still attack with a light or one-handed weapon or take any other action that doesn't require two hands.

Helping an Ally Grapple

You can help an ally establish or maintain a grapple by taking actions that improve the result of her combat maneuver check. One of the easiest ways to accomplish this is by taking an aid another action (see page 135). You can also use spells or abilities that boost your ally's attack bonus, Strength, or size (such as *bull's strength* or *enlarge person*). Conversely, applying penalties to the opponent's Strength, Dexterity, AC, or size will lower its CMD, making the grapple easier for your ally.

You have more diverse options for helping an ally escape a grapple. Casting *freedom of movement* will end a grapple outright, and casting *grease* on your ally's clothing adds a +10 bonus on his attempts to escape. Dazing a grappler prevents her from attempting a grapple combat maneuver check, thereby ending the grapple on her turn, and stunning her causes her to drop anything she's holding (including your ally), ending the grapple instantly. You can also use some of the same techniques discussed above; adding bonuses to your ally's checks with the aid another action, bardic performances, or ability-boosting spells could give him the edge he needs to escape.

See page 567 of the *Core Rulebook* for more on the grappled condition.

WHEN TO ATTEMPT A COMBAT MANEUVER CHECK

You must succeed at a combat maneuver check to grapple a creature, but you have to succeed at that same check each round if you want to continue the grapple. Failing it means that your foe breaks free.

See page 199–201 of the *Core Rulebook* for more information on these combat maneuvers.

See page 175 of the *Core Rulebook* for the typical hardness and hit points of objects.

BULL RUSH

Moving your foes around the battlefield can give you an edge or help you get out of a difficult situation. The bull rush combat maneuver allows you to push a foe in a straight line. You can even use this maneuver to push your enemy off a cliff or into a pit of molten lava!

If you succeed at your combat maneuver check, your foe is moved 5 feet plus an additional 5 feet for every 5 by which the result of your combat maneuver check exceeds your foe's CMD. If you haven't taken your move action yet, you can even choose to move with your foe, maintaining the same relative position to it as you move.

When You're the Target: If you're the target of a bull rush, you don't have much choice except to go along for the ride. After it's done, you might want to move back into a more favorable position.

DISARM

Some enemies are just as skilled at using weapons as player characters, capable of dealing deadly wounds round after round. When you're facing such a foe, knocking the weapon from its hand can put a stop to the onslaught and put your opponent at a serious disadvantage.

If your combat maneuver check to disarm a foe is successful, it drops an item that it's carrying of your choice. If your combat maneuver check exceeds the foe's CMD by 10 or more, you can make it drop two items it's holding in its hands, but if you fail by 10 or more, you drop your own weapon. Since picking up a dropped weapon provokes attacks of opportunity from all nearby foes, use this tactic carefully.

When You're the Target: If you're forced to drop an item, whether or not it's a good idea to pick it up depends on the situation. If you're surrounded by foes, provoking attacks of opportunity from all of them might not be worth it. Consider drawing a new weapon or changing tactics.

OVERRUN

Sometimes you may need to move through a foe's space to help an ally or get close to an enemy spellcaster. If you aren't skilled at Acrobatics (which allows you to move through foes' spaces with a successful skill check), you can always try to overrun your enemy—this combat maneuver allows you to move past the creature and maybe even knock it down.

When you initiate an overrun combat maneuver, the foe can opt to let you pass without forcing you to attempt a combat maneuver check. If it doesn't and your check is successful, you push your way past your foe. If the result of your check exceeds your foe's CMD by 5 or more, you also knock it prone.

When You're the Target: When a foe tries to overrun you, it may be better to get out of its way than to risk being knocked prone. Of course, if it's trying to get past you to attack a vulnerable ally, you might want to stand your ground and force it to attempt the check.

SUNDER

When disarming a foe isn't thorough enough, you can try to destroy a weapon or item held by your enemy by making a sunder attempt. If successful, you deal damage to the item, which could destroy it. Sunder is riskier than disarm, though, because even if you succeed at the combat maneuver check, you could still fail to deal enough damage to destroy the item, leaving your foe with a functional weapon to use against you.

Any damage you deal to an object is reduced by an amount equal to its hardness, a rating that represents how tough that object is. A glass vial shatters easily (hardness 1), but a steel sword is much more difficult to break (hardness 10).

When You're the Target: Losing a weapon or other valuable item might put you at a serious disadvantage for the rest of the fight, but there are plenty of spells, such as *mending*, that can fix an item after the battle is over.

TRIP

Knocking down an enemy can give you a big advantage; it both reduces your foe's Armor Class and gives the foe a penalty on any attacks it tries to make. Furthermore, standing up provokes attacks of opportunity from everyone within reach, meaning that any nearby allies get a free swing when your opponent gets back up. If you fail your trip attempt by 10 or more, though, you'll be knocked prone.

Take stock of your target before deciding whether to trip it. Enemies that fly, have more than two legs, or slither along the ground are often significantly harder to trip, if not outright immune to this maneuver. You just can't trip a snake, so it would probably be best for you to pick another course of action.

When You're the Target: If you find yourself flat on your back, its best to try and find a way to get back up. Provoking an attack of opportunity is a small price to pay compared to the penalties for being prone: a –4 penalty to your Armor Class against melee attacks and a –4 penalty on any melee attacks you make.

OTHER COMBAT MANEUVERS

Later rulebooks introduce additional combat maneuvers you might hear mentioned at the table. More information on the maneuvers below can be found on pages 320–322 of the *Pathfinder RPG Advanced Player's Guide*.

Dirty Trick: With this maneuver, you can hinder foes by throwing sand in their eyes, pulling down their pants, hitting them in vulnerable spots, and so on. Although the distraction doesn't last long, it can make a huge difference at a critical moment.

Drag: The opposite of bull rush, the drag combat maneuver allows you to pull a creature in a straight line, moving it into a more advantageous position for you and your allies.

Reposition: While the bull rush and drag combat maneuvers both move a foe in a straight line, the reposition maneuver forces a creature to move to a different spot adjacent to you, setting it up for a flanking attack or moving it away from an ally who's in trouble.

Steal: While disarm lets you knock an item out of an enemy's hand, the steal combat maneuver lets you snatch a small item from a foe's body. Great for grabbing a brooch, a magical hat, or a holy symbol, this combat maneuver lets you take something valuable from a foe in the middle of a fight.

SPECIAL ATTACKS

There are a few other special attacks you might want to consider while embroiled in a battle. These are simpler to use than combat maneuvers, and in some cases are less risky.

Aid Another: As a standard action, you can take the aid another action (*Core Rulebook* 197) to give an ally a +2 bonus on his next attack roll or to his AC for 1 round. To do this, you make an attack roll against an AC of 10—if it's successful, your ally gains the +2 bonus. You can also use this action to grant an ally a +2 bonus on a skill check.

Charge: With a charge (*Core Rulebook* 198), you can move up to twice your speed and make a single melee attack at a +2 bonus. Charging is a reckless move, though, so you also take a –2 penalty to AC for 1 round after making a charge. Some weapons, such as lances, deal additional damage when used to make a charge attack.

Feint: As a standard action, you can attempt to trick a foe into lowering its defenses, rendering it flat-footed against the next melee attack you make against it. This ability is most useful for rogues and characters who can take advantage of enemies that are flat-footed. For more information on feinting, see page 201 of the *Core Rulebook*.

Mounted Combat: Fighting from horseback is difficult—to be adept at it, you need to invest in a few feats (such as Mounted Combat), plenty of ranks in the Ride skill, and a mount that is trained for battle—but being mounted lets you move around the battlefield much faster, and you receive a +1 bonus on attack rolls against foes who aren't riding a mount. For more information on mounted combat, see page 201 of the *Core Rulebook*).

See page 568 of the *Core Rulebook* for more information on the prone condition.

USING THE RIGHT MANEUVER

Which maneuver you should attempt depends on the foe you're facing. If it wields a weapon, disarm might be the right choice, but trip is better if it's attacking with its claws or teeth.

IMPROVISING

The rules in the *Core Rulebook* can't cover every situation that might occur during combat. Don't feel constrained by the options presented in that book or consider them an all-inclusive list of what your character can do. You might find yourself in a situation where you want to grab hold of a dragon as it soars off into the air. While the grapple rules might seem like a good fit here, they come with some hindrances that might not be appropriate to the situation. In such cases, work with your GM to figure out how best to represent the action. Remember that the GM is always the final arbiter in such situations.

BIG HITS AND BONUSES

Pathfinder's combat system has a lot of rules that describe how chance, characters' skills, combatants' conditions, and other battlefield factors affect combat. The rules you're likely to use most often are those describing bigger-than-usual hits, and how different bonuses and penalties affect your attack and damage rolls.

Critical Hits

Sometimes, a combination of chance and skill allows a character to get in a great hit that does more damage than usual. These **critical hits** (or **crits** for short) can do a lot more damage than a regular hit, but they require you to make an additional attack roll to "confirm" the critical hit. Below is a breakdown of how critical hits work.

> **1. Threatening**: When you make an attack roll, if the roll is a **natural 20** (meaning the die actually shows a 20), that attack is a **critical threat** and has a chance to do extra damage.

> **2. Confirming**: Roll the attack again at the same bonus—this is called the **confirmation roll**. If the confirmation roll would hit your opponent, then you have **confirmed the critical hit** and the attack is indeed a critical hit. If the confirmation roll would miss, then the attack is a normal hit instead of a critical hit. Rolling a natural 1 on the confirmation roll always fails to confirm the critical hit. Rolling a natural 20 on the confirmation roll always confirms the critical hit.

> **3. Damaging**: If you confirm the critical, you deal double damage. Treat this as if you had hit twice: roll your damage dice and add the damage modifiers, then do it again and add it all together. For example, if your longsword normally hits for 1d8+2 and you critically hit with the longsword, you deal 2d8+4 points of damage. Extra damage dice from a class ability or special effect (such as a rogue's sneak attack) are rolled only once, not twice. Some weapons grant a ×3 or even ×4 multiplier to critical hit damage.

> **Spells**: Any spell that requires an attack roll and deals damage (including ability damage and ability drain) has a chance to be a critical hit.

Bonuses, Penalties, and Stacking

Bonuses and penalties are everywhere in the Pathfinder RPG, affecting how likely you are to hit, the amount of damage you do, skill checks, and more. These bonuses and penalties come from a wide variety of sources, such as feats, spells, magic items, conditions, or even just the environments and situations you find yourself in. For the most part, bonuses and penalties are simple—just add or subtract them from the associated scores or rolls. There's one notable exception, however: stacking.

Stacking is the act of applying multiple bonuses to the same roll or attribute. Whether or not bonuses can stack depends on their **bonus type**—there are many different type of bonuses, such as luck bonuses, enhancement bonuses, armor bonuses, and more. (If a bonus doesn't say what type it is, it's considered an **untyped bonus**.) You don't need to know all the different bonus types, just how they interact. You can benefit from multiple bonuses of the same type as long as they're affecting different things (such as a +1 morale bonus on saves and a +2 morale bonus on attack rolls), or different bonus types affecting the same thing (such as a +2 armor bonus to AC and a +2 deflection bonus to AC). However, you can never benefit from multiple bonuses of the same type on the same thing. If you end up with two bonuses of the same type on the same thing, use only the higher bonus—so a +2 enhancement bonus to Strength and a +4 enhancement bonus to Strength only gets you +4, not +6.

In addition, bonuses from the same source never stack. If a spell is cast on you twice, you don't add its bonuses or penalties twice, even if they're untyped bonuses. This also applies to conditions, effects, and magic items.

Exceptions: Dodge, racial, and untyped bonuses always stack with themselves, and circumstance bonuses may as well, at the GM's discretion. Penalties stack with everything, but can never reduce an ability score below 1. The only way to go below 1 on an ability score is by taking ability damage or drain equal to or in excess of your ability score (including any bonuses). There are occasional exceptions to the "penalties stack with everything" rule, such as penalties from poisons (*Core Rulebook* 557), but these are relatively rare.

> **TIP** You should always keep a piece of scratch paper handy while playing so you can easily track the bonuses and penalties affecting your character. It's also a good way to note what spell effects are affecting you and how long they will last before coming to an end.

Some weapons threaten critical hits on a natural 19 as well as a natural 20, or even on a natural 18–20. See Table 6–4: Weapons on page 142 of the *Core Rulebook*.

Some weapons deal triple or even quadruple damage on a critical hit. The Critical column in Table 6–4: Weapons on page 142 of the *Core Rulebook* gives the critical multiplier for each weapon.

Spells, traps, and special abilities often cause a character to gain a condition, such as frightened or paralyzed. These conditions are detailed on page 565 of the *Core Rulebook*.

CRITICAL MISSES

As an optional rule, when a character rolls a natural 1 (often known as critical fumble), a character doesn't just miss, but also suffers some sort of damage or penalty at the GM's discretion. For instance, the GM might rule that you drop your weapon, hit an ally, or fall prone! If you enjoy such rules, consider using the *GameMastery Critical Hit Deck* and *Critical Fumble Deck*!

DEATH

The hazards of the adventuring life always take their toll sooner or later. As you take damage in combat, you gradually lose hit points. For the most part, this loss doesn't actually affect your character's functioning, but once you reach 0 hit points, things get dangerous in a hurry! Below is a summary of the rules for death and dying.

 If you're getting close to 0 hp, get out of melee! Healing a character in a threatened space is difficult.

How to Die

Character death can be stressful, but it can also be a fun and dramatic part of the game, adding tension and a sense of danger to combat. In order to keep the game properly heroic, Pathfinder has been designed so that characters rarely die instantly. Presented here in order are the various stages of the dying process—characters may pass through all of them or skip over early stages, depending on how much damage they've taken.

Disabled (Zero Hit Points): When you reach 0 hit points, you're hovering on the edge of unconsciousness—the slightest strain can tip you over into true danger. At this stage, you're **disabled**, which means you get only a single action each round, and they can't be strenuous (as determined by the GM). Move actions are always safe, but standard actions and any other actions the GM deems strenuous are too much for your injured body—you can take one, but if so, you take another point of damage, fall unconscious, and start dying (see below). Note that the act of healing yourself (such as via a spell or potion) does not cause you to fall unconscious and start dying, so long as its effects are immediate.

Dying (Negative Hit Points): In Pathfinder, if an amount of damage would take your hit points below 0, you continue to count down into negative numbers. (For example, if you have 10 hp and get hit for 15 points of damage, you're now at –5 hp.) When your current hit points are below 0, you're **dying**. You're unconscious, and continue to lose 1 hp each round until you either die or **stabilize** (meaning you stop actively losing hit points but remain unconscious). Stabilizing on your own requires a successful Constitution check as outlined on page 190 of the *Core Rulebook*, but any sort of healing, even for a single point of damage, automatically stabilizes you, as does someone else succeeding at a DC 15 Heal check made to stabilize you (a standard action).

Dead (Negative Constitution Score): If your hit points ever drop so far that their negative value is equal to or greater than your Constitution score (for example, –10 if your Constitution is 10), you die. This is exactly as bad as it sounds—unless the rest of your party brings powerful magic to bear (see below), your character is permanently out of the game (though this doesn't mean that you can't join in again with a new one). A few game effects bypass hit points and kill instantly, including ability damage that reduces Constitution to 0, magical death effects, and drowning.

Death Isn't Always the End!

In the Pathfinder RPG, even death can be overcome, but bringing a dead character back to life usually carries a heavy cost, and the deceased character can't do it on his or her own. The following spells can bring characters back from the dead.

Raise dead requires 5,000 gp just for the material component, and imposes you 2 negative levels (*Core Rulebook* 562) for being brought back from the dead.

Resurrection works in certain cases when *raise dead* doesn't, but it costs twice as much, and also gives you a negative level.

Reincarnate is cheaper, but may change your race.

Removing negative levels from death requires a *restoration* spell and a 1,000 gp material component per negative level. In addition, *restoration* can be used this way only once per week on a single character, so fully recovering from *raise dead* takes at least two weeks.

Before asking the other players in your group to raise your character, consider that character's place in the campaign's ongoing story. If the death was a fitting end or bringing the PC back is too expensive, starting a new character may be the best option. Coordinate with the GM about appropriate ways to introduce a new PC into the campaign—your new PC could be a friend of your deceased character, a replacement sent by a patron, a prisoner rescued in the next room of the dungeon, and so on.

Nonlethal Damage

Some special attacks do damage that can knock you out with no risk of death. Don't deduct this from your normal hit points, but rather keep track of this amount separately—if the amount of nonlethal damage you've taken ever equals your current remaining hit points, you're staggered (*Core Rulebook* 568), and if it exceeds them, you fall unconscious. See page 191 of the *Core Rulebook* for more information.

DOWN THE HATCH

Drinking a potion to heal yourself while at 0 hit points likely requires two actions and thus two rounds: one round to retrieve the potion from your bag (a move action), and one to drink it.

See pages 206–221 of the *Core Rulebook* for complete rules on spellcasting, including dispelling and counterspells.

SPELL DESCRIPTIONS

For information on how to read and understand a spell's description, see page 35.

SPELLCASTING

Many of the player characters, monsters, and NPCs in the Pathfinder Roleplaying Game have the ability to cast a wide array of spells. With such magic, characters can soar through the air like a bird, unleash scorching balls of flame, and eventually even alter reality with the power of a single wish. Regardless of what spell you're casting, each spell is cast in the same way using the following rules.

Types of Spellcasting

From the simplest cantrip to the mightiest of evocations, each spell follows the same basic principles. Every creature with the ability to cast spells has a list of spells that it can cast. In the case of player characters, this list typically takes one of two forms: a list of spells prepared that day (for clerics, druids, rangers, paladins, and wizards), or a list of spells known (for bards and sorcerers). Certain creatures have the innate ability to cast certain spells—these are known as spell-like abilities.

Prepared Spells: The list of spells a spellcaster has prepared represents all of the spells that character can cast that day. Each prepared spell can be cast only once and then is used up. If the character wants to cast a specific spell multiple times in one day, he must prepare multiple copies of that spell.

Spells Known: Some casters—called **spontaneous spellcasters**—learn their spells by heart, and don't need to prepare them daily. A spontaneous spellcaster can cast only spells from her list of spells known, but she can cast them in any combination, limited only by the spell level and total number of spells she can cast per day.

Spell-Like Abilities: Some creatures have a list of talents called spell-like abilities (*Core Rulebook* 221). These use mostly the same rules as spells do, and each one notes how many times per day it can be used.

Schools of Magic

Each spell belongs to a school of magic that helps define that spell's theme and overall purpose. In some cases, a spell's school also provides guidelines to help you adjudicate the spell's effects during a game. There are eight schools of magic in the Pathfinder Roleplaying Game.

Abjuration: Spells of this school protect their targets. They can create physical or magical barriers, negate magical abilities, or ward an area to harm intruders or raise the alarm.

Conjuration: Spells of the conjuration school can summon creatures from other planes of existence. They can also manifest energy to harm your foes.

Divination: By peering into the future or across vast distances, casters of divination spells can discover the world's forgotten secrets or communicate with beings in faraway lands.

Enchantment: These spells affect the minds of others, influencing their actions or even controlling them for a period of time. Enchantment spells can even turn a foe into short-term ally.

Evocation: Spells of this dangerous school manipulate magical energy to create a variety of explosive effects, dealing large amounts of damage to creatures in the affected area.

Illusion: Capable of deceiving all of the senses, illusion spells can hide your appearance, create fantastical mirages, and even make you invisible.

Necromancy: Manipulating the powers of life and death, spells of this school can create hideous undead creatures or snuff the life from those who stand in the way of their casters' intentions.

Transmutation: Spells of this school can change the properties of objects and creatures. They can grant great strength or even entirely alter someone's form, turning a scrawny villager into a powerful beast.

Subschools: Some spells also possess a subschool that helps to further define their roles within their respective schools of magic. In particular, spells that belong to the conjuration, illusion, and transmutation schools have subschool rules that come up more often. See pages 209–212 of the *Core Rulebook* for more information.

How To Cast a Spell

1. **Choose which spell you're going to cast.** You should have the *Core Rulebook* open to your spell's description, at least until you've cast the spell a few times and become familiar with it.
2. **Concentrate on the spell.** If something interrupts you while you're concentrating on casting a spell (such as an attack), you must attempt a concentration check. If you fail, you don't succeed at casting the spell, but the spell is used up as if you had cast it. To attempt a concentration check, use the following formula.

 Concentration check = d20 + your caster level + your casting ability score modifier + any other bonuses or penalties

The check's Difficulty Class can vary wildly depending on the source of the interruption. The most common is damage, in which case the DC is equal to 10 + the damage dealt + the level of the spell being cast. Some abilities and feats may give you bonuses on concentration checks. Although the character sheet doesn't have a specific box for your concentration bonus, some players write it down in the Skills section since it's used in a similar way.

3. **Cast the spell.** Most spells have components, which are requirements for casting that spell. You must be able to speak to cast a spell with verbal components—if you're under the effect of magical silence, for example, you can't cast such a spell. You must have at least one hand free to cast spells with somatic components. You must have the appropriate material components to cast spells, though you can safely assume you have all you need if you have a spell component pouch. To cast a spell has needs a focus component, you must have the item it calls for (or a holy symbol, in the case of a divine focus component).
4. **Spend the time to cast a spell.** A spell's description will tell you how long it takes to cast; some spells take only a standard action to cast, while others take 1 round or longer to complete.
5. **Determine the effects.** These may include the damage the spell deals, how many creatures it summons, the area affected by it, the Difficulty Class to resist it, and so on. Any saving throws granted by the spell are attempted at this point. Apply the spell's reduced effect (see below) to any targets whose saves are successful.

Caster Level

Most spells reference your caster level when determining their range and effect. This is generally the same as the number of levels you have in your spellcasting class—except for rangers and paladins, whose caster levels equal the number of levels they have in their respective classes - 3.

Spellcasting and Ability Scores

Each spellcasting class has a key ability score to which its spellcasting is tied. For example, wizards' spells are tied to Intelligence, but clerics' gain spells are tied to Wisdom. This key ability score (and its modifier) affects things like how many spells you can cast per day, whether or not you can cast a particular spell, and the Difficulty Class for saves made to resist the effects of your spells. Pay attention to which aspects of spellcasting depend on your ability score (such as spells per day) and which ones depend on your modifier (such as Difficulty Classes and concentration checks).

Saving Throws

Many spells grant a saving throw to reduce or entirely negate their effects on a creature. Each spell dictates which saving throw is used and what the effects are if the saving throw is successful.

- Spells that affect the body—causing disease, poisoning, or even death—usually call for Fortitude saving throws, which represent the creature's ability to resist such influences.
- Spells that conjure flame, unleash lightning, or otherwise create blasts of energy usually call for Reflex saving throws to avoid some of the damage. A successful save usually results in the damage being reduced by half, as the creature shields itself from harm or dives out of the way.
- Finally, spells that befuddle the mind or snare the senses are resisted using Will saving throws. A successful saving throw usually negates the effect entirely as the target's mind resists the influence.

   Attempting a Saving Throw: To attempt a saving throw, roll a d20 and add the appropriate save bonus plus any other applicable modifiers. If the result is equal to or greater than the spell's Difficulty Class, then you succeed, which generally reduces or negates the effects of the spell. See page 121 for more on saving throws.

 Saving throw = d20 + base save bonus + ability modifier + class ability bonus + racial trait modifiers + any other bonuses or penalties

For a complete list of Difficulty Classes for concentration checks, see the table on page 207 of the *Core Rulebook*.

CASTING ON THE DEFENSIVE

Generally speaking, casting a spell provokes attacks of opportunity from all enemies within reach. If they hit you as a result of this attack of opportunity, you might fail to cast the spell. You can avoid this risk by casting the spell defensively. To do this, you must attempt a concentration check with a DC equal to 15 + twice the spell's level. If you succeed, you cast the spell without provoking an attack of opportunity. If you fail, the spell is lost, but you still don't provoke an attack of opportunity from your enemies. See page 207 of the *Core Rulebook* for more information.

HIGHER ATTACK BONUS

One of the best ways of dealing with foes who have a high AC is to ensure that you have the highest attack bonus you possibly can. At higher levels, this often involves magic weapons and spells, but even low-level characters can give themselves a boost by purchasing a masterwork weapon and investing in the Weapon Focus feat. Not only will a high attack bonus serve you well against a foe with a high AC, it will allow you to use feats like Power Attack to deal more damage to a foe with a lower AC by taking a penalty to hit.

CASTER COMBAT

Spellcasters often have a hard time hitting with their weapons since they mostly rely on magic. If you're playing one of these classes and need to hit with an attack roll, look at the spell *true strike*. It gives you a +20 bonus to hit!

TACTICAL CONSIDERATIONS

When you're in the midst of battle, how you react to surprises can spell the difference between victory and defeat. No one book can detail the myriad tactical situations a PC might face during an adventuring career, but here are a few of the challenges you might encounter and methods for overcoming them.

Foes You Can't Hit

An opponent's high Armor Class may make her hard to hit. Which approach you should take to dealing with that depends on the source of the enemy's superior AC and the options you have available. Below are some common weaknesses that often accompany different types of high AC, as well as tactics for exploiting them.

Fighting Foes with High AC

ADVANTAGE	WEAKNESS	TACTICS
High armor or shield bonuses, natural armor	Low touch AC	• Use touch and ranged touch spells. • Alchemical items such as acid flasks and alchemist's fire use touch attacks, and tanglefoot bags entangle foes and lower their Dexterity to help later attacks succeed (*Core Rulebook* 160).
High Dexterity or dodge bonuses	Low AC when flat-footed (or against any attack that denies a foe its Dexterity bonus)	• Attack while invisible or otherwise unseen. • Blind of stun an opponent to negate its Dexterity bonus to AC (*Core Rulebook* 565, 568) • **Feinting** negates a foe's Dexterity bonus for a single attack (*Core Rulebook* 201).
Spells or potions that boost AC (e.g., *mage*	Dispelling magic or spell duration	*Dispel magic* can remove a single spell, and *greater dispel magic* can handle more than one.

Additional Tactics

CIRCUMSTANCE	TACTICS
You're fighting with an ally who does significantly more damage than you can.	• Use the **aid another** action to give your ally a +2 bonus to their next attack roll (*Core Rulebook* 197). • **Flank** your opponent with your ally (stand directly opposite your ally on the other side of your foe) to give both of you a +2 bonus to hit (*Core Rulebook* 197).
You are or are allied with a spellcaster who can cast spells to boost allies' attack rolls or lower an opponent's AC.	• *Haste* gives allies an extra attack (when making a full attack) as well as a +1 bonus to hit and to AC. • Even low-level clerics can cast *guidance,* which gives allies a +1 bonus on attack rolls.

Foes You Can't Hurt

Some opponents resist being damaged. Typically, this takes the form of damage reduction, an incorporeal or otherwise insubstantial form, or the swarm subtype. Regeneration (*Pathfinder RPG Bestiary* 303) and fast healing (*Pathfinder RPG Bestiary* 300) can fall into this category too.

Fighting Foes That Are Difficult to Damage

ADVANTAGE	WEAKNESS	TACTICS
Foe has **damage reduction (DR)**. DR reduces damage taken unless the attacker has the right kind of weapon. A creature with DR 5/bludgeoning subtracts 5 points of damage from each attack unless the attacker is using a bludgeoning weapon.	Weapons that overcome DR.	• Use the right weapons, if you can—front-line combatants should gear up with bludgeoning, piercing, and magic weapons to overcome different types of damage reduction. • Use aid another (*Core Rulebook* 197) to bolster an ally who hits harder or has the right weapon. • Drop your shield, if you have one, and wield your weapon two-handed for a damage boost. If you wield a one-handed weapon with two hands, you add 1-1/2 × your Strength bonus to your damage roll (instead of the normal 1 × your Strength bonus). • Use Power Attack, if you have it (*Core Rulebook* 131). • Switch to energy damage like alchemical weapons or spells.
Foe is **incorporeal**. Incorporeal creatures are bodiless monsters such as ghosts and animated shadows. These creatures take reduced damage from most magical attacks and ignore non-magical attacks entirely.	Magic and magical weapons.	• Use a magical weapon. • Use aid another (*Core Rulebook* 197) to help an ally hit. • Provide flanking for an ally (though it may expose you to incorporeal touch attacks). • If your foe is undead, remember **positive energy**—the magic that powers good-aligned divine casters and items like *wands of cure light wounds*—harms them. • While alchemical items can't harm incorporeal creatures, holy water can if it's splashed on them (*Core Rulebook* 160). • Force effects like *magic missile* can damage incorporeal foes.
Foe is a **swarm**. A swarm is a group of small creatures that become dangerous when gathered together. The rules treat them as one creature that damages anyone in its space, and can potentially ignore weapon damage.	Spells and other effects that damage an entire area.	• Use area-affecting attacks. Swarms take extra damage from area effects (*Core Rulebook* 214). • Swarms of Fine or Diminutive creatures ignore weapon damage, making splash damage like acid and alchemist's fire more effective than wood and steel (*Core Rulebook* 160). • If the swarm is made up of Tiny creatures, it still takes weapon damage. • Without splash or area damage, fleeing may in fact be the only option!

PREPARATION

As you grow in power and ability, so will the foes you face. Some of these abilities will make it very difficult for you to hurt your foe unless you come prepared. As you gain levels you should always be on the lookout for options that allow you to counter the special abilities and defenses of your enemies. Carrying a silver dagger, for example, can really come in handy when you're facing off against a werewolf. It might not do as much damage as your longsword, but its ability to penetrate the lycanthrope's DR will more than make up for its smaller damage die.

Need to buy alchemist's fire or holy water? You can find the prices and descriptions on pages 158 and 160 of the *Core Rulebook*.

For information on how splash weapons like acid and alchemist's fire work in the game, see page 202 of the *Core Rulebook*.

COMBAT TRICKS

Think creatively in battle. While rushing over to the nearest enemy and hacking at it can win the day, it's not the only way to fight, and other strategies may be even more effective. Besides potentially catching an opponent off-guard, you'll have more fun in combat if you try some of the tricks below.

BE THEATRICAL

If you think something might give you a bonus, ask your GM. Climb onto a boulder, topple objects on your opponents, and try other tactics to keep the battle engaging.

CENTER AREAS FOR BEST EFFECT

Positioning an area of effect spell carefully will let you leave allies or opponents (as preferred) out of the effect. Cone areas come in two varieties (*Core Rulebook* 215); one may do a better job for a particular situation, so consider both choices.

FEEDING THE FIRE

If a foe's already on fire, there's no need to waste alchemist's fire if you have oil at hand. Any flask of oil thrown at a burning foe ignites automatically without the need for a fuse.

HEIGHT ADVANTAGE

Attacking from higher ground gives you a +1 bonus on attack rolls. Being mounted gives you a height advantage against an unmounted foe of your size, as does flying above your opponent or fighting opponents who are lower on a slope or staircase.

Barbarian

Rage early and often, but once the fight is a foregone conclusion, stop raging to save some of your fury for the next fight.

Berserker: Meet your opponents head-on, and overwhelm them with raw ferocity and frequent use of Power Attack. Use Intimidate to scare your foes, making them take penalties on many types of rolls.

Smasher: Sundering works best against opponents like clerics and rogues who rely on weapons but lack your prowess with them. Shields make great targets, but break them early in the fight or not at all. An adamantine weapon is an excellent investment.

Bard

Open fights by inspiring courage; at higher levels, add a spell like *good hope* or *haste*.

Trickster: Lurk around the edges of battle, striking where it will do the most good. Use your spells to confound foes who notice you and to keep your allies in the fight.

Troubadour: Fight shoulder-to-shoulder with your friends in melee, relying on your performances and spells to keep you whole.

Cleric

Your spell selection shapes your role in battle: combat caster, front-line combatant, or support and healing.

Battle Priest: Use a buckler, light shield, or two-handed weapon to be able to cast without stowing your weapon. In rocky areas, watch for opportunities to surprise enemies with a sudden *stone shape*.

Healer: Position yourself carefully and use Selective Channeling to heal only your allies. Against undead opponents, your healing magic becomes a potent weapon.

Stargazer: Information gathered with divination can shape your tactics before the battle even begins. Cast area enhancement spells early in the fight, while your allies are close together.

Druid

Consider casting long-duration enhancement and protective spells, including those which buff up your animal companion, before combat breaks out.

Animal Friend: Focus your in-combat casting on enhancing and healing your companion. Remember that you can target your animal companion with personal spells (spells that have "you" in the Target section of the spell description).

Fury: Prepare spells with a range of energy types, so you can tune your damage to your foes' weaknesses. *Produce flame* hits more easily and does better damage than most ranged weapons. Use Natural Spell and mobile forms of wild shape (like birds) to stay out of melee range while casting.

Nature Warrior: Save on weapon costs with spells like *magic stone* and *shillelagh*, or let summoned creatures do your fighting for you. Use wild shape for tough fights, and keep a careful eye out for animal forms that have abilities you can duplicate.

Fighter

High hit points, high AC, and great combat capability make front-line melee a natural fit for the fighter.

Brute: Cleave gives you the option to move to a pair of enemies and still get two attacks per round. Use Power Attack often to finish your foes faster.

Shield Fighter: Use your high AC to maneuver safely between foes into flanking positions with your allies. Against poorly armored enemies, use your shield bash (*Core Rulebook* 152) to get an extra swing in.

Monk

Flurry whenever you can; not only do you get extra attacks, but they're at a better attack bonus than your normal attacks.

Martial Warrior: Carry a variety of weapons made of many materials to help overcome damage reduction. It's good to remember that shuriken can be used with your flurry of blows ability if your enemies step out of range.

Maneuver Specialist: Grapple negates most spellcasting and neutralizes mobile foes. Trip puts melee combatants at a crippling disadvantage. Disarm is also great, but works poorly against weapons held in two hands.

Paladin

Though you're less adept with weapons than a fighter, your high saves and healing ability give you better staying power.

Crusader: Save your smites for the most fearsome opponents. Lead from the front and protect those less able in battle. Heal your allies as well as yourself; you can use lay on hands to heal yourself as a swift action and still make an attack on your turn.

Knight: On open ground, use Ride-By Attack, setting yourself up for your next charge with your remaining movement. In tighter conditions, bring your mount's attacks to bear along with your own. Consider magic items or scrolls as a source for an emergency mount if yours is unavailable.

Ranger

When fighting a favored enemy, your damage output is truly devastating. Against other foes, though, you're not quite as impressive. Pick your targets with that in mind.

Archer: Rapid Shot nearly always works better than taking single shots. Try to keep melee-capable allies between you and your foes. Focus your arrows on wounded targets for quick takedowns.

Dual-Weapon Warrior: Fighting a favored enemy offsets your two-weapon fighting attack penalties. Your lack of heavy armor makes staying in the thick of battle risky, so stay on the edges of the fight. Plan your attacks so you can 5-foot step to the next foe if the current one drops.

Rogue

You deal dramatically more damage when sneak attacking. Take advantage of flat-footed foes, flanking, invisibility, and Stealth checks to roll your extra damage dice as often as possible.

Shadow: Roll in and out of combat with Acrobatics checks, Mobility, or Spring Attack, always looking for an opportunity to flank. Fight defensively or with Combat Expertise when pinned down. If you have warning before battle, consider taking a concealed position for sniping.

Thief: Make sure your blows count. It's often better to use a round to get into position for a sneak attack than to take an attack without your extra dice. Keep a thrown weapon in hand, so you can get a quick sneak attack against flat-footed opponents.

Sorcerer

Cast freely in battle; you have enough spell slots that you won't run low often, and you can use your bloodline powers if you do run out of spells.

Angel-Born: Superior damage reduction makes your summoned creatures potent against evil foes. Once you gain wings, flying up out of reach protects you from melee opponents, but makes you an obvious target for ranged attacks.

Dragon-Child: Keep your defenses up outside of combat with enhancement spells from potions, scrolls, or wands. Your claws deal as much damage as most manufactured weapons, and you don't have to deal with two-weapon fighting penalties. Your breath weapon ignores spell resistance.

Fire-Blooded: Look for clusters of opponents for *burning hands* and other area of effect spells. If creatures fail their saves against your elemental blast, immediately follow up with another fire effect to exploit their temporary vulnerability.

Wizard

Leave melee combat to those suited for it. Keep an eye on your spell slots—you don't need to cast a spell every round to be effective.

Conjurer: Summon monsters into flanking positions for an attack boost, especially if there's a rogue in your party. Don't always pick the same creatures; tune your summons to the enemies' weaknesses.

Illusionist: Coach your party members on your favored illusions, so they can help sell your deception. Save enchantments for brutish or dim-witted foes. Spellcasters usually have high Will saves, so they'll be harder to fool or control with your magic.

Traditional Mage: Area of effect spells work best against weaker foes in a cluster. If targeting a single foe, cast damaging spells if the target is already wounded, and use incapacitating magic against a fresh opponent. Warn your allies if you plan to drop an area-affecting spell, so they can stay out of that area on their turns.

PREEMPTIVE PROVOKING

If you trick an enemy into using its attack of opportunity early in your turn, it probably won't be able to take another attack of opportunity during that round. For example, you could move to provoke an attack of opportunity, then cast a spell without worrying about losing the spell when the opponent makes an attack of opportunity. If you have a summoned creature, you could have it provoke the opponent instead!

READYING FOR FLANKING

If you have an ability that hinges on flanking (such as sneak attack), move and ready an attack for when an ally flanks your opponent. Be sure to let your party members know that you want them to get into position. This method risks losing your attack entirely (if no ally can reach that flanking spot), but the extra damage and bonus to hit make it a strong strategy.

SLIPPING INSIDE REACH

Instead of moving up to a foe with increased reach and only getting to attack once, let the opponent move to you. Then, on your turn, you can take a safe 5-foot step adjacent to it and still take your full attack.

TAKING TURNS

Although narrative play doesn't use initiative, that doesn't mean you shouldn't take turns. Give every player at the table a chance to contribute to an encounter. If one character's Diplomacy attempts aren't working, another character might succeed at Intimidation. Even if they don't have much to add, it still gives them a chance to engage in the story and make their character a part of the scene.

NARRATIVE PLAY

Playing Pathfinder is all about interactive storytelling—that is, narrative. Thus, some of the most memorable moments when you're playing the game aren't battles, but rather narrative interactions: unexpected, funny, or even moving moments between characters. Narrative in the game is more free-form than combat, but it still has rules and can be just as important as your character's statistics. When done right, narrative play is full of suspense, danger, emotion, and humor, both advancing and enriching the ongoing storyline of your campaign.

Give Your Character a Personality

Characters with distinct personalities make game sessions lively and entertaining. When a dryad charms a normally stoic barbarian into performing silly tricks or a lighthearted and frivolous rogue goes deadly cold upon seeing a child threatened—that's when a character truly comes alive. Establishing a framework for your character's attitude, as well as typical reactions to common situations, can help provide inspiration for roleplaying. Below are some tips for coming up with a personality for your character.

- *Flesh out your character with real-world archetypes.* The world is full of archetypes and stereotypes—the absentminded scientist, the hard-nosed cop, the grizzled sea captain, the vivacious starlet, and so on. Consider how you can adopt—or subvert—one of these concepts, or combine several.
- *Pay homage to your favorite TV, film, or literary characters.* Put your own spin on one of your favorite childhood heroes by basing elements of your character on him or her.
- *Reimagine modern roles in a fantasy setting.* What if a high-powered CEO found himself dependent on a mysterious mercenary to help him find his missing brother? What if a jittery, agoraphobic hacker was forced to go on a dangerous adventure in the hostile wilderness? Change "CEO" to "noble" and "hacker" to "alchemist," and you've got characters who are believable in the setting, but still fish out of water.

Relationships with Other Party Members.

Party members need to work together if they're going to get anywhere in the game. But why are they working together? What do they think of each other? Your character might view the naive young sorcerer as a younger brother of sorts, have a friendly rivalry with the grizzled fighter, admire the remote and silent druid from afar, and openly distrust the sly ranger. Before the campaign starts, talk with your group to determine whether any characters already know each other, and what their relationships are like. As you come to understand the personalities of the other characters in your party, ask yourself how spending every day with them and risking life and limb together might change the ways they view and interact with one another.

Catch Phrases and Habits

Battle cries and oaths help make combat colorful and entertaining. Your character's habit of always getting an ally's name wrong can provide comic relief for the other party members, and be surprisingly touching when, in an important moment, she finally gets it right.

Character Backgrounds

Making an NPC someone from a PC's past generates drama and raises the stakes. Ask your GM if you can give her a short write-up of your character's history, and call out a few important people and secrets from his past that the GM can bring introduce at her discretion to add interesting wrinkles to the plot.

Roleplaying Is a Team Effort

There's a rule in improvisational theater that when a performer says something, the other performer should reply, "Yes, and..." That is, the second person should add something new to the scene the first performer is creating, rather than shutting it down. That approach is great for roleplaying as well. Support what other players do with their characters' personalities by having your character react to the others' quirks, and build those reactions into a dynamic relationship with the other characters.

EXPLORATION AND DUNGEON DELVING

One of the best parts of any roleplaying game is exploring weird and wonderful places—deep crystalline caves, trap-filled dungeons, untamed elven forests, and abandoned monuments of lost civilizations. Different characters rely on different abilities depending on their strengths and character options. A ranger might use Knowledge (dungeoneering), a rogue might use trapfinding, a bard might use his special bardic lore, and a cleric or wizard might use Knowledge (history). Below are some notes to keep in mind while exploring.

Strange-Looking Creatures Aren't Always Foes

Before you attack a bizarre creature, consider bribing it, intimidating it, or sweet-talking it into telling you where the important elements of a dungeon level are. Questioning intelligent monsters or prisoners can save you a lot of time, and gives your GM a chance to enrich the scene with fun and interesting new characters.

Sneak and Scout

Use characters good at traveling unseen, such as rangers and rogues, to learn what dangers lurk around the bend, and what your party might want to do to prepare for them—or avoid them entirely.

Don't Just Fight—Investigate!

Leave one monster alive to tell you where the chieftain keeps the loot. Use a *comprehend languages* spell or the Linguistics skill to read the ancient books of lore in the library. A lot of dungeon exploration goes more smoothly if you actively seek out information rather than charging straight ahead, and even an unsophisticated fighter can still taunt, mock, and bluff a foe in combat to provoke it into revealing important clues! (Remember, speaking is a free action, and taunting a monster usually gets a reaction from the GM.)

Use Your Background

Just as you know things your character doesn't, your character knows things you don't. Don't be afraid to ask the GM for extra lore based on who your character is in addition to what skills your character has, as long as it's a logical extension of your character's backstory. After all, a dwarf probably knows a thing or two about dwarven strongholds even without studying them!

 TIP **Don't Be Afraid to Ask**: It's okay to ask out-of-character questions like, "Does this seem familiar to my character?" The GM may give you extra information relevant to your race, class, and history.

GET A CLUE

While exploring the world, your character will pick up a lot of information. While much of this is just flavor to give you a sense of immersion, many GMs include subtle clues about the quest you're currently undertaking, sometimes hidden in plain sight. For example, if the GM mentions that your city seems to be unusually flush with foreign visitors, it might not seem important at first. But if you later discover that there's a spy in the queen's court, knowledge of the recent influx of travelers may guide your subsequent investigation, perhaps leading you to uncover an assassination attempt or planned invasion.

Knowledge skills are always useful when exploring a city or dungeon. See page 99 of the *Core Rulebook* for more information.

FOREIGN TONGUES

Knowing an additional language or two can help you understand your foes—sometimes without them realizing it—and speaking to your allies in a language that your foes don't know might prevent enemies from listening in on your secret plans.

DIPLOMACY AND GATHERING INFORMATION

Engaging in diplomacy and information-gathering can help your group figure out its next steps, gain allies, prepare for challenges, and learn more about the surroundings, often by listening to NPCs roleplayed by the GM and chiming in at the right moment. The primary goal of an information-gathering encounter is—obviously—getting the right information, and the best way to do that is for everyone to have fun and be creative with the questions and answers.

Social Skills

Sometimes called a **face**, a **social character** is a PC with a high Charisma score, and often one who has put ranks into social skills like Diplomacy, Bluff, Intimidate, and Sense Motive. Most often, social characters are bards or rogues, since these classes get a lot of skill points and can afford to spend them on social skills. Charisma-based spellcasters like paladins and sorcerers also make good faces, since most social skills are Charisma-based. When your partying to make a deal with mistrustful NPCs or having a high-stakes audience with powerful rulers, it makes sense to let the character most likely to score high on social skill checks take the lead, though all party members can contribute.

 Silver or Sharp-Edged Tongues: The key skills for convincing NPCs to do things your way are Diplomacy, Intimidate and Bluff. Persuasion can take many forms, including clever negotiation, scare tactics, or even lying.

Knowledge Is Power

You can be the most charming person in the world, but if you don't know the customs of the place you're in, or don't know what information you're trying to get, you're going to get tripped up eventually. It never hurts for your character to know a little something about where she's going.

Social skills like Diplomacy are far more effective when paired with Knowledge skills like Knowledge (local), which gives you information about local practices and culture, or Knowledge (history), which can guide you to the right questions to get key—and even life-saving—information about the ruined temple or foul dungeon you're about to explore.

Sometimes a single character has the right combination of skills to obtain the information your party seeks. Often, however, two or more PCs must work together to gather information. For instance, your party's charming face might flatter the lady of the land and steer the conversation toward the answers the party needs while a knowledgeable character quietly feeds the face the right questions to ask.

Combat might be grim and serious when the stakes are high, but there's certainly no requirement for diplomacy, gossip, and bluffing to be dark, formal, or moody. Jokes, wit, and silly comments are all welcome.

How to Help

Even if you're playing a fighter or a ranger with limited charm, you can always contribute to roleplaying scenes that involve gathering information, regardless of whether you're the one doing the talking. Keep the following points in mind.

- Pay attention.
- Remember what the GM says.
- Put the pieces together yourself and share discoveries with the group.
- Remind the character leading the interaction about forgotten clues ("Hey, didn't the GM tell us...?" or "Seoni, what about the goblins who burned down that house?").
- Take notes on names and events.

 What do they really want? A high Sense Motive score can allow your character determine the best approach for dealing with an NPC, even if someone else does the talking.

MEETING IMPORTANT PEOPLE

A lot of adventures begin in a meeting with a ruler, the head of a guild or faction, or some other local leader. A GM may set the stage with the leader asking the adventurers for help, and the more experienced your adventuring group is, the greater the status and wealth of the authority asking for help tend to be. An adventure's opening roleplaying encounter is often a big opportunity for your character, and you might gain great rewards, learn important information, and have a lot of fun if you really go for it. Below are some thoughts on how to handle these kinds of encounters.

Run With It

You may be tempted to skip the talking and go straight to the sword-swinging, but "Sure, whatever, we'll slay the dragon" isn't a strong negotiating position. Keep the following in mind before you rush out the door.

- The NPC calling you in to present the adventure hook often needs your character to take care of a problem. This puts you in a good position to ask for extra equipment, servants, and pack animals, and maybe even a title—whatever might reasonably help the odds of the expedition succeeding or suitably reward you for the risks you're taking.
- A character who's commissioning your party to perform some task or mission might have a lot of information that's not presented in the initial job offer, so ask questions. Ask for a map to the location, and whether there are any witnesses, or experts on dragonslaying, or local bards who know a little about the creature in question.

Bragging and Negotiating

If your patrons want the best, then they should pay for the best. Try playing up your accomplishments in order to drive up the offered reward. This might be more natural for some character types (such as rogues and fighters) than others (particularly paladins), so feel free to let those characters take the lead, but it's worth making a point of how important your character is to the kingdom. (Plus, in-character bragging can be fun!)

Disruption and Dismay

Sometimes, encounters with important NPCs can end up feeling boring or formulaic. On such occasions, the urge to spice things up by picking the minister's pockets or enchanting the court wizard might be hard to resist. This is often a bad idea, however, and can potentially derail the entire campaign (much to the GM's annoyance). Be cautious when considering such actions, even if they seem appropriate for your character—if you get caught, you might find yourself with a prison-break or escape-the-execution scenario to work through.

HIGHER POWERS

No matter how formidable your character is, there are always going to be those in higher positions of power or authority. Even if you could swat the king like a fly, it's probably not worth having his entire kingdom come looking for you—especially as there may be high-level assassins his heirs could hire to punish you. Remember, nobles don't know anything about your statistics—all they know is that they're of a higher social station and command respect. Showing them that respect will go a long way toward helping you achieve your goals. This doesn't mean you should give in to every request, of course. When a noble is asking you for a favor, make sure she understands that you expect to be repaid in kind.

MORE THAN GOLD

One of the advantages of dealing with nobles and other leaders is that they can offer you rewards above and beyond simple gold. A lord may grant you a keep and title. An archmage could be convinced to cast powerful spells over your hideout, giving you valuable defenses. No matter the form that they take, these rewards add to your prestige, and possibly even to your legend.

STEALTH AND SCOUTING

Most adventuring groups are big on busting down doors and smashing up the monsters in as loud and aggressive a way as possible, but some situations call for a subtler approach.

Options for All Classes

Sometimes an adventure is all about being sneaky, such as when you're attempting a jewel heist or trying to rescue a prisoner without waking up an orc army. The following tactics can help members of your party scout effectively.

- Rogues and rangers have class abilities that help them sneak effectively, and should put ranks into Stealth if your party needs a scout.
- Sorcerers and wizards with *invisibility* and *fly* spells can get eagle's-eye views of the terrain ahead, or vanish from sight to get a closer look with a low risk of discovery.
- Consider buying some potions and scrolls that can make it easier to retreat, disappear, or walk by dangerous encounters unnoticed.

How to Use Stealth

How do you sneak past a foe? It boils down to the following:

 d20 + your Stealth bonus + any additional modifiers (from *invisibility*, *silence*, etc.) versus your opponent's d20 roll + your opponent's Perception bonus + any additional modifiers

If your opponent's result is equal to or higher than yours, he notices you. Certain elements can give you character advantages or disadvantages when sneaking, as listed below.

- **Moving**: Moving makes you easier to hear. You can move up to half your normal speed while using Stealth and not take a penalty. Moving at full speed gives you a −5 penalty. You can't use Stealth while running, attacking, or charging.
- **Invisibility**: When you're invisible, you gain a +20 bonus on Stealth checks if you're moving, and a +40 bonus if you're immobile.
- **Size**: Smaller creatures gain bonuses on Stealth checks, and larger creatures take penalties. The ones you're most likely to use are +4 for Small creatures, +0 for Medium creatures, and −4 for Large creatures.

Scouting Styles

Different styles of scouting make more sense in different situations.

Lone Scout: Some situations simply require one party member to sneak ahead and reconnoiter while the others hang back.

Advantages: If your party employs the lone scout style, you'll need only one character who is effective at Stealth. Further, this scouting style requires fewer uses of spells such as *invisibility*. While the lone scout is sneaking about, the other members of your party will have time to prepare for whatever challenge or danger awaits.

Disadvantages: If the lone scout is found, she's on her own. There's little more disconcerting than stumbling across a terrifying foe when you're totally alone and no one has your back.

Strategies: If you think you're going to be your party's lone scout, consider taking ranks in Use Magic Device (assuming it's an option for you) and equipping yourself with a scroll of *expeditious retreat* or *levitate* so you can escape sticky situations. Also, if you're scouting ahead on your own, always plan an escape route. In such situations, a fast mount can save your skin.

Party Scouting: While party scouting isn't effective in every situation, sometimes it's better for everyone in your adventuring party to stick together while you're sneaking about.

Advantages: If one of you gets caught, the entire party is there to fight.

Disadvantages: All party members need to succeed at being stealthy if you're scouting together, and you'll need a lot of resources to make that possible.

Strategies: If your adventuring party is scouting together, consider using spells like *silence* to neutralize noisy armor and sounds caused by clumsiness. Further, it's often advantageous to have one member of your party who has ranks in Diplomacy or Bluff distract guards while the others in the party sneak by.

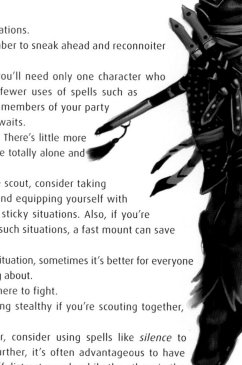

MYSTERIES

Mysteries are a fairly common element of the Pathfinder RPG, even if they aren't always simple murder mysteries or whodunit sorts of tales. Often, to progress the story, your group needs to find answers: What's killing the town's livestock? Who unleashed the plague of zombies? Why are the saint's bones missing? Even if they're not the highlight of the adventure, some mystery elements or hidden secrets are included in many fantasy campaigns that make the whole story come alive.

The Game's Afoot

So how do you go about investigating? The GM, of course, knows all the answers, and you'll need to come up with creative ways to pry the crucial nuggets of information free from the NPCs roleplayed by the GM. This could involve gauging the way that the GM portrays certain characters: Are they trustworthy? Are they holding back? It could also involve using critical spells like *speak with animals*, *speak with dead*, or *commune* to uncover information you can't get otherwise. Of course, it might simply be a matter of seeking out characters who have information you need.

Two Keys to Solving Mysteries

Once you have a general strategy, use these tips to see the search through.

Persistence: The more persistent you are, the better your odds of success.

- Talk to every NPC who seems knowledgeable.
- Visit every location that seems relevant.
- Be willing to spend days of in-game time on tasks like research or waiting to follow a suspect if necessary.

Keep Good Notes: Decide who'll keep records in your group, and ask her to write down things you notice.

- Remember that clues may appear on the first session of an adventure but not pay off until the tenth.
- Pay attention to clues, puzzles, names, and dates—anything that seems out of the ordinary or relevant.

Don't Be Afraid to Ask

If your group is really stuck and the mystery has gone from a fun diversion to an annoying mess, you can always prompt the GM to provide a hint, a helpful NPC, or a reminder of some item of gossip that gets the party back on the right track. Some GMs may be reluctant to make it too easy, but if you have been paying attention, have gone through the available options, and don't see any path forward, ask for a hint.

TIP If you're stymied and the GM won't give you a hint, move on to some other portion of the adventure. It's possible the mystery isn't meant to be solved yet.

PUZZLES

Sometimes you'll come across an actual puzzle that needs to be solved. These are usually accompanied by handouts, and they require you, the player, to figure out how to solve them. Of course, you might feel that the character you created has a better chance at solving the puzzle than you do, in which case it isn't out of the question to ask the GM for a relevant skill check to give your character a clue if you're feeling stuck. Make sure you've recorded everything you know about the puzzle if you run into a dead end. You may find you overlooked some vital clue that will help solve the puzzle.

THE TROUBLE WITH DEDUCTION

In a world of magic, it can be very difficult to deduce the cause of any given mystery. If an elf is found dead in his locked room at the inn, you might suspect the innkeeper who has a spare key or the shifty rogue downstairs, but the killer could be almost anyone. A wizard could have used *teleport* to gain access to the room. A druid might have cast *wood shape* to get through one of the walls. Even the town drunk could have used a *potion of gaseous form* to enter undetected. Since magic might be involved, you must consider the impossible.

MONOLOGUES AND FLASHBACKS

Some live-action roleplaying games and free-form games use a technique that lets other players get inside a character's head: at a certain moment in the game, you can declare that your character has a monologue for the group, or your GM might ask you act out an incident from your character's past in the form of a flashback. The monologue or flashback might be about your character's family, her youth, a horrible memory, or a moment of closure or vengeance—anything you like. Once you've given the speech or acted out the flashback, play resumes as normal. Getting some time in the spotlight can be a nice change of pace from discussing tactics, clues, and loot.

GIVE THE GM A HEADS-UP

While springing your cool lines, taunts, and battle cries on the GM can be a lot of fun, sometimes you may want to let her know ahead of time that your character has it in for some of the monsters in the upcoming game session. If you and the GM compare notes, it's possible she'll share a line that she intends for the villain to speak so you'll be able to respond to it in character.

OTHER NARRATIVE ELEMENTS

There's no limit to the different techniques you can use to play your character and add to the story. Here are a few other ideas for using your character to make your game sessions colorful and fun.

Taunts and Challenges

In movies, the hero often has a good one-liner as he's battling the villain. Sometimes he roars a challenge, and other times he taunts his foe to get it to make mistakes. It's possible to come up with a good exclamation on the spur of the moment, but a bit of preparation can make your quips even better.

Before combat—it could be any fight, but the big finales are ideal—think about one or two things your character might say.
When the other players aren't around, practice your exclamation out loud to see how it sounds.
You can modify battle cries from history if you like. "For England and St. George!" is pretty easy to rework to suit a paladin, but there are lots of other historical options, such as this dramatic Viking battle cry: "An axe-age, a sword-age, shields shall be cloven; a wind-age, a wolf-age, ere the world sinks in ruin!"
Whether your foes are giants, fallen knights, or simple goblins, you can insult their size, their brains, their battle prowess, their ancestors, and their taste in armor and weaponry.
Pure, unbridled mockery can be a lot of fun. You can find some entertaining archaic insults by consulting Internet resources—searching for "Shakespeare's insults" is a great place to start.

Write down one or two of these challenges or taunts for your character, and save them for the right moment—such as when you first spot the villain, when you score a critical hit, or when a party member strikes the killing blow after a particularly tough combat. Better yet, use challenges, taunts, and mockery to enrage foes and lure them into positions where you gain bonuses for being on the high ground, where they fall into a pit or mire, or where you can simply hammer at them with ranged attacks and they are unable to reach you. Yes, taunting foes is fun—and it can also be effective.

Looting and Dividing the Spoils

Pathfinder is a game of heroism and triumph over fearsome enemies, but it's also a game of looting valuable treasures from ancient tombs.

The division of the loot is a roleplaying opportunity, and a time for bargaining, bartering, and haggling. Many groups conduct this activity out of character, making comments like, "Well, my character could really use a magical sword, and you already have one. Do you want the wand instead? They're worth about the same amount." This simplifies things and speeds up play.

At the same time, there's no reason you can't have fun by handling some of the loot-dividing in character. Once in a while, you might also want to haggle with NPCs whom you encounter during the adventure (guides, hirelings, mercenaries, and so on), and those discussions might be better done in character. If you play a party loudmouth or leader of some type, you can shout demands for what you want most. If you're a barbarian who rarely has interest in anything other than magical great axes, it can make quite an impression when you exclaim, "This magic horn belonged to my people's ancient enemies—I claim it by right of conquest!"

BEHIND THE SCREEN

There comes a point when every player thinks, "I wonder what it's like to tell my own story, invent my own villains, and help shape the saga of a new band of heroes?" Being a Game Master comes with its own set of unique challenges and difficulties, but it can be very rewarding when your players interact with the adventures you've designed, coming up with their own solutions to the difficulties you've set before them. They might curse the daunting challenges that confront them, but they'll be back next week for more!

Where to Begin

Learning to be a Game Master isn't as hard as it might first appear. A number of resources are readily available to help you get started. The *Pathfinder RPG Beginner Box* is specifically designed to make things easy for new GMs and players alike, teaching the basics without loading you down with some of the more complicated rules concepts until you're ready. The *Beginner Box* also includes a sample adventure and tips on making your own.

Your next step should be to pick up the *Pathfinder RPG GameMastery Guide*. This invaluable tome is loaded with rules and advice to make your job as a GM easy, including tips to help you formulate your campaign, put together encounters, and reward your players appropriately.

Your First Game

As a GM, your most important job is to tell a good story. Getting your players engaged in the world and the plot of the adventure is far more critical than ensuring that you get every ruling just right. That said, because the GM is the final arbiter of the rules of the game, your second most important job is to be an impartial judge. It isn't "you" versus "them." Everyone is participating together to tell a good tale, no matter what side of the GM screen they happen to be sitting on.

Remember that the game is designed in such a way that the characters have a high chance of success, but that doesn't mean you should make it easy for them. The players should feel like they earned their treasure and experience points. Making things too simple cheapens the reward. Here are a few other tips you might want to keep in mind.

Consider running a published adventure for your first game. All of the work is already done for you and all you need to do before the game is read the adventure and familiarize yourself with the story and encounters.
Come prepared with your own dice, scratch paper, pencils, rulebooks, and miniatures to represent the monsters.
Shortly before the game, reread the part of the adventure that you can safely assume the PCs will encounter in the upcoming session. This will refresh your memory and allow you to plan ahead for how you'll handle areas that you think might be problematic.
Make sure your players are ready for the adventure. Remind them to make their characters beforehand and to arrive promptly at the start of the session. Once they arrive, give them a chance to introduce their characters to one another, and if the adventure calls for it, devise a backstory that explains why they know each other and have decided to adventure together.
During the game, try to be as descriptive as possible. The players are relying on you to paint a picture of the world around them. Your job is to give them the information they need to interact and play in your story.

TIP Remember, everyone playing the game is there to take part in a good story. As GM, it's your job to narrate the tale and give your players the opportunity to interact with the adventure.

Creating Your Own Adventures

If you're creating your own adventure, start by drawing up an plot outline. This could be as simple as "A merchant needs protection as she travels to a nearby town with valuable goods." Next, design encounters that plug in to the plot. Perhaps brigands attack on the road, or the merchant's wagon breaks down, forcing the PCs to deal with a hostile farmer for replacement parts. Make notes about the other characters the PCs will encounter, including the NPCs' appearances and personality quirks. By following these steps, you'll have a basic adventure in no time.

Once you've got a first draft of your adventure, it's best to go through it again and see if there's anything you missed. Did you award enough treasure? Are the planned combat encounters of an appropriate challenge for the PCs in your game? After you run the game, you should look back over your work and consider how the adventure went. Did the players have fun? Were the players challenged and engaged in the story? What might you do differently next time? Given enough practice, anyone can become an expert Game Master!

GM SCREEN

Many GMs use a screen to hide their notes and die rolls from players. The *Pathfinder RPG GM Screen* is designed for this purpose and includes many handy charts and tables on the back side for the GM to reference during play.

For more information on being a Game Master, see page 396 of the *Core Rulebook*.

For rules and advice on how to create challenging encounters for your players, see page 397 of the *Core Rulebook*.

One way to reward characters is to give them valuable magic items. See the Magic Item chapter starting on page 458 of the *Core Rulebook* for more information.

ADDITIONAL RESOURCES

More information on Game Mastering can be found in the *Pathfinder RPG Bestiary* volumes, the *GameMastery Guide*, *Ultimate Campaign*, *The Inner Sea World Guide*, and any of our Pathfinder Adventure Paths.

ADVICE FOR BETTER GAMING

Whether you're a GM looking to hand out some pointers to your players or a new player who wants to better navigate the social aspects of roleplaying games, the following principles will help everybody fit in and have a good time when sitting down at the table to play Pathfinder. Each group has its own social standards and play style, but the near-universal tips below will help you and your friends have a more enjoyable gaming experience.

Playing RPGs Is a Social Experience: This is the foundation of every other recommendation in this section. If someone's not having fun, something's gone wrong. If your actions are making the game unrewarding or uncomfortable for others, step back and consider if there's anything that you can do to make sure others have a good time as well.

Make a Good Impression: Aim to be a person who's fun to sit with at the table. Act with courtesy and patience in all of your interactions, and feel free to ask questions when you don't understand something!

Be On Time: You can't start the game without the players! When you're late, you make everyone wait. If you're frequently the last one to the game table, chances are good the rest of the group will be irked.

Be Respectful of the Host: Observe any non-game rules that the host sets, even if they're not about playing the game, such as keeping your voice down after a certain hour, leaving your shoes at the door, or not using profanity. Be a considerate houseguest.

Be Respectful of the GM: It's customary in RPGs for the GM to be the final judge of what actually happens in the game world. This is important for keeping the action moving, so be respectful of GM decisions, even if they don't match your own interpretation of the rules. Pathfinder doesn't actually pit players against the GM in "win-lose" scenarios; a game session is a success if everyone has fun.

Take Turns: During combat, each character takes one turn, waits for everyone else to have a turn, and then gets to act again. Respect that process, even though it may be tempting to tell other players what to do when they're struggling with decisions or doing things that ruin your strategy. Brief requests and polite suggestions are entirely reasonable, but having one player reign over all of the others tends to get old quickly. Let others play their own characters.

CHIP IN

Gaming groups frequently order food or break out the snacks. Be a good guest by chipping in to help cover the costs, whether it's by bringing something to share or tossing some money into the group's snack fund. Of course, when the food is all eaten, help the host to clean up and put things away. You might also want to consider helping out with gaming supplies. Players may own a few books, some dice, and maybe a character miniature, but GMs typically need monster books, extra miniatures, maps, published adventures, and more. Those costs can add up. Many players share their own books and gaming resources with the GM, chip in to cover the GM's share when food is ordered to help defray her costs, or even buy the GM a new gaming book as a thank-you gift after a great campaign.

Taking turns also happens from a narrative perspective. If one player always tries to be the main character in the story, all of the other players gradually fade into a team of sidekicks. Every player should have an opportunity to shine, so don't forget to share the spotlight with others.

It's a Team Effort: Regardless of how good your character is, she'll probably be even better if you coordinate her actions with the other PCs. For example, if you dash into a pack of enemies without warning, your sorcerer ally can't throw her favorite explosive spells without hitting you. If you step in front of a character whose strength is charging into melee, he can't be effective. Be open to working with other players to improve your teamwork.

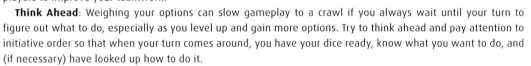

Think Ahead: Weighing your options can slow gameplay to a crawl if you always wait until your turn to figure out what to do, especially as you level up and gain more options. Try to think ahead and pay attention to initiative order so that when your turn comes around, you have your dice ready, know what you want to do, and (if necessary) have looked up how to do it.

Don't Betray Everyone: Narrative games are different in some ways from other forms of storytelling. Betraying your party might seem like a cool twist to the story, but if your character kills another player's character in his sleep, you've effectively told the other players at the table that your desire to insert a "twist" is more important than whether they have fun. This can lead to hurt feelings for both players and characters, and betraying the others might be the last thing your character does. If you feel the need to betray the party, talk to the GM about your idea and see if it can be woven into the game in a way that would be enjoyable (or at least not hurtful) for everyone.

Similarly, character alignment is not an excuse for ruining other players' experience. Even if your *character* sheet says "evil," you as a *player* should be a considerate and collaborative gaming partner. Remember that even evil people generally cooperate when it's necessary to achieve their goals. Your character doesn't have to love her allies to see the necessity of keeping them alive in combat.

Avoid Metagaming: "Metagaming" refers to actions or strategies that take advantage of things that you know as a *player* but your *character* doesn't know. Using that knowledge to direct your character's actions is typically taboo. For example, you might know from reading the *Pathfinder RPG Bestiary* that mummies are vulnerable to fire, but if your character has never encountered a mummy before, having her reach immediately for the alchemist's fire is bad form. (Asking to make a Knowledge check to see what your character knows, however, is good gaming!)

Leave Your Baggage at the Door: Between gaming sessions, people go to work, attend classes, experience loss, and have arguments. For many, gaming is a way to relax, socialize, and have fun. Leave your non-gaming baggage outside your gaming sessions. If you recently had a dispute with another player, it might be *really* tempting to have your character kick the tar out of that player's character. On top of being immature and rude, though, this makes for bad storytelling. If you have a problem that doesn't involve the game, don't bring it to the gaming table.

Consider Your Disagreement Style: Sometimes people disagree about how to interpret a rule or how two rules might interact. Discussing how the rule should work is a time-honored tradition in RPGs, but it can quickly escalate into a shouting match. Remember that it's possible to disagree without fighting, and a calm, logical argument tends to keep things nice and move the game along, whereas yelling, demanding, insulting, or accusing just makes everyone angry or uncomfortable. If someone is getting worked up over how a rule works, take a step back and consider whether winning an argument is more important than everyone having fun. As always, the GM has the final say—if you disagree with a GM ruling, wait to discuss it privately and politely *after* the game, rather than interrupting the action.

Understand the House Rules: A gaming group sometimes devises extra rules—called house rules—for the game that they all agree to follow. When you join a group, be sure to ask about house rules early on so that you know what, if anything, will be different about how the game operates.

Be Awesome: Nothing compares to being in a group of excited roleplayers having fun together. Fun is contagious, and if you're outgoing, friendly, and engaged, there's a good chance that everyone else at the table will be, too.

LEVEL UP YOUR GAME

The main point of narrative play is to amuse yourself and everyone else at the table. It's okay to ham it up a little. Take a few chances—try talking your way out of trouble, bribing the infernal secretary in Hell's waiting room, or bluffing your way into the presence of the archmage. You might find that a taste for adventure doesn't always mean a taste for blood and combat, but simply a taste for daring deeds and bold words. Sometimes, that's enough. Other times, those bold words lead you right into a fight—getting into trouble is a specialty of many adventurers. The world is there for you to play in, so don't be afraid to see what wild possibilities exist!

PAY ATTENTION

If the players aren't willing to listen to what the GM has to say, then there's really no game. Discipline yourself against constantly checking your electronic devices for anything but game-related material. A moderate level of "table talk" is usually fine, but when off-topic chatter starts to drown out the action, the game slows to a halt. In the end, wouldn't you rather be hunting monsters and seeking treasure anyway?

Pathfinder Society Organized Play brings together roleplayers from around the world to participate in a single campaign in which the PCs are all members of the Pathfinder Society, an organization of explorers dedicated to seeking out lost relics, forgotten knowledge, and ancient sites scattered about the world of Golarion.

So far, everything you've read in this volume has had to do with what are commonly referred to as **home games**. In a home game, you can tell any type of story that you want to, and your character can conceivably do anything that the story (and GM) permits.

The **organized play** gaming format is a shared campaign in which large numbers of players participate in one shared story. Members of the organized play campaign volunteer to GM adventures that each last a single session, but contribute to an ongoing narrative. These GMs then report the results of that session to a central campaign manager and hand out a certificate to each player to show what rewards he or she earned, such as gold, experience points, magic items, and more. By earning these certificates, your character will grow in power and participate in increasingly epic adventures.

Pathfinder Society agents can have nearly any background, and the organization recruits adventurers of all talents. Anyone who wants to join the campaign can sit down at a table, form a group, and be playing through an adventure in a matter of minutes. Because anyone can play, you also get to choose when you want to play and with whom, participating as often or as infrequently as you want.

Pathfinder Society Organized Play is free and easy to join, and has two separate wings: the Roleplaying Guild for players of the roleplaying game, and the Adventure Card Guild for players of the Pathfinder Adventure Card Game. While the following section focuses on the Pathfinder Roleplaying Game program, the two guilds have many similarities, and you can play in both!

Why Organized Play?

Sure, meeting new players and participating in convention games is fun, but why play in a Pathfinder Society campaign rather than a normal Pathfinder game? Here are a few benefits to organized play.

Explore a Living World: Every Pathfinder Society character exists in a common setting shared by thousands of other gamers. In each Society game, characters experience the same adventures as Pathfinders the world over, sharing experiences, rising in prestige among their peers, and participating in ongoing stories unique to the Pathfinder Society campaign.

Find Allies and Further Your Goals: Not only does every Pathfinder Society character belong to the illustrious ranks of the Pathfinder Society, but each is also a member of a faction within the organization, working toward goals shared by only a subset of any given adventuring party. Over the course of a given season of play—the yearlong span between August of one calendar year and July of the next—members of each faction tirelessly work to see their factions' goals achieved, all while adventuring as Pathfinder field agents. Those factions who achieve their goals see their influence in the Society increase, paving the way for unique rewards and plot developments, while those who fail might see their faction diminish in importance.

Win Fame and Use It: Throughout a Pathfinder's career, she not only gains wealth and experience as all Pathfinder Roleplaying Game characters do, but also earns fame and prestige, representing her renown as a Pathfinder and adventurer. This fame allows her to call upon her allies within the Pathfinder Society and her respective faction for special favors, unique character abilities, free spellcasting services, powerful magic items, and other rewards.

Your Actions Matter: Every character's actions help guide each yearlong plot arc of the Pathfinder Society campaign. Over time, decisions made at Pathfinder Society gaming tables can determine the direction of future adventures and even the canon of the Pathfinder campaign setting.

Finding a Game

There are several common venues for playing Pathfinder Society games.

Play in Your Area: Game stores, comic book stores, local conventions, and libraries are among the most common locations where you will find Pathfinder Society games being run. To locate games in your area, you can ask at these locations, check online at **paizo.com/pathfinderSociety/events** using the Pathfinder Society event finder, or post on the Pathfinder Society message boards to see if anyone in your area is coordinating an event.

Play at Home: Just because Pathfinder Society encourages and facilitates playing at public events in pickup groups doesn't mean that you can't play in the comfort of your own home. Some players prefer to play with the same group consistently, but they can still be part of the overall campaign so long as they use the Pathfinder Society rules for character creation, rewards, and adventures to structure a home game.

Play Online: You can also enjoy Pathfinder Society online with your friends, running a game together even if everyone is in a different time zone. Perhaps you prefer the narrative opportunities of play-by-post, in which players use email or a message board to post their character's actions. Virtual tabletop (VTT) programs are also an excellent option, as they allow you to draw maps, track stats, roll dice, and move figures, all in an online platform that every participant can see. Break out some webcams, and you'll have much the same experience as if you were all at the same table.

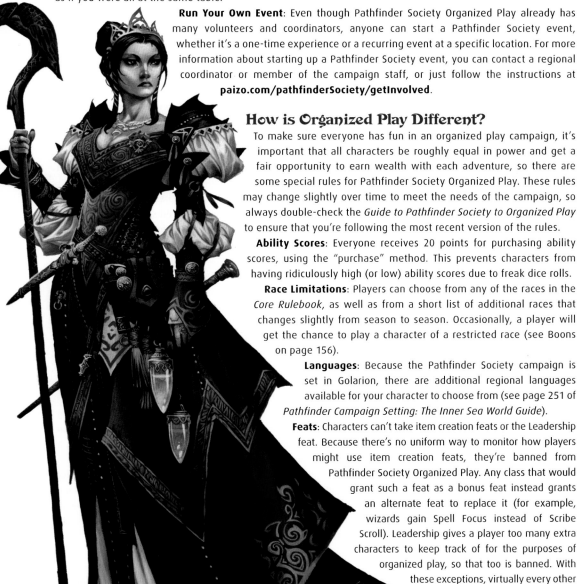

Run Your Own Event: Even though Pathfinder Society Organized Play already has many volunteers and coordinators, anyone can start a Pathfinder Society event, whether it's a one-time experience or a recurring event at a specific location. For more information about starting up a Pathfinder Society event, you can contact a regional coordinator or member of the campaign staff, or just follow the instructions at **paizo.com/pathfinderSociety/getInvolved**.

How is Organized Play Different?

To make sure everyone has fun in an organized play campaign, it's important that all characters be roughly equal in power and get a fair opportunity to earn wealth with each adventure, so there are some special rules for Pathfinder Society Organized Play. These rules may change slightly over time to meet the needs of the campaign, so always double-check the *Guide to Pathfinder Society to Organized Play* to ensure that you're following the most recent version of the rules.

Ability Scores: Everyone receives 20 points for purchasing ability scores, using the "purchase" method. This prevents characters from having ridiculously high (or low) ability scores due to freak dice rolls.

Race Limitations: Players can choose from any of the races in the *Core Rulebook*, as well as from a short list of additional races that changes slightly from season to season. Occasionally, a player will get the chance to play a character of a restricted race (see Boons on page 156).

Languages: Because the Pathfinder Society campaign is set in Golarion, there are additional regional languages available for your character to choose from (see page 251 of *Pathfinder Campaign Setting: The Inner Sea World Guide*).

Feats: Characters can't take item creation feats or the Leadership feat. Because there's no uniform way to monitor how players might use item creation feats, they're banned from Pathfinder Society Organized Play. Any class that would grant such a feat as a bonus feat instead grants an alternate feat to replace it (for example, wizards gain Spell Focus instead of Scribe Scroll). Leadership gives a player too many extra characters to keep track of for the purposes of organized play, so that too is banned. With these exceptions, virtually every other feat published by Paizo is allowed.

VENTURE OFFICERS

Along with Paizo staff, there's also an extensive network of campaign volunteers and regional coordinators (referred to as venture-captains and venture-lieutenants) whose job it is to promote Pathfinder Society events in their area, welcome new members, and help players find their first game. In the back of the *Guide to Pathfinder Society Organized Play*, you'll find a list of all of these regional coordinators as well as contact information so you can write an email to your nearest representative for more information.

PAIZO.COM

You can find a wealth of information about the Pathfinder Society on our website at **paizo.com**. In addition to complete rules for character generation and play, we also feature messageboards. There you will find a thriving community of Pathfinder Society players, along with news about upcoming events, game days, and conventions. There are also reviews of scenarios, recaps of events, and even events that are played online. You can find all of this and more at **paizo.com/paizo/messageboards**.

Alignment: No Pathfinder Society character can have an evil alignment. This is primarily to prevent someone from using alignment as an excuse for antisocial behavior.

Hit Points: You don't have to roll hit points at each level; instead, you gain a specific amount each time you level up. At each level after 1st you receive the statistical average roll of your Hit Die, rounded up to the nearest hit point. For example, a ranger normally gets 1d10 hit points every level, so in Pathfinder Society a ranger gets 6 hit points every level (slightly above the 5.5 average value of 1d10), plus whatever hit point adjustment he would normally get from his Constitution bonus or penalty.

Factions: Each character is part of a faction. Each faction has interests that you can promote as you perform missions for the Society. In return, the factions offer you special rewards, and you get to shape that faction's ongoing story. At the date of this publication there are seven available factions to choose from; see the *Guide to Pathfinder Society to Organized Play* for details on each.

Traits: Traits are part of an optional rules set that Pathfinder Society uses. Think of each trait as a half-feat that emphasizes your character's background. For example, you might have been a bully and have a trait that gives you a bonus on Intimidate checks, or be especially devoted to your deity, granting you a bonus on Will saves. Pathfinder Society characters each get two traits. Your choice of a faction also opens up new trait choices, helping you to distinguish your character from others.

Starting Gold: Every character receives 150 gp as starting wealth.

Chronicle Sheets: As mentioned above, completing a scenario earns you a certificate of your progress, called a Chronicle sheet (a written record of what you did and what you earned). You'll need to keep these with your character sheet, as they're your proof that your 9th-level cleric really did complete certain adventures. If you happen to lose your Chronicle sheets, your regional coordinator can help you replace them using your Pathfinder Society number and online records.

XP: Earning experience points is simplified in Pathfinder Society. Every scenario grants you 1 XP, and every 3 XP earned allows you to gain a level. This means that you never have to worry about ending an adventure when you're just a few experience points shy of gaining a level.

Gold Earned: Pathfinder Society Organized Play gives each of the participants a set amount of gold (depending on character level) for completing each adventure. With that money you can then buy any of the cool magic items your party found during the session.

Prestige Points and Fame: As you succeed at missions, your character will earn Prestige Points, which are like a separate form of currency. You can exchange Prestige Points for favors from the Pathfinder Society itself, which will heal your character's wounds, give you minor magical items, or even cast *raise dead* to allow you to keep adventuring if you should happen to die during your exploits!

Fame is a measure of the total number Prestige Points your character has ever acquired. Your Fame total never goes down even if you spend Prestige Points. Fame is important for determining what types of items your character can purchase beyond those you find during an adventure. The higher your Fame, the more interesting the equipment you'll be offered by merchants.

Boons: Boons refer to non-gold, non-item rewards that you might receive on a Chronicle sheet. Typically, these represent special favors or blessings that you acquired as part of an adventure, such as earning the everlasting friendship of a region's dwarves or winning a future favor from a fey noble. Each boon will tell you exactly what it does.

One other type of boon is the convention boon, which is a special award a player can win when attending a larger event that hosts Pathfinder Society games. These special awards might be unique benefits for an existing character or access to a special option for when you make a new character (such as creating a character of a normally unavailable race). You're allowed to trade this type of boon to other players.

Additional Resources: Nearly everything in the *Core Rulebook* is legal for play, and Pathfinder Society campaign leaders also add most options from each new Paizo publication to the list of legal options—typically leaving out evil items and other features that aren't appropriate for the campaign for one reason or another. To find out whether something from another Paizo book is legal for use in Pathfinder Society events, check **paizo.com/pathfinderSociety/about/additionalResources**.

Get Started Now

Pathfinder Society Organized Play offers you all the fun of a normal Pathfinder game, plus the chance to connect with new players and participate in a huge, constantly evolving story in which your character can shape the world. So join up now and give it a try!

QUESTIONS ABOUT PATHFINDER SOCIETY?

In many ways, participating in Pathfinder Society Organized Play events is the same as playing in a game at home, but the far-reaching community elements do create some differences. Here are answers to a few common questions about the Pathfinder Society.

What does "Organized Play" mean?

Pathfinder Society members volunteer their time to schedule and host public events, and participants report the results of their games to Paizo's campaign staff. This way, everyone's playing with the same rules and assumptions, allowing you to play the same character in events all over the world and collect unique Pathfinder Society boons and other benefits.

When and where can I play?

Call your local game store and ask when they run their Pathfinder Society events, or check out the event locator at **paizo.com**. If you want, you can even play at home! Check out **paizo.com/pathfinderSociety/getInvolved** for details on sanctioning your own campaign.

Are there prizes or rewards for playing?

Every time you participate in an official Pathfinder Society game, your character receives the loot he or she has won as part of the adventure. Often this is gold or other treasure, but in some special events it might be access to new races, cool powers, or other rewards unique to the Pathfinder Society.

Do I have to know all the rules?

No! Not only does Pathfinder Society regularly run events custom-made for starting players, but even regular games are perfect places for players who only know the basics to have fun, get more experience, and learn some awesome new techniques!

Is Pathfinder Society right for me?

The Pathfinder Society is an accepting, safe, and fun community of gamers that gives players of all ages, genders, ethnicities, and sexualities the opportunity to share their love of roleplaying adventures. Everyone is welcomed, and regional coordinators and the Paizo campaign staff are dedicated to creating fun places to play, mediating concerns, and ensuring that you have the best gaming experience possible.

I have other questions. Where can I find answers?

You can find tons of other Pathfinder Society Organized Play resources online at **paizo.com/pathfinderSociety**. Among these are everything you need to sign up, the free downloadable *Guide to Pathfinder Society Organized Play*, and messageboards full of active Pathfinder Society members and the Paizo campaign staff. Stop by, introduce yourself, join in the discussion, and ask away!

CONVENTION PLAY

Attending a game convention can be daunting for a new player. Here are some tips and tricks to help you navigate your first convention experience.

Register

Many conventions or game days require you to register to attend the event. For larger events, you will be given a badge that grants you entry to all the show has to offer.

Signups and Tickets

Most shows that offer Pathfinder Society events have a limited number of tables and GMs. As such, they often require you to sign up to play so you can be assured a seat at a table. Some larger shows use tickets, which can be purchased at a nominal fee. You might even be able to preregister for your games, allowing you to organize your convention experience before you even arrive.

Marshaling

Pathfinder Society players often have a number of characters of various levels. To ensure that your table has a group of characters around the same level, most conventions will marshal their players before seating them at a table, allowing them to organize into balanced groups for adventuring.

INDEX

This index offers you a quick reference for key terms and concepts.

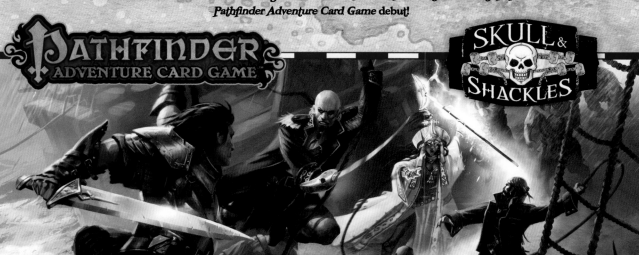

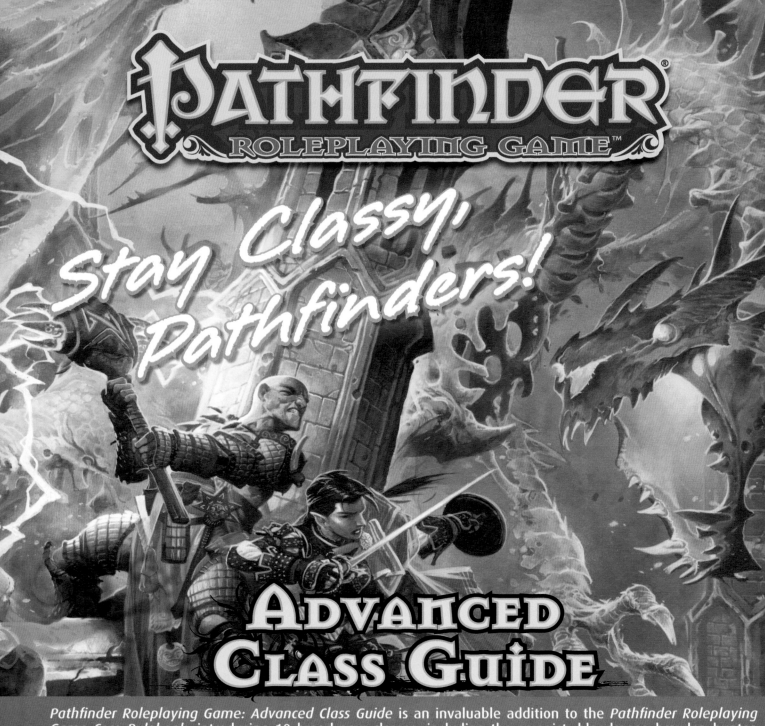

PATHFINDER
ROLEPLAYING GAME

Stay Classy, Pathfinders!

Advanced Class Guide

Pathfinder Roleplaying Game: Advanced Class Guide is an invaluable addition to the *Pathfinder Roleplaying Game Core Rulebook*, introducing 10 brand new classes, including the arcanist, bloodrager, brawler, hunter, investigator, shaman, skald, slayer, swashbuckler, and warpriest.

Pathfinder Roleplaying Game: Advanced Class Guide also includes:

• Archetypes, feats, and spells for all of the new classes, as well as a wealth of options for every existing character class in the Pathfinder RPG
• Gear to kit out your character and plenty of new magic items to fill up the GM's treasure chest
• Plenty of advice on how to construct a new character class, archetype, or prestige class, giving the GM powerful tools to make the rules they need for their game